EYE OPENER BOB

THE STORY OF BOB EDWARDS

Grant MacEwan

annotated by
James Martin

introduction by
Will Ferguson

BRINDLE & GLASS

First published by the Institute of Applied Art, 1957.
Second edition: Western Producer Prairie Books, 1974.

Library and Archives Canada Cataloguing in Publication

MacEwan, Grant, 1902-2000.
Eye Opener Bob : the story of Bob Edwards / Grant MacEwan ; introduction by Will Ferguson ; notes by James Martin.

First published: Edmonton : Institute of Applied Art, 1957.
Includes bibliographical references.
ISBN 0-9732481-6-5

1. Edwards, Bob, 1865-1922. 2. Eye opener (Newspaper) 3. Newspaper editors—Alberta—Calgary—Biography. 4. Calgary (Alta.)—Biography. I. Title.

PS8459.D8Z75 2004 070.92 C2004-904866-X

Cover image: Provincial Archives of Alberta, P5238.
Interior images: Please see list of images on page 209.
Cover and interior design: Ruth Linka

The editor and publishers would like to extend grateful thanks to James Martin, Fiona Foran, Bonnie Shedden, Paul Shreenan, Cory Wilson of Alberta Theatre Projects, Dr. Donald Smith, Jim Bowman and Doug Cass at the Glenbow Archives, and especially to Heather MacEwan Foran and Dr. Maxwell Foran. We cannot thank Dr. Hugh Dempsey highly enough for his work in keeping Edwards's spirit and memory alive this past half-century. His scholarship has been essential in preparing this volume, and without his delightful and invaluable books (*The Best of Bob Edwards*, Hurtig Publishers, 1975, and *The Wit and Wisdom of Bob Edwards*, Hurtig Publishers, 1976 it is inconceivable that this new edition of *Eye Opener Bob* and its companion, *Irresponsible Freaks, Highball Guzzlers and Unabashed Grafters: A Bob Edwards Chrestomathy*, would have ever been published.

Canada Council for the Arts — Conseil des Arts du Canada

Brindle & Glass acknowledges the support of the Canada Council for the Arts and the Alberta Foundation for the Arts for our publishing program.

Brindle & Glass Publishing
www.brindleandglass.com

Brindle & Glass is committed to protecting the environment and to the responsible use of natural resources. This book is printed on 100% post-consumer recycled and ancient-forest-friendly paper. For more information please visit www.oldgrowthfree.com.

1 2 3 4 5 07 06 05 04

PRINTED AND BOUND IN CANADA

Some men spoil a good story by sticking to the facts.

—Bob Edwards

CONTENTS

INTRODUCTION
by Will Ferguson

BOB EDWARDS WAS A GENIUS. That's all you really need to know, but that would make for a very short introduction, so let me also say this: he was a failed genius. Or rather, an *unfulfilled* genius.

Edwards arrived in the Canadian West in the 1890s and set up shop as a one-man newspaper operation, launching the *Eye Opener* a few years later in High River. He was a soft-spoken man with a slight lisp and a Scottish lilt in his voice, not the sort of person you would peg as a hellraiser or a firebrand, but brand fire and raise hell he did.

> An editor who started about twenty years ago with only 55 cents is now worth $100,000. His accumulation of wealth is owing to his frugality, good habits, strict attention to business and the fact that an uncle died and left him the sum of $99,999.
>
> —Bob Edwards

Edwards was a wandering soul, and the *Eye Opener* moved six times between five different towns in its first ten years of operation. In spite of this, the paper was a raging, albeit unlikely, success. Circulation soared from 250 to 35,000, though as historian Hugh Dempsey has pointed out, "the *Eye Opener* was not a newspaper, but Bob Edwards's personal platform for social comment and humour."

Edwards fought for minimum wage legislation, old age pensions, provincial rights, increased Canadian curriculum in schools, agricultural co-ops, prison reform, and a system of public hospitalization that would give equal access to all. Health care, he argued strenuously, was a basic human right. He opposed the racial restrictions placed on Chinese immigrants and warned Canadians about "the prospect of becoming hewers of pulpwood and drawers of waterpower for the Americans." He led a campaign to abolish the Senate, or at the very least reform it, labelling Canada's Upper House an "impotent relic," "a Refuge for fallen political prune-eaters," "a Haven for the discredited," "a Home for pensioners who don't need the money" and "an Exhibition of ill-visaged wax-works." He was also a great admirer of that other prairie hellraiser, Nellie McClung.

About the slowest way to settle an argument is to get two women interested in it.

—Bob Edwards

In *The Eye Opener*, Edwards teased women mercilessly and with the same unbridled gusto with which he mocked men, but he was also a staunch supporter of women's rights, and he urged women to run for political office. "It is our firm conviction," he wrote, "that the blending of women's ideas with those of reasonably thoughtful men will some day bring about an era of common sense." This was the essence of what Edwards believed in, dreamed of, fought for. *An era of common sense.*

These were exciting times and the Canadian West, especially in its formative years, was very much a self-selecting venue. The West attracted misfits and outcasts, dreamers, schemers, eccentrics and oddballs, mountebanks and moneymen. The restless. The lonely. The thirsty. Thirsty for something more, something better. Thirsty for life. Thirsty, in Edwards's case, for rot-gut whisky and that elusive "era of common sense." The young city of Calgary, where Edwards eventually settled, was a boomtown rife with robust individualism and larger-than-life characters: the cattle king Pat Burns, the irascible Irish lawyer Paddy Nolan, the thundering, hard-drinking fire chief Cappie Smart—and right in the thick of things, Bob Edwards, social crusader.

The most distinctive attributes of a large, bustling city are streetcars, crooked gamblers, confidence men, and a "complacent" police force. Hurry up with those streetcars, will you?

—Edwards's assessment of Calgary in its early years

Bob Edwards wielded truth like a weapon. He abhorred pretension and was capable of blowing his opponents out of the water with a barrage of verbal brickbats. When a Presbyterian minister in High River began harassing a local hotel-keeper, Edwards let loose a blast of calumny, describing the priest as one of those "tactless, offensive, conceited, self-sufficient, arrogant young parsons with no experience of men and things, uncultured by travel or reading, with absolutely no knowledge of the world, possessing a highly developed faculty for making themselves ridiculous and obnoxious, troubling the waters of a peaceful village, and sowing discord broadcast, having no rational argument in favour of their own existence."

Whew! You wouldn't want to get on the bad side of Bob Edwards. More often than not, though, Edwards preferred to employ a withering and devastating sense of humour when taking down the high and mighty:

> We understand—ha ha!—that—haw haw!—R. J. Stuart—ah-yaw-haw—ha ha ha!—is going to run oh oh ha ha—for alderman—ha ha ha ha ha ha!—Ha ha ha ha ha ha!—ha ha ha ha ha ha ha ha ha ha!

How do you recover from something like that?

Edwards even took on the Almighty CPR, which was a law unto itself in those days. The railway treated public safety with a disdain that bordered on contempt, and in response Edwards launched a campaign of "ridicule and awkward truth." Awkward truth, indeed. That was Edwards's forte. The *Eye Opener* began running headlines reading "No deaths caused by the CPR this week!" and "Not a single life was lost at the CPR rail crossing on First Street West!"

In a similar vein, Edwards once sunk a local greed merchant by reporting what *hadn't* happened. Yet. "The many friends of Alex B. Munson, who amassed a comfortable fortune in Calgary during the oil boom, will be glad to learn that he is still out of jail."

The CPR finally relented and Edwards, true to his word, ended his campaign. In all his years as a windmill-tilting, dragon-engaging, underdog-defending knight errant, Bob Edwards was only ever successfully sued for libel once, and that was over an obvious spoof. Edwards published an apology and continued on, undaunted. (In *Eye Opener Bob*, Grant MacEwan states that Edwards was never successfully sued for libel, but in fact he was, though admittedly the lawsuit and the repercussions were minor.)

When cautioned to use the word "alleged" more often, Edwards replied with a news article that ran: "J. W. Pringar of Cayley, with his alleged daughter, paid High River a visit last week. After putting his alleged horse in the barn, Mr. Pringar filled up on some alleged whisky which seemed to affect his alleged brain." (The humour here is incredibly deft; note how each "alleged" Edwards employs carries with it a slightly different nuance and a slightly different meaning, suggesting in turn: infidelity, a stolen horse, cheap moonshine, and a lack of intelligence.)

The *Eye Opener* offered its readers a wealth of advice—almost all of it bogus, whether it be health tips or points of etiquette and fine dining. A typical recipe for Rabbit Stew begins: "Take a good fat cat and give it a bat over the head in the cellar."

Edwards also published wildly popular and equally bogus "society notes," which perfectly lampooned the pretensions of Calgary's social-climbing set. The comings and goings—and drunken excesses—of such upstanding citizens as Annabel McSwattie, Mrs. Bucklewhackster, Lottie McGlory, Peter O'Snuffigan, and Mrs. T. Tinglebuster were duly reported in deadpan style, leaving readers guessing as to which events being alluded to were true and which were not.

Some of Edwards's "Society Notes" were at the level of schoolboy humour: "The Okotoks Methodist Ladies' Aid will give a bean supper from 6 to 8 PM to be followed by a musical program." Others were not-so-subtle digs at the presumed respectability of the middle class: "Peter F. Ayer, who has been absent from the city for over a year, returned home last week to find himself the proud father of a bouncing boy just a few weeks old."

My personal favourite? One from 1922: "Society Note—Mrs. J. B. Scluff, of Fourteenth Ave W., entertained some of her neighbours informally last Monday afternoon. That is to say, she and her cook had a quarrel on the front porch."

In one of the most cutting examples of political satire ever penned in Canada, Edwards once ran a "transcript" of a debate in the House of Commons, in which the Members of the Opposition raise the matter of a high-ranking inspector in the Liberal government who, it has been proven beyond a shadow of a doubt, has killed his mother-in-law and chopped her into pieces, and then laced her remains with strychnine and fed them to the wolves, and then sold the pelts back to the government for a tidy sum.

The Liberals brush aside the Opposition's questions as irrelevant. "The honourable member is surely aware that the department lays down no hard and fast rules as to what kind of bait shall be used in the case of wild animals on whose pelts a bounty is paid by the government . . . It seems a pity that the honourable members do not obtain more exact information on which to base their charges against the government."

"But the minister killed his mother-in-law and fed her to the wolves!" the Opposition shouts with growing exasperation. "Surely such a monstrous piece of business should be looked into. Will the government take steps to remove the inspector from his position?"

The government refuses, stating that the inspector's work within the department has been exemplary and that any pelts he sold were done so in perfectly good faith. The Prime Minister himself eventually rises to scold the Opposition for besmirching the inspector's good name and to protest against the time of the House "being frittered away in this manner." It is as laugh-out-loud funny today as it was when Edwards wrote it in 1907. But beyond his devastating use of satire, Edwards was also capable of a remarkably light-handed approach. He even penned a playful verse or two:

> She frowned on him and called him Mr.
> Because in fun he went and Kr.
> So out of spite the next good night
> The naughty Mr. Kr. Sr.

After sitting through an especially effusive eulogy, one that managed to elevate a recently deceased alderman from the realm of mere politician to that of statesman, Edwards mused: "Now I know what a statesman is; he's a dead politician. We need more statesmen." It is probably Edwards's best-known quip.

The aphorisms of Bob Edwards are on par with those of Ambrose Bierce, and indeed, one could easily recast many of Edwards's sayings as definitions, akin to those in Bierce's *Devil's Dictionary*. I have done this with a few of Edwards's aphorisms as an example below:

Illusions: the grand ideas we have about ourselves.
Delusions: the silly ideas other people have about us.
Remorse: memory that has begun to ferment.
Bachelors: men who still have illusions about women.
Lawyer: someone who gets two men to strip for a fight and then runs off with their clothes.
Marriage: two people promising at the altar with perfectly straight faces to feel, think and believe for the rest of their lives exactly as they do at that minute.
Highbrow: a person whose education is generally beyond his intelligence.
Cynicism: the art of seeing things as they are, instead of as they ought to be.

The philosopher Santayana may have warned "Those who cannot remember the past are condemned to repeat it." But it took Bob Edwards to enter a plea on behalf of the common man. "If it's all the same to history," Edwards wrote in the aftermath of the First World War, "it need not repeat itself anymore."

Over time, Bob Edwards's fame spread to Great Britain and the United States. A New York literary journal hailed the "clear judgment and common sense" of Edwards's writing and held up a theatre review he had written as a "specimen of dramatic criticism that might well serve as a model for some of our more pretentious critics on the New York press." In the British papers, Calgary was referred to, by way of explanation, as "the place where the *Eye Opener* comes from."

> Applause has made a fool of more men than criticism.
>
> —Bob Edwards

The tragedy of Bob Edwards was that he failed to live up to his larger literary talents. In the pages of the *Eye Opener*, he penned brilliantly comedic tales about characters like Peter J. McGonigle, the fictional editor of the equally fictitious *Midnapore Gazette*—an irascible but oddly charming horse-thief and boozehound who was constantly being thrown in and out of jail; as well as the wonderfully inventive British remittence man, Albert Buzzard-Cholomondeley of Skookingham, England—whose letters home, trying to inveigle funds from his gullible parents, stand with the best of Stephen Leacock and Mark Twain.

Bob Edwards was an alcoholic and a binge drinker who went on week-long benders that often ended with Edwards checking himself into Calgary's Holy Cross Hospital to be treated for delirium tremens. It was his battle with the bottle that ultimately undermined Bob Edwards.

> One of the worst stings of defeat is the sympathy that goes with it.
>
> —Bob Edwards

In his final few years, Edwards tried his best to stay sober. He married, settled down and even ran for the provincial legislature—as an Independent, natch. But by then, Edwards's health was already failing. He attended only one session of government and made only one speech in the legislature.

Bob Edwards died on14 November 1922 and was buried in Calgary's Union Cemetery at the alleged age of fifty-eight. (There is a discrepancy between the date of birth Edwards had given and the dates inscribed at his grave.) His widow tucked a flask of whisky and a couple of copies of her late husband's newspapers into the headstone. And thus, Bob Edwards was laid to rest alongside his greatest strength and his greatest weakness.

A toast. A toast, I say! To Bob Edwards, muckracker, hellraiser, social crusader, and man-of-letters, in appreciation and admiration.

PREFACE

by James Martin

NO NICEY-NICE TALE of petticoats and butter-churns, *Eye Opener Bob* is a foot in the keister of bloodless history. It's a two-fisted tale of cheeky iconoclasm, bitter rivalry, human frailty.

But excitement ain't the half of it. In fact, *Eye Opener Bob* is downright essential.

Grant MacEwan recorded the histories no one else thought capital-i important, plucking from obscurity the mighty women and mighty men (to pinch his descriptors of choice) who shaped the Canadian West of the nineteenth and early twentieth centuries. It is through his sizable efforts—writing forty-eight books in sixty-four years, in addition to myriad other pursuits—that the names Nolan and Fulham, Jaques and Haultain, have a life beyond the boneyard.

Add Bob Edwards to that list. And how.

By the time of *Eye Opener Bob*'s publication in October 1957, Edwards had been pushing clouds for thirty-five years, his literary legacy reduced to yellowing newspapers haphazardly scattered in attics and garages across the continent. (Hugh Dempsey's groundbreaking anthologies, *The Best of Bob Edwards* and *The Wit & Wisdom of Bob Edwards*, would not appear until the mid-seventies.) As his original readership single-filed into the Great Unknown, a rapidly widening generation gap threatened to swallow Edwards whole. *Eye Opener Bob* bridged this chasm by educating neophytes and satisfying longtime converts. (My own first-edition copy of *Eye Opener Bob*, my grandfather's name carefully inked atop the fly-title, speaks to this double duty.) "BobMania" may be overstating the case, but MacEwan's tome reinstalled Edwards in the popular imagination. A series of CBC made-for-TV movies (1959–1964), the Dempsey books, at least two stage plays, Alberta Theatre Projects' annual Bob Edwards Luncheon . . . there but for the grace of *Eye Opener Bob* go not we.

None of which is to say it's a perfect book. MacEwan worked at a breakneck pace, his passion for "getting it down" often favouring vigour over rigour. Dates are occasionally flubbed, compelling threads left unexplored. (To be fair, MacEwan's task was greatly complicated by Edwards's truth-obscuring self-mythology and erratic publishing schedule, as well as the lack of complete collections of *Eye Openers*, *Free Lances*, *Breezes*, and Edwards's other literary endeavours.) Eschewing the temptation of revision, this volume treats *Eye Opener Bob* as a historical document, presenting herein a warts-and-all reproduction of the 1974 second edition. There are, however, some additions. Where applicable, I have annotated MacEwan's original text with footnotes stemming from my research for *Irresponsible Freaks, Highball Guzzlers & Unabashed Grafters: A Bob Edwards Chrestomathy* (the first collection of Edwards's writings in nearly thirty years, published in a handy companion volume by Brindle & Glass) and I have silently corrected a few dates and quotes. I humbly submit these additions in the hope of contributing, in some small way, to the appreciation and enjoyment of MacEwan's seminal history.

Viva Bob!

FOREWORD

AT A MEETING of the Men's Canadian Club of Calgary in 1954, this question was presented to the members: "Considering intelligence, originality, and public influence, whom would you name as Alberta's Prize Personality?" In the balloting which followed, Bob Edwards, founder, publisher and one-man staff of the *Calgary Eye Opener*, received the highest number of votes, followed in order by Rt. Hon. R. B. Bennett, Father Lacombe, Pat Burns, and Hon. Frank Oliver. A few weeks later, the same question was submitted to the Men's Canadian Club of Edmonton, and again Bob Edwards received the most votes; but this time, Edmonton's pioneer publisher, Hon. Frank Oliver, was second, and then Dr. H. M. Tory, Nellie McClung, and Pat Burns. After the Edmonton ballots were counted and the results announced, one venerable club member came forward to confess: "I had to vote for Bob Edwards, but, really, I think he was a bad egg."

To anyone familiar with Western story, neither the voting nor the confession will come as a surprise. For years, Bob Edwards was the West's most controversial character, and even after his death in 1922, the arguments about his qualities continued to rage. That he made his mistakes and rather many of them, nobody could deny; he drank too much whiskey, as he admitted readily; he wrote some editorial rubbish, and he recorded a few stories which should have been omitted from the columns of his famous paper.

But whatever sins may have been laid at his door, his heart was big; his mind was clear; and, altogether, he was a most fascinating part of early Alberta. One of the great misfortunes is that a man with his talent for creativeness did not devote himself to the writing of Canadian novels or something else which would have made a lasting contribution to Canada's living literature.

Evidently it never occurred to Bob Edwards that somebody might one day wish to write the story of his storm-beaten career, and he left nothing by way of personal records apart from what appeared in copies of the *Eye Opener*. To make matters worse for a person attempting his biography, not all issues of the paper have survived. Happily, however, many of the pioneer citizens have good memories.

Hence, the author desires to thank the scores of "Old Timers" who patiently shared their recollections of Bob Edwards; those who "dug up" odd copies of the *Eye Opener* which had been hidden away in old trunks; Bob Edwards's widow, Mrs. Kate McKeen; Leishman McNeill, who can find an answer to any question about early Calgary; and lastly, the *Calgary Herald* for permission to use its microfilm library.

Grant MacEwan, Calgary, 1957

CHAPTER ONE
The Early Years

"Cheer up! Happy New Year! All the good people don't die young. Lots of them live to a ripe old age and die poor."

(1 January 1910)[1]

"The path to success is paved with good intentions that were carried out."

(22 November 1919)

"Most of our tragedies look like comedies to the neighbours."

(*Summer Annual*, 1921)

AS MATERIAL FOR a success story of the conventional kind, the life of Bob Edwards, creator and editor of the famous *Eye Opener*, would be a poor and indefensible choice. Although this maverick of the Alberta country had some admirable qualities, he was no Puritan and nobody considered him as a shining example of virtue. His was a strange and stormy career. "Heaven and Hell really do exist," he insisted (18 December 1909); he had been in both, and his writings seemed to confirm it.

Taking stock of financial progress during his first twenty years as an editor in Western Canada, he noted that he began publishing with "cash on hand of $1.47," and twenty years later could show total liquid reserves of "sixty-seven cents and half a bottle of Scotch." (*Summer Annual*, 1922) If personal wealth was the measure, Bob Edwards was a failure. "If money talks," he commented, "all it ever said to me was 'goodbye.'" (21 February 1920) But during those years in which western people were reading his columns, he furnished a million dollars' worth of entertainment, and that was not all; while amusing the many and annoying the few, he exerted a public influence which probably surpassed that of any western editorial or political figure of his time.

Even at the peak of his career, not many people would recognize the name of Robert Chambers Edwards; but all true westerners knew "Bob Edwards" and most of them had strong views, good or bad, concerning the man. He was loved by the fortunate ones who knew him well, enjoyed by thousands who read his humour and recognized traits of genius, and feared and hated by any who did not care to face the truth. That was Bob Edwards, archenemy of all that was spurious and snobbish, one of Alberta's outstanding personalities.

[1] Unless otherwise specified, in-text date citations refer to the *Eye Opener.*

Yes, only a few people knew him well enough to understand the thinking which made him the great enigma of his time. On the surface a strange complex of contradictions, he seemed as mixed up as second-hand barbed wire. Although fearless eloquence flowed from his pen, he was a quiet and retiring fellow; he drank heavily at times but supported temperance, as his famous editorials prior to the provincial plebiscite of 1915 would show; his writings, on occasion, were those of a low-brow and roughneck; but the real Bob Edwards was a humanitarian, a cultured scholar, a lover of the theatre, a musical critic, and a student of classical literature. He castigated politicians, yet entered actively into politics; and though criticizing many churchmen of his time, there was no reason to conclude that Bob Edwards did not possess his own staunch brand of religious faith.

Hypocrites, "stuffed shirts," and phony figures in public life inspired his sarcasm. Any society placing good clothes ahead of good ideas "is founded on humbug." No social eccentric can completely escape disapproval; and almost constantly somebody was after him. Ministers preached sermons of condemnation; for a while the railroad company refused to allow the *Eye Opener* to be sold on its trains; and there were times when even the mails were denied him for his paper. And though threatened with libel suits, only once was he actually involved in court action, and that time he was the plaintiff rather than defendant.[2] Once he was challenged to fight a pistol duel "in the foothills, back of Millarville racetrack," but he declined acceptance, explaining that "In the present state of Western Canada, a frequently-sober editor can do more good than a permanently-dead hero." But happily, his troubles didn't weigh very heavily upon him, especially when convinced he was in the right.

He was Bob Edwards of Alberta, and there was nobody like him. Had he lived longer, consumed less whiskey, and possessed more ambition for personal advancement and fame, he might have shared immortal honours with the like of Mark Twain.

As might have been expected, the *Eye Opener* was no less unusual among newspapers than Bob Edwards among men. Publishing fortunes rose and fell, but like the Jerusalem-bound pilgrims who reached their destination by taking two steps forward and one backward, the *Eye Opener* achieved the largest circulation of papers published west of Winnipeg. Coming out "semi-occasionally," it broke all the accepted rules of

[2] MacEwan alludes to the McGillicuddy trial of 1908 (see Chapter 10), which—if his long-lasting vendetta is any indication—undoubtedly shook Edwards to his core. But it wasn't his only trip to the courthouse. *The Winnipeg Free Press* (31 March 1910) reported that Edwards "was committed for trial on a charge of assisting in the making, publication and distributing of obscene literature" and released on $1,000 bail. (It's worth noting that the charges came within mere weeks of his relocation to Winnipeg—see Chapter 11.) Whether due to the charges being dropped, or the short-lived nature of his Winnipeg sojourn, there is no evidence that the case ever went to trial. Two years later, E. P. Davis charged Edwards with criminal libel. These charges were dropped when Edwards published an apology (*Calgary Herald*, 12 October 1912). See *Irresponsible Freaks, etc.* for details of this case.

journalism and should have gone down to ruin. When the "Great Moral Weekly" failed to appear, a subsequent issue might carry the editor's unblushing explanation that his old enemy, booze, had overtaken him, and readers were ready to forgive.

At one stage, Edwards did forsake Calgary with the idea of publishing in Eastern Canada, but after a year he returned to find the local market for his paper more eager than ever. Perhaps he was right when he concluded that one reason for *Eye Opener* survival was that, "We have not bored our readers with regularity."

The paper's journalistic status was strange to the point of appearing ridiculous. It had no subscription list, no printing plant, and according to critics, not much conscience. It classified as a newspaper, yet carried little or no news. A "Journalistic Hermaphrodite," was what fellow editor Dan McGillicuddy called it,[3] while a more scholarly judgment was: "A daring adventure in satire."

But call it what they would, most western papers envied its popularity and its influence. When an election was in the offing, the power of the *Eye Opener* was coveted and sought by all political groups. R. B. Bennett blamed the *Calgary Eye Opener* influence for his defeat at the polls in 1905,[4] and one of Calgary's mayors admitted to friends that he could not be re-elected because Bob Edwards was opposed to him.

Skill in blending sense and nonsense explained much of the editor's appeal. To be sensible all the time is to be dull, he reasoned, and people across the West needed entertainment. Each time there was an epistle from Remittance Man Bertie Buzzard-Cholomondeley or a story about the editor's other fabulous brainchild, Peter McGonigle of Midnapore, the *Eye Opener* became Western Canada's top entertainment; and where moral objection did not forbid, the paper was passed from one frontier home to another so that neighbours might share the antics of an *Eye Opener* hero. Oh yes, there were homes in which the freewheeling *Eye Opener* was not allowed—lots of them; also, there were folk who "wouldn't be seen" reading the *Eye Opener* in public, but who sought opportunity to study its crisp stories behind closed doors.

When, from the *Eye Opener*'s "Society Column," it was reported that "J. P. Q——, the local evangelist who fell into an open sewer and broke his flask, has fully recovered and is now able to be about,"[5] (8 April 1916) people on the street enquired of each other: "Who is this J. P. Q.?" And when it was noted that "Pete Johnson, who is held for cutting his wife's throat, is not P. T. Johnson, the well-known haberdasher

[3] This is from McGillicuddy's "Nemesis" letter. See Chapter 10.

[4] Bennett harboured ill feelings about Edwards's constant abuse—James H. Gray says as much in *R. B. Bennett: The Calgary Years* (Toronto: University of Toronto Press, 1991)—but there's no official record of him crediting his early defeat to Edwards.

[5] In fact, Bob explicitly named "John P. Quigley."

whose spring stock is now on view,"[6] (30 March 1918) the ordinary society page editors could not compete for reader interest, and other haberdashers had to watch their trade going to Johnston.

In his makeup there was much of the "rolling stone," and Calgary was the only place that succeeded in holding him for more than a few years after he reached maturity. Only in his last five years did he have the restraining influence of a wife, and hence for most of his life he was free to move when he felt so inclined. He lived for spells in Scotland, England, France, the United States, and various parts of Canada; but after returning from the East in 1911, he announced that Alberta would be "Home" until he was "getting his mail in Heaven."

He was born in Edinburgh on 12 September 1864,[7] the son of Alexander Mackenzie Edwards and wife Mary Chambers. When Bob was only weeks old his mother died; and in 1868, while on a world cruise, his father died.[8] The responsibility of rearing the infant Bob and brother Jack was assumed by maiden aunts, strict disciplinarians, ardent Sabbatarians, and pious rooters for the Ten Commandments. Young Bob was a robust youth with round face, sparkling black eyes, and a look of cherubic innocence which disguised an inherent predisposition to mischief.

And yet some people wonder why the paper doesn't come out more regularly.

In the home, household economy was both a necessity and a virtue and porridge was standard fare. The "parritch" was made at night and stirred with a professional touch at just the right times. It was at the peak of its goodness at the breakfast hour, and there was only a trace of deterioration by noonday. At any time it was a "first class poultice for the inside of a human stomach." Now and then it was varied slightly: neep brose was made from oatmeal cooked in turnip water;

[6] Edwards further clarified that the Johnson haberdashery was located on First Avenue West.

[7] It seems Bob flattered himself with a spot of self-reinvention. He may have claimed the above date as his birthday, but his birth certificate lists 17 September 1860.

[8] The *Eye Opener* of 25 November 1922 claimed that Alexander Edwards died, and was buried, in New Zealand.

and Atoll brose, fit for kings but not for bairns, contained oatmeal, water, honey, and whiskey.

Notwithstanding the colossal misfortune of being left fatherless and motherless, Bob Edwards secured a good education in the best Scottish tradition. He attended Clifton Bank Private School at St. Andrews and learned to play golf; Royal High School at Edinburgh and learned to fight; and ultimately, Glasgow University,[9] where students of his generation fared sumptuously on the classics. Of the formal education prescribed for him at school and university, he was quite critical. Even in his youth it was not in his nature to accept anything that could not stand against his reasoning. He believed students should receive more instruction which would fit them for day-to-day living. In a practical sense, he was leaving school "a veritable ignoramus." "True," he said, "nobody could fool us on Horace and Virgil and we could conjugate the Greek verb Tupto with our hands tied behind our backs, but outside of that we knew practically nothing." At the University, "All the students had to do was . . . sit out dreary lectures on Moral Philosophy, Logic, Metaphysics[10] . . . which were deemed of vital importance by frowsy professors . . . No pretense at useful instruction." (27 January 1917)

However Bob Edwards appeared in later years, there was very little evidence of scholarly qualities until he began to mature. He had time aplenty for soccer and boxing and student pranks. When the professor couldn't find his spectacles, or when the pages of his textbook were glued together at a crucial point, angry glances were cast toward Bob Edwards. Conversation and reading were his greatest sources of satisfaction, and rather often he was still reading when he should have been attending classes. During those university years Sir Walter Scott was his literary idol; but gradually his affection shifted to Robert Burns, and the influence of Scotland's beloved bard became increasingly clear in Edwards's life.

Extramural interests and a show of indifference, however, did not prevent the young fellow from distinguishing himself at University and he emerged as a gold medallist from Glasgow's proud seat of higher learning. Said Glasgow teachers, "A young rebel, with traits of literary genius."

The quest for adventure took him to Paris, Berlin, and Rome; and then he was ready to go to work. But work at what? There was a family tradition for publishing, and the young man was faintly interested. His mother's father, Dr. Robert Chambers, had been a founder of the Scottish publishing house of W. and R. Chambers, while another relative was the Scottish artist, Sir Joseph Noel Paton. If

[9] Edwards's academic history is taken from the posthumous *Eye Opener* of 25 November 1922.
[10] Tellingly, MacEwan spares the academy additional insult by omitting the phrase "and other rot."

his mother "had been a gentleman," Bob Edwards, so he himself said, "would have been in the publishing business."

Most of all, this stoutly constructed young Scot with built-in determination wanted to do things for himself. His first business venture was a gossipy newspaper called *The Traveller*,[11] published at Boulogne, France, mainly for the entertainment of wealthy tourists to the Riviera. It was popular enough, and its editor was a frequent visitor on the boulevards of Nice and Monte Carlo where education for a young man assumed an entirely new form. He had his fun on the Riviera, but the experiences there made him see the shallowness of high society. Gorgeous hats on empty heads made him realize that much of society is founded on false values and humbug. Madam Holidayer's gay gown and expensive ostrich plume, bought with money she did nothing to earn, gave her no right to lord it over other women who were mentally and morally her equal. What he saw at those stylish resorts left him rather disgusted and cynical.

The paper was short-lived,[12] and back in Scotland Bob Edwards worked briefly with Sir James Marwick, city clerk in Glasgow. It was a time when no adventuresome young Britisher was overlooking the alleged glories of life in a Texas stock saddle. In neither education nor experience did Bob Edwards have the slightest of qualifications for the role of rancher, but he and brother Jack resolved to find out for themselves. It was 1892, and the boys set out for Texas "to ranch and be away from relations."

They went to Wyoming instead of Texas, and if they were looking for excitement, the choice at that particular time was good. They arrived at Cheyenne, in the southeast corner of the State, just after the Johnson County Range War of 1892, while forty-four of those who led the offensive were still in jail and awaiting trial. Cheyenne, with half-hearted law enforcement, was a wild city at the best of times, and it offered a rude initiation for young Scots whose knowledge of Plato's *Republic* far exceeded that of the cattle frontier. Rustling, conducted by organized bands, had reached its peak on the Wyoming ranges and cattlemen concluded they must take the law in their own hands. There were quiet hangings now and then, but they did not stop the cattle thieving. Early in 1892 cattlemen met at Cheyenne to organize reprisals; and in the spring a special train carried cowboys, horses, and guns from

[11] This period of Edwards's life is hazy. By his own admission (e.g., *Eye Opener* 9 January 1904), Edwards lived in France as a young man. According to the first posthumous issue of the *Eye Opener*, he published a Riviera tourist rag titled *The Channel*. [For excerpts from *The Channel*, originally published in 1881, consult *Irresponsible Freaks, etc.*] But this *Traveller* business is a bit of a mystery; the title is oft cited in reference to Edwards, but the source appears to have been *Eye Opener Bob*. It's unclear where MacEwan found this information. There was, however, an English newspaper called *The Traveller* published in Milan in 1879. The date fits an Edwards timeline, and the location isn't much of a stretch—but the only extant copy is held by the Bibliothèque nationale de France, which is loath to grant access to the fragile volume.

[12] The British Library holds issues of *The Channel* for the period June 1881 to October 1882.

Cheyenne to Casper in the central part of the state. From the latter point, the armed party rode north into Johnson County where rustling was known to be serious. On the way a couple of alleged rustlers were killed and another suspect escaped capture, arousing alarm locally about the impending "invasion" of cattlemen. Rustlers and settlers banded together to resist, and a major war was in prospect when military troops were called out to halt the "invaders." Cattlemen were arrested and taken back to Cheyenne. At midsummer they were released on bail to await trial, but Cheyenne sympathy was all on their side and the authorities found it difficult to find an acceptable trial jury. Finally the charges were dismissed, and Cheyenne, including the newcomers from Scotland, celebrated for days.

The Edwards brothers hired with a rancher on Crazy Woman Creek; but Bob admitted that his cowboy experience did not go beyond the Cheyenne celebrations, and he was instructed to help the cook. Later, however, both boys were riding the Wyoming range and liking the life. The free life in the saddle inspired eager enthusiasm in the young cowboys, until Bob witnessed the lynching of a suspected cattle rustler. It was all so revolting that Bob Edwards quit that part and went to Iowa. At Sioux City he wasted some time and some savings, and then accepted a job with Aberdonian Alec Mitchell on a mixed farm four miles east of the town of Spencer in Clay County.

Corn Belt farming lacked the glamour of the cattle country and hours were long—5:00 AM to 11:00 PM. He was working about fourteen hours a day and then doing four hours of chores, which were not considered work, after that. He didn't rise with the birds—he "got up early enough to awaken them." Those never-ending chores he could not forget; the memory of them brought forth sympathy for anyone who rated as a "hired man," and dispelled any illusions he might have had about the grandeur of farm life. Years later (19 April 1919) he wrote:

> It is all bosh to suppose that living close to nature ennobles a man's thoughts and imparts a serenity of mind. One may wax poetic and slushy when paying a spasmodic visit into the country where the scenery happens to be striking but the farmer himself does not give a damn for scenery. His mind is engrossed in the drudgery of his daily life which is composed of an endless chain of chores . . . The farmer cannot go anywhere "until the chores are done," and he always has to "get back to do the chores." A farmer on his death bed hastens his end by worrying about the chores and wondering if they will be attended to properly when he is gone. Chores are the great obsession on a farm.

> At Ponoka [Mental Hospital] they have a fake barn with dummy horses, cows and pigs, where insane homesteaders and crazy farmers have their hobby humored. They always feel better after pitching three or four tons of hay to a wooden horse. The thing that struck us as most extraordinary in the farming game was that chores were not considered work at all, only a side line, so to speak. The real hard work was supposed to be done between morning and evening chores. Feeding and watering horses, milking a lot of cows and chopping up a cord or two of wood, hauling water to the house, and chores of a like nature were not looked upon as work at all. . . . By the way, were you ever a hired man on a farm? Morning and evening chores and one loud call for thee.

After the Iowa harvest was off and Bob Edwards was growing tired of his greedy farmer employer, he wrote to his brother Jack, who had remained in Wyoming, to come and buy the farm. "Out he came," wrote Bob (29 July 1922) "and bought up the whole bloody outfit, lock, stock and barrel. He even kept the housekeeper who was not bad looking at all." The deal was completed without disclosing a relationship between the purchaser and the hired man, and Bob had the pleasure of personally booting the former owner off the farm.

But rather soon Bob was leaving the farm too, and never again was he on good terms with mules. It was haying time and Bob was driving the little mule on the rake. Having finished raking after dark one night "between 10 and 11 as usual," he put the mule in the barn, expecting the animal to go right to its stall without needless direction because the mule knew its way around that farm better than the human residents. Well, it seems the old milk cow had been sick that day and left her supper in the manger and the mule went to the cow's stall instead of its own. "Later, in the darkness," Bob wrote, "I came with milk bucket in hand and entered the stall and started to milk the animal standing there. Three hours afterward I recovered consciousness and my farming days were over."

Bob Edwards had been thinking about Canada. Now he would see what it had to offer.

CHAPTER TWO
Sixteenth Siding

"Some people might as well be crazy for all the sense they have."

(11 May 1918)

"The things that come to the man who waits are seldom the things he waited for."

(27 January 1912)

"Most people who are old enough to know better often wish they were young enough not to."

(20 April 1912)

"SO THIS IS WINNIPEG," Bob Edwards murmured as he stepped off the train from the south after two days of travel; "I can tell it's not Paris."[1]

More than at any time in his life, he was alone. In Denver or Cheyenne he could find people he knew; but in Winnipeg and the vast new land beyond, there was nobody whose name he could even recognize. But why dwell on thoughts which could foster loneliness? He seized his grip and strode boldly onto Main Street, not knowing where it would take him.

The personality of Winnipeg was quickly evident. Here was a robust frontier city through which scores of land-seeking immigrants were passing daily. The population was 35,000, predominantly male, but with enough women to make family clotheslines fairly commonplace and ensure a good battle between liquor interests and the Women's Christian Temperance Union. Half-breeds and Indians leaned heavily against store fronts, oxen on the streets outnumbered horses, and one of the main topics of conversation was typhoid fever. Winnipeg was getting some modern notions, however. Parts of Portage Avenue and Main Street were block-paved to offer protection from the putty-like gumbo; and, just two years before, electric streetcars had been introduced to supplant the old horse-cars.

Even in the motley Main Street crowds through which Bob Edwards made his way, he was not inconspicuous. Although his total assets consisted of a copy of the Kilmarnock Edition of Burns's poems, the contents of his small grip and thirty-five dollars, he looked and walked more like a St. Paul banker than a homestead-hunter.

[1] Here, and elsewhere, MacEwan seems to indulge in some proto-New Journalism, ascribing speculative inner monologue to Edwards.

His clothes were neat and tailored to fit his five-foot-seven-inch frame; well-shined shoes betrayed him as a stranger to Red River mud, and a stiff felt hat with a Glasgow trademark topped everything off like tailfeathers on a peacock. Winnipeggers turned for a second glance as he walked by with all the boldness that loose planks in the sidewalk would allow. Turning in at the Queen's Hotel, he registered, noted that this, the twelfth day of September, 1894, was his thirtieth birthday,[2] and enquired, "Where's the bar?"

Nobody knew better than this well-dressed young man that he could not live long in idleness. The choice was between finding employment in the city and pushing on into the country offering farm work and homesteads. At the office of the *Manitoba Free Press* he was told, "No help wanted;" and from the *Winnipeg Tribune* he heard the same. The only work available seemed to be in railroad construction, and his brother's parting words when leaving Iowa came back to him: "If the country looks good, I'll join you and we'll get homesteads."

At the bar of the Queen's Hotel, Bob Edwards met up with a rollicking cattleman from the far west, a narrow-hipped, sharp-featured, weather-beaten cowboy who could talk, drink or fight with the best of them. His name was Stimson—Fred Stimson—and he was manager of the big ranching spread known as Bar U, west of High River. After listening to tales about cattle drives and round-ups, Bob Edwards sought Stimson's advice.

"Where should I go to find the best homestead land?" was his question.

"You'd like High River," Stimson told him in a voice that could be heard across Main Street. "After you lived there," he went on, "you wouldn't be satisfied in the Garden of Eden. But that country's for ranching and we don't want any more sodbusters with their damned barbed wire and ploughs in there. Tell you what—if you want to see good farmland, go along the new railroad between Calgary and Edmonton. Trains have been operating only three years, but that's the place for homesteading. Stuff grows so fast, well, you gotta jump out of the way when you put seed in the ground. A fellow at Red Deer didn't jump fast enough and he got hooked on a corn stalk—would've starved up where he was if the neighbours hadn't come and cut him down. If I were you, I'd go all the way to Edmonton and look it over."

This man Stimson was an extravagant talker, quite obviously, but he was a good companion and seemed to know the country. And so, before many days, Bob Edwards was westbound by CPR. At Calgary his remaining money was in one-dollar bills, and not enough of them to pay for a train fare all the way to Edmonton.

[2] Again, if his birth certificate is to be believed, 12 September 1894 was actually five days shy of Bob's thirty-fourth birthday.

"How far can I travel for $3.25?" he asked the ticket agent at Calgary.

The man behind the counter studied his schedule and replied, "Sixteenth Siding."

"All right, a single to Sixteenth Siding. And if you have any tips about how a man without money can eat up there, you might let me have them."

Travelling north from Calgary, Bob Edwards was counting sidings. It helped to pass the time and it helped forget an absence of food in the face of mounting hunger. But the train conductor told him where to get off and wished him luck. From the station platform it was difficult for a newcomer to see either beauty or challenge in this place. The town was split by the railroad tracks, with most of the business section confined to a couple of street blocks on the west side. There were two stores and one butcher shop, but the little town had three hotels: Walker House, Queen's, and Royal, and each had a flourishing bar.

Any way one looked at it, Sixteenth Siding was a shabby shack-town. The only paint about the place was on the outdoor toilet at the rear of West's General Store. The three hotels were constructed like oversize egg-crates and a livery stable was the busiest place on the street. To a young fellow with a violent appetite and no money, nothing in sight was inviting. He took a short walk to get his bearings, and just as the sun was setting stopped at the livery stable to enquire about jobs.

Bill Eggleston, with homespun face and muscles like a buffalo bull, was the stable operator. His reply about work wasn't encouraging: "Farmers aren't hiring any men just now." But somehow the liveryman sensed this stranger's need and added in a drawl: "I'm cooking supper soon's I throw down some hay. Might as well hang that New York hat on a harness-peg and eat with me." Bob didn't have to be coaxed. Never before—while sober, at least—had he gone so long without food.

Dining in the renovated box stall Eggleston called his "house," not even the penetrating odour of harness oil and sweating horses could lessen the enjoyment of the simple fare. As they consumed beans, bread, and tea, Bob learned more about Sixteenth Siding. It had good farmland about it. Bill Eggleston was sure of that. It would be a great city some day and its real name was Wetaskiwin, called after the nearby Hills of Peace, where Crees and Blackfeet had fought one of their last battles and then got together to smoke a pipeful of kinnikinnick and seal a truce. We-tusk-awin, the Indians called those hills.

Then Bob heard about the fire which had destroyed the one building in which every Wetaskiwin citizen would have had pride. "If you had been here a few days ago, you'd have seen the damnedest fire." It was the new school. Almost completed at a cost of $1,900, it was a total loss. Now, the liveryman explained, townsmen were organizing to rebuild, hoping the new structure would be ready for use before Christmas.

"By the way," Eggleston asked, "you any good at pounding nails?"

Bob thought a moment, recollecting that he hadn't driven a dozen nails in his life; but he recognized the point of the question and answered, "Yes." After a good meal like that, he felt that he could pound anything—even to a John L. Sullivan. Immediately Eggleston proposed that his guest get a job rebuilding the school. "If you promise not to smoke or light matches, you can shake down in my hay for a night or two. But, by golly, those'll be the best clothes that ever hung in my hayloft."

And so Bill Eggleston, liveryman and horse dealer, was Bob Edwards's first friend in the West; and the barn, half full of partly tamed broncos which the horseman had herded in from Montana for sale to homesteaders, was his first residence.

On Bob's second day at Wetaskiwin, Indians from the nearby reservation came to town to spend treaty money; and the two storekeepers did everything possible to make it easy for them. It was as though the Indians from Hobbema had timed their celebration as a welcome to the newcomer. At once the tempo of the town quickened. The tribesmen making camp beside the railroad didn't try to hide their Indian appetites; and the two storekeepers, who had most to gain, presented them with a fifteen-dollar steer bought from a homesteader. While Bob Edwards watched in silence, the steer was shot, bled, and dressed, and the Indians prepared for a feast to be followed by a powwow on the street at night. It was an occasion to remember, as braves, bloated with beef and a little rum, shrieked and danced around their fire at the centre of town until after midnight. For the merchants, the steer worth a cent and a half a pound by values of that year was an excellent investment; and the Indians remained until their treaty money, and simultaneously, their welcome, were exhausted.

Wetaskiwin, c. 1900. The building on the left is the Walker House Hotel.

When the Indians departed, life at Wetaskiwin returned to normal. Able to earn a dollar a day on the school building, Bob Edwards went to live at Jerry Boyce's Walker House Hotel—named for Col. James Walker of Calgary who helped finance it. Edwards and the hotel-keeper were attracted to each other at once. To help pay for his room, Bob, in off hours, would work behind the bar or elsewhere; and, as Jerry Boyce soon discovered, the Bob Edwards personality drew business to his hotel and bar. So great was the business advantage that Boyce began to plan another hotel at Wetaskiwin—one which he would call the Driard.

The school was finished in December; but Edwards had a place at the hotel for the winter, and by springtime he knew everybody within a day's drive. He wrote to his brother to sell out in Iowa and come to Wetaskiwin. By midsummer Jack Edwards was there, looking for a homestead location. But before the farming idea was carried out, Jack met up with W. A. Stoughton, an Englishman starting a cattle ranch just west of Bittern Lake. Stoughton wanted an active partner; and Jack Edwards, who knew everything about livestock, was his man.

The ranching enterprise flourished, and during the first year, when Bob wasn't living and working with Jerry, he was at the ranch. The ranch life was not all work; with a number of young bachelors farming and ranching in that Bittern Lake area, there were some lively parties. It was in the morning after one of these gay affairs that Jack Edwards became seriously ill. Story had it that in taking his morning medicine he got the "wrong bottle," with fatal results. He lived only a short time.

Carefree and reckless as Bob Edwards had been, the tragedy of Jack's death made him conscious of his own failure. For the first time during his stay at Wetaskiwin, helping behind Jerry Boyce's bar was not good enough. He considered going back to Scotland, but the idea was abandoned as quickly as it was conceived. At any rate he was determined to do something useful. He had seen enough easy living with no goal. He admitted to Jerry that he had been squandering time but would do better. "A man who acknowledges that he is a chump has begun to acquire wisdom." (*Summer Annual*, 1923) The idea of a weekly newspaper struck him. Jerry Boyce, not knowing what was involved, was skeptical. But gripped with a sense of serious determination, Bob went to Strathcona and made an arrangement with the *Plaindealer* Printing Office to print the paper he proposed to call "The Wetaskiwin Bottling Works" because it was sure to be a "corker." Before any official launching on the rough sea of journalism, the editor was persuaded against using that ribald name; and on 26 March 1897, his four-page paper appeared with the more conventional name of *Wetaskiwin Free Lance*. It was the first paper published between Calgary and Edmonton, and if the name finally adopted was conventional, nothing else about the paper was that way.

By this time, according to the editor, Wetaskiwin had a population of "287 souls plus three total abstainers." (23 October 1902) During the next year there was no net increase, because the number of people leaving to seek fortune in the Klondike gold fields just equalled the incoming settlers. But the prospect of a local paper was well received by all except the few who looked with suspicion upon Bob Edwards.

The first *Free Lance* office, if such it could be called, consisted of a table and chair and a corner of the waiting room in Bill Eggleston's livery stable. There the homesteaders asked if they might borrow a copy of the paper, promising to subscribe as soon as they sold some eggs.

After a few months, when the bankrupt meat merchant vacated his shop, Bob Edwards moved in. The butcher's sign remained over the door, however, and the editor wrote his "stuff" while sitting at the counter on which the former occupant, L. T. Miquelon, chopped his meat.

"We take this opportunity," the editor wrote, "of announcing that the beautiful painting of a bull's head over our new office does not signify that it is still a meat market. It was once, but not now. People wandering through our portals in search of pork chops will have to go empty away. Our patience is well nigh exhausted by children coming in and rapping on the counter with a dime, while we are dashing off an editorial on CPR atrocities, and calling for ten cents worth of liver." (6 May 1898)

Wetaskiwin, c. 1900. Miquelon's Meat Market is the one-storey building in the centre.

From the very beginning, the "Local News" as reported in the *Free Lance* had a sardonic twist, and few local personalities and institutions escaped the editor's treatment. In acknowledging receipt of a pass from the railroad company, he offered some nice compliments, saying the "service of the CPR is undoubtedly the most perfect in the whole of the civilized world. Trains run like clockwork at a phenomenal rate of speed." (27 January 1898) But in the same column was another item: "Lots of trains—all late." And for the district's would-be statesman with more ambition for himself than the community:

> Mr. S——, our talented fellow townsman should be elected to the onerous office of dog-catcher. It is only fitting that all these years of

unremitting toil in the political arena should culminate in Mr. S——'s appointment to this high office and we feel sure he is eminently fitted for the place. That Mr. S—— may pass down through the vista of life with joy and happiness and fulfil his solemn trust as dog-catcher with satisfaction to himself and the dogs is the earnest wish of the *Free Lance.* (27 January 1898)

Of course, Charlie Klob's mules furnished cause for a journalistic kick now and then, because Bob Edwards hated mules and "couldn't forgive a jackass for fathering them." And George Turner's new billy goat, "arriving on Monday's train from Calgary," made homestead-shaking news:

> It is a thoroughbred, by Jupiter and out of Sight, and winner of many prizes . . . Mr. Turner has a herd of nannies on his ranch and calculates on going into the manufacture of Swiss cheese . . .
>
> There will be an ideal Alpine scene from now on out at Little Pipestone, with Mr. Turner roaming on the mountains, alpenstock in hand, at the head of his goats, leaping from crag to crag and yodelling all day long. (27 January 1898)

Before long the *Wetaskiwin Free Lance* was winning smiles and frowns from as far as Edmonton and Calgary. "Who is this fellow Edwards?" folk were asking. The *Calgary Herald* made the mistake of publicizing one exchange item from the *Free Lance* too soon. The story was about an earthenware jar, globular in form and Etruscan in style, which a Wetaskiwin farmer was reported to have discovered when digging a well. It was an archaeological curiosity, most certainly, and was to be sent to the Smithsonian Museum for examination. Most astonishing of all was the inscription on the rim around the top—obviously in an ancient language: "Iti sapo tandab igone." The report stated, "No one in Wetaskiwin can decipher it."

Well, according to Bob Edwards's account of the events, the *Herald* editor not only gave the story front-page prominence but wrote an editorial showing how these western prairies must have been peopled by a strange race of Latin origin.[3] That was really a shocker for the scientists, who had never considered such a theory. The newsmen could hardly contain themselves in their enthusiasm until Paddy Nolan, who knew all about Latin, was invited to the newspaper office to study the inscription.

[3] This story doesn't appear in any extant copies of the *Herald* from that period, or in the *Eye Opener*, suggesting that Edwards's "account of the events," whenever this appeared, may have been apocryphal.

Lawyer Nolan pondered unsuccessfully until the office workers got to speculating about what sort of strange bird this man Edwards was. Paddy Nolan got an inspiration, looked again at the inscription, and decoded it to read simply: "It is a pot and a big one." Then, according to Bob Edwards, "The whole staff went on a bat."

But the journalistic struggle was not an easy one; and noting that Frank Oliver was obliged to reorganize his *Edmonton Bulletin*, Edwards wished him luck, adding: "If Mr. Oliver has as much fun with his 'company' as we are having with ours, he'll wish he had died in infancy." (19 August 1898) Most settlers clamoured to read the *Free Lance* but there were those inevitable folk who bruised easily. And then there was the problem of financing. Things improved somewhat when Pioneer Druggist J. H. Walker, offering "the best horse medicine for cure of coughs, heaves, and thick and broken wind," accepted the role of business manager with the *Free Lance*. Still, it was difficult to meet printing and other expenses. A homesteader would exchange a bag of potatoes, or a dressed hen with a long life of egg-production behind her, for a year's subscription; but an editor needed some cash. When a subscriber did come to the office prepared to part with a dollar, he expected to be taken to the hotel at once, where the entire price of a year's subscription would be spent at the bar.

Under the circumstances, an editor could be pardoned for taking unusual measures to keep expenses at a minimum. The butcher whose shop Bob Edwards inherited for use as a combination residence and office providentially left a chair and a pot-bellied heater, but getting winter fuel for the stove remained a problem. It so happened that Constable Ketchen of the North West Mounted Police had his barracks next door, and all his wood was provided by the government and sawed to proper stove-lengths by prisoners. On the other side was an Englishman named Keble, who bought and sawed his own wood. On dark nights, when the town was asleep, "also Ketchen and Keble," fuel was purloined for the editor's premises. Neither of the neighbours sensed depredations until spring, when the editor acknowledged his gratitude:

> Now that winter has come to a close we beg to thank the various owners of woodpiles in the vicinity of our office for all the wood we have stolen. Although not caught on any occasion, we consider it our duty to express grateful appreciation. It was all right. The only improvement we can suggest for next winter is that Mr. Ketchen get his wood cut a little shorter and Mr. Keble, his a trifle longer.

Years later, when reminded of his wood rustling, Bob Edwards explained:

> Ketchen the Mountie, not having to saw his own wood, was easily placated. All we had to do in his case was to set 'em up a few times down at the hotel. Keble, on the other hand, who had to saw his own wood and didn't drink, was rather inclined to grumble at first, but beyond remarking that he thought it damned cheek on our part, he soon got over it. (*Summer Annual*, 1922)

To some people Bob Edwards was still "that awful man," but life at Wetaskiwin, with an occasional trip to Calgary, suited him pretty well. Wetaskiwin could keep him occupied and that was important. He promoted a horse race and almost lost his shirt; he judged a school debate and awarded the decision to the best debater rather than the popular side; and now and then he attended parties at which people danced until close to sun-up. Being about the worst dancer in the community, however, he was inclined to seek other pastimes and sometimes they led to mischief. On one of those party nights at Heric's Hall, two local mothers took the wrong babies home after the dance; and however innocent the editor may have been, he was unable to clear himself of suspicion.

By some strange circumstance, the clothing on the two tots, who had been packed away in a back room to sleep while mothers danced, was changed; and when the evening program was over, unsuspecting mothers, identifying their sleeping cherubs by clothing alone, went home with the wrong ones. With proper identification after the drives home, there was great consternation until next day. When the wee ones were sorted out, Bob admitted nothing, but saw a moral, nevertheless: "Clothes are deceivers and mothers and bachelors should know it."

"Why is the blame for these little local tragedies always directed at me?" he asked Jerry Boyce; and Jerry's reply was: "Because you're usually guilty."

Folk thought they understood him. They knew he had been drunk more than once and that he was unorthodox in his thinking and writing. Women who met for a mid-week meeting at the church reached agreement that he had his points though the town would be better without him. His acts of charity he managed to keep hidden, except now and then when exposure was accidental. On one of these occasions he was taking a Sunday afternoon walk. Unlike the Cheyenne he had known, Wetaskiwin didn't offer much else to do during that part of the week. But he liked walking. Before going far this day, he heard a boy crying. To investigate, he turned off the trail where a mound of fresh clay showed that somebody had been digging a well. There, beside the hole and leaning precariously over it, was a tousle-headed six-year-old, sobbing so bitterly that he couldn't explain the reason for his grief. A glance into the dry hole, with the digger's windlass and rope over it, showed Bob Edwards the reason for the lad's distress—there at the bottom, twenty feet below, was a small kitten sitting frightened and helpless.

Either the wee cat had fallen in or had been thrown in. But how it happened didn't really matter at this point; the important thing was that two creatures were in trouble—the boy at the top and the cat at the bottom. It would have been easy for an adult on a Sunday afternoon stroll to say, "It's too bad, little man, but I guess you've lost your cat," and walk on. But it was not in Bob Edwards to do that. He wanted to sob too, or do something about a rescue.

There were anxious pleadings in the boy's watery eyes; and without considering the hazards in an uncribbed well, Bob removed his coat and placed his beautiful derby hat beside it, made the rope secure on the windlass shaft, gripped the rope and slid to the bottom. That much was easy and the kitten was quite willing to be picked up and perched on human shoulders. Now, however, was the problem of getting out. A twenty-foot rope-climb is all right for those accustomed to such exercise, but for a man who makes his living with a pencil it can be a severe test. Anyway, the crying stopped as the boy gazed more hopefully. Bob shouted at him to keep back from the edge in case he too might fall in. Then he began to climb. Bob Edwards was muscular and fairly athletic, but this was something he had never done and he was awkward about it. He drew himself up a few feet without difficulty and a few more feet with difficulty. Halfway up he was obliged to slide back and rest before another attempt. The kitten clung tenaciously, with claws anchored in shirt and flesh, and the boy stared with urgent hope. After resting a few moments, Bob studied the best way of gripping the rope between his legs, spit on his blistered hands, and started again. This time his head and shoulders reached the ground level, but he was exhausted and just couldn't make the remaining two or three feet to the shaft of the windlass. But before he slid back, the anxious boy reached from his place at the edge of the hole to grab his precious cat from Bob's shoulders. The cat was saved and the boy's red eyes laughed; Bob laughed too, but he was still down the well.

No use becoming excited, Bob told himself; might as well take it easy and hope for success next time. After a good rest mingled with some fears, he tried again, but with even less success than on the previous try. Now, he realized, the boy's face was missing from the well top; and Bob surmised what had happened: with his kitten in his arms the boy had run for home.

Naturally one would suppose that the little fellow would tell his father about a man in the well, and very soon somebody would come to the rescue. But the boy, for reasons best known to himself, said nothing. Perhaps he wasn't supposed to be at the well on Sunday and considered it best to keep quiet. Anyway, the man in the well tried again and again to pull himself out, but with diminishing encouragement. Darkness fell. Without coat or hat, he shivered and accepted the cold and cruel necessity of remaining there till morning.

It was a long and most unhappy night; but a couple of hours after sunrise the well-diggers came to resume their work, and to their surprise found a man in their well. With rope and windlass they soon brought him out—a dejected spectacle. Bob Edwards felt as though his blood had turned to ice and his blistered hands pained brutally, but what hurt most was the insinuation that the kitten story was a fabrication—that he was really intoxicated when he fell in. That really hurt.

"Never exaggerate your faults," he wrote (5 February 1921); "your friends will attend to that." It might be a reasonable theory, but he practiced the exact opposite and told the world about his mistakes. When Bob Edwards was drunk everybody would know about it; but when he nearly killed himself working for a small boy and his cat, the only reward was the satisfaction of bringing laughter to a boy in tears.

And so, early in 1899, Bob Edwards decided to leave Wetaskiwin. Having no printing equipment, moving was not difficult. Friends at Leduc persuaded him to come there, and for a short time he published the *Alberta Sun* with a Leduc dateline. Though absent from Wetaskiwin, he lost none of his affection for the place and Jerry Boyce's hotel. He liked to go back to visit the old friends.

"Last week," he wrote, concerning one of those return trips, "we took a run up to Wetaskiwin. . . . They are the same as ever. Those who were not passing in through the folding doors, were coming out, wiping off their chins. . . . There is a pleasant air of prosperity about Wetaskiwin and her citizens which makes her stand out alone from other towns along the line north of Red Deer. Edmonton is but a snide place which gives everyone the blues. . . . Calamity has no terrors for Wetaskiwin. She has come through the rabbit era with smiling face, had a cycle of summer frosts, been hailed out on several occasions and burned up once. The only thing left in the calamity line is an earthquake. Like a child that has had all the ailments from mumps to measles, she may be considered immune. This is possibly why the air is so full of the divine spirit of optimism." (13 May 1905)

Leduc, of which the world was to hear much in later years, was little more than a flag-station on a new railroad and totally unconscious of the oil wealth in its subterranean limestone. But the Leduc stay was short; in just a matter of months Bob Edwards was packing again and going to Strathcona—not yet called South Edmonton. Intention was to publish the *Strathcolic*, because it would probably produce the equivalent of abdominal pains for pious readers. It did; but very shortly the editor restored the more respectable name—the *Alberta Sun.*[4]

Strathcona was rather hectic, the temptations to drink coming too often. He shared a small house east of the CPR tracks and south of Whyte Avenue with Bill Halliday, a tailor. Both men were Scots; both liked porridge and both yielded to drink now and then.

The editor declared that his purpose would be "simply and entirely to amuse. It is the best we can do with oats at eighteen cents." But the vicissitudes of small-time publishing did not diminish. Temperance workers, and self-appointed morality officers who could not comprehend, were making it hot for him. There was also the ever-present problem of money. At no time was he a successful collector of debts, and once again his main reward was in experience.

After that third journalistic venture in the Alberta country was failing, Bob Edwards accepted the necessity of working for somebody else; and late in the year 1900 he went to Winnipeg to take a position with the *Free Press.*[5] But it wasn't satisfactory. The fact of the matter was that Bob Edwards was not cut out to work for others. He had to be his own boss so he might work all night when he felt so inclined and neglect his duties at other times if there was a compelling urge.

Moreover, Winnipeg might be the Gateway to the West, but it wasn't the real West he had grown to love. The birds in the trees didn't sing to suit him; the people in the offices were altogether too diligent, and the ink refused to flow evenly from his pen. He wrote to Jerry Boyce—loyal Jerry—who by this time was located at High River, and confessed to unhappiness. Jerry knew what to suggest: "Come back to these parts—where nobody locks his door—and try again."[6]

Bob replied that he was coming; he'd start a paper. The next attempt at publishing might be a success. "It's the last key in the bunch that opens the door." (5 September 1912)

[4] The offices of the Strathcona incarnation of the *Alberta Sun* were located at 10345 82nd (Whyte) Avenue, on the upper floor of the Hub Cigar building. MacEwan's chronology is a little off in this section; Edwards published the *Alberta Sun* after his return from Winnipeg (see below).

[5] Spring of 1899, actually. "R. C. Edwards, the sage of Wetaskiwin, left this morning for Winnipeg," reported the *Calgary Daily Herald* of 17 April 1899. "A number of admiring friends saw him off at the station. Tears flowed copiously during the parting 'feature.'" Edwards had been living in Calgary, but publishing the *Free Lance* with a Wetaskiwin dateline, since the autumn of 1898.

[6] Edwards returned to Alberta after six months in Winnipeg. According to the *Herald* (23 September 1899): "R.C. Edwards, the erstwhile editor of the *Wetaskiwin Free Lance*, was a passenger on Monday's westbound train. It is understood that he will again enter journalism in the Territories. Mr Edwards is one of the cleverest writers in the Dominion and while under his control the *Free Lance* was the most quoted paper between Winnipeg and the coast. Mr. Edwards comes of good literary stock, being related to William and Robert Chambers, the famous Edinburgh publishers. He was educated at the Edinburgh Royal High School, which from Sir Walter Scott down has produced many famous literateurs." After his stint in Leduc and Strathcona, Edwards returned to Wetaskiwin and once again opened shop, this time under the banner the *Wetaskiwin Breeze*. About a year later, Edwards moved to High River.

CHAPTER THREE
High River Hijinks

"While some of us have more ups and downs in this world than others, we'll all be on the dead level sooner or later."

(11 November 1916)

"Meanwhile, the meek are a long time inheriting the earth."

(16 September 1916)

"What with whales at Edmonton, sharks at Calgary, lobsters at Okotoks and suckers everywhere else, Alberta bids fair to become an interesting aquarium of marine curiosities."

(5 September 1903)

"People always laugh at the fool things you try to do until they discover you are making money out of them."

(31 May 1918)

HIGH RIVER TOWN, as Bob Edwards saw it in 1902, was a rangeland capital with a reputation for light hearts and heavy hangovers. Social rank was indicated by the degree to which a man's legs resembled the contour of a saddle-pony's ribs. It was fascinating although Bob Edwards was not a stranger in cattle country; having worked on a Wyoming ranch, he was not to be fooled by such technical expressions as "blowing a stirrup," "busting a steer," and "pulling leather." At once he felt at home here on this distinctive island in a vast sea of grass.

High River at its best, however, was the welcome from Jerry Boyce—Jerry who had been Bob's friend and "banker" in the Wetaskiwin years and was now operating the Astoria Hotel in this cattlemen's town. Bob had corresponded with Fred Stimson, the hell-popping manager of the Bar U Ranch, and he knew others thereabouts; but it was Jerry and no other who induced his coming. When close to Jerry he felt security, a feeling born of experience that at least he wouldn't be hungry. As Bob expected, Jerry had a place for him—a room in the hotel annex built over the livery stable. It wasn't fancy, but who cared? It had a bunk with blankets, a chair with rockers, and a table with three legs. The aroma of horses leaked through from the stable below, but that was all right too; Bob reminded himself he was in High River where a man's real worth would not be judged by the elegance or smell of his residence.

The town could boast of one general store known as the High River Trading Company, one drug store, a blacksmith shop, and a barbershop. But it had two hotels—Jerry's and the one operated by Jack Matheson—and their saloons were the busiest places in the community. The doors to the bars were big enough to admit a cowboy on his horse; and with a few customers entering that way, parking problems around the hitching posts were eased considerably.

Bob Edwards knew that, next to Fort Macleod, no place in the Chinook belt held richer cow-country traditions. With ranching woven inextricably into its fabric, the High River country was the dream of nearly every lad whose ambition was to be a cowboy.

A few miles to the west of town was the site of old Fort Spitzee, one of the lawless whiskey posts, built in the late sixties by T. C. Powers and Company of Fort Benton. Close to Spitzee, Howell Harris and Fred Kanouse had erected a trading post in 1871 and wintered work oxen there. It was on the choice grass along the river that George Emerson and Tom Lynch had released a thousand cattle in 1879, the first big herd to be given the freedom of the open range. And in 1902, when Bob Edwards moved in, ranching was still without rival among local industries. In the hills to the west were some of the biggest ranches, and on all sides men pulled leather chaps over their bowed legs and worked in stock saddles.

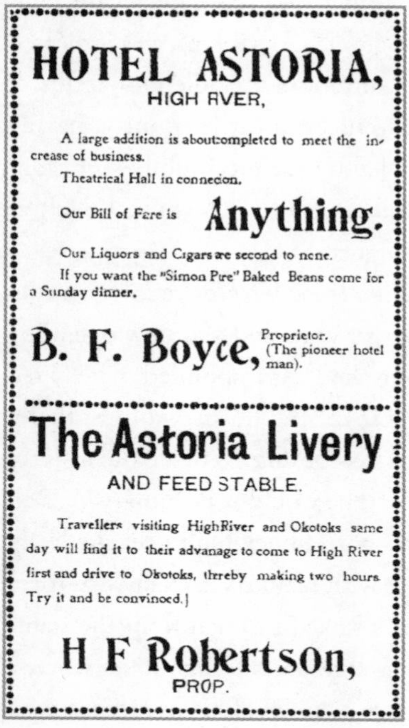

HOTEL ASTORIA,
HIGH RVER,
A large addition is aboutcompleted to meet the increase of business.
Theatrical Hall in connecion.
Our Bill of Fare is Anything.
Our Liquors and Cigars are second to none.
If you want the "Simon Pure" Baked Beans come for a Sunday dinner.
B. F. Boyce, Proprietor. (The pioneer hotel man).
The Astoria Livery
AND FEED STABLE.
Travellers visiting HighRiver and Okotoks seme day will find it to their advanage to come to High River first and drive to Okotoks, threby making two hours. Try it and be convinced.]
H F Robertson,
PROP.

Nor was it all work at High River. Polo was the acknowledged king of outdoor sports and poker ruled on the inside. Bob's friend and medical adviser, Dr. G. D. Stanley, told years later of some of the marathon games that went on at Jerry's, but couldn't say if Bob Edwards was present at them. The young Englishmen receiving remittances from "home" were usually the biggest losers. There was one twenty-four-hour game in the course of which a team of Clydesdale horses, a residence in High River, and thirty acres of townsite changed ownership. In another game sat a well-known local cowboy and a Calgary shark with one glass eye. The cowboy sensed something irregular, and standing erect, drew his six-shooter and made a pretty little speech: "I ain't accusin' nobody of nothin' crooked," he said, “an’ I ain’t mentionin’ any names, but there’s some funny work agoin’ round this table an’ I’m only sayin’ that if it don’ stop, somebody’s agoin’ to lose his other eye.”

Without thought of personal gain, Jerry Boyce placed his old friend on display with resulting increase in hotel business. Bob could see himself serving the same purpose as the tame bear Jerry kept behind the hotel at Wetaskiwin. He didn’t mind that, however; and almost at once, everybody knew him. “High River is going to be all right,” he assured himself, coming under the spell of the range. This place would be tolerant and forgiving. His enthusiasm to start another paper mounted, and with Jerry providing a small loan, the *Eye Opener* made its appearance on March 4, 1902. It was the town’s first weekly paper, and the reception was something to bring joy to an editor’s heart. Temporarily at least, it seemed that the editor and this foothills community were created for each other. Unfortunately, as time was to show, the compatibility was rather brief—but that is another part of the story.

The first issue of the *Eye Opener* carried its own introduction to a reading public quite overjoyed at the prospect of having a paper—any kind of a paper.

> In the quiet cove of High River we anchor the *Eye Opener*, hoping it won’t bust like the Maine. Clothed in righteousness, a bland smile and a lovely jag, the editor of this publication struck town two weeks ago. The management has decided on the name, ‘*Eye Opener*’ because few people will resist taking it. It will be run on a strictly moral basis at one dollar a year. If an immoral paper is the local preference, we can supply that too but it will cost $1.50. (4 March 1902)

The *Eye Opener*’s paths would be those of “pleasantness and peace,” avoiding controversial and unpleasant topics such as cattle mange. Such genteel intentions did not last long, but the *Eye Opener* did work diligently for High River. In its first issue the editor urged that a bid be made for settlers. Ranching, he argued, is all very well, but mixed farming should be encouraged in certain areas where it is appropriate and the railroad company’s assistance in getting settlers should be enlisted.

“Remember,” he wrote, “the Trinity of Canada is the CPR, Clifford Sifton and the Almighty. So it would be just as well for High River to start moving up to the pie counter for more settlers. Never let it be said that we surrender the cream of Ontario’s sod-busters to hilarious Cayley or the bustling water-tank town of Nanton.” (4 March 1902)

Whatever criticism there might be about Bob Edwards’s conduct at High River, nobody could say he failed to boost the abundant grass, good soil, and unsurpassed scenery. His enthusiasm was genuine: ". . . favored by location and nature with everything calculated to make it one of the most delightful places in the West. Beautiful for situation with a health-laden breeze floating down from the mountains, High River has little to complain of in regard to her share of nature's bounty." (17 October 1903)

Not all of the *Eye Opener*'s promotion was as well received; there was the contention, for example, that High River was the logical site for a new educational institution which the editor would call Tanglefoot University. It would fill a long-felt need for a training college at which young commercial travellers from the East would become "acclimated to the fearful and wonderful varieties of Western whiskey before going on the road. . . . As Calgary will most likely get the Presbyterian College, it is only fair that High River should be chosen as the logical site for this new seat of boozing. . . ."

Students would be instructed in the delicate art of drinking without getting drunk, and "mopping up" countless drinks with customers without reducing their chances of securing large orders.

> Lectures on Alcoholic Hallucinations will be given once a week by one who has been there, accompanied by colored illustrations of alligators, pink rats, performing elephants . . . snakes and reptiles of every description. Tanglefoot University should make a hit. It will save many a good man from going wrong. We are willing to accept the presidency and a thoroughly qualified staff of teachers can be procured right here in High River. (25 July 1903)

To people he considered fair-minded and "free from dinky little prejudices," Bob Edwards admitted readily that there was too much drinking in High River, especially among his friends. But booze was there in all its killing fury, and Bob Edwards contended that the people who could get a laugh out of it would do at least as much toward curbing the evil as the ones who remained righteously aloof to it. And so, what happened to the High River Mounted Policeman who decided to leave the force after nineteen years and get married might as well be told. The policeman was a friend of the editor and plans were made for the wedding to be at the bride's uncle's home in Calgary on the following week. But unfortunately, High River insisted upon tendering the popular Mountie a final send-off in the form of a banquet.

> It lasted three days and nights without let-up and dragged on till the

> day fixed for the wedding which everybody, including the prospective bridegroom, apparently forgot all about. Then somebody remembered that the Mountie was billed to appear in Calgary the following day and get married. Bill Bersche, the local bank manager, and a sympathetic soul, decided to journey to Calgary himself and explain to the bride and her folks that the bridegroom was stormbound at the Bar U ranch, where he had been sent at the last moment to serve some summonses. Bersche made the trip to Calgary on the evening train but he too was still 'litup' and he returned confessing he had forgotten the purpose of his trip. Anyway, the wedding was postponed for a couple of weeks, the bridegroom got sobered up and the happy couple left these parts to reside in Southern California. (13 May 1922)

The editor considered it his privilege to tease local people, and there was additional reason why he should humble the proud neighbouring towns—Okotoks in particular. Not realizing how he might live to regret it, the editor of the *Okotoks Times* made frivolous references to the *Eye Opener* being denied the use of the mails. (22 August 1903) Bob Edwards struck with retaliation that continued for months. He could "parry and thrust" with any writer and enjoy it. The result was that Okotoks received a lot of publicity—not all to the liking of the town's Board of Trade. The *Eye Opener* announced that Okotoks was planning to hold the next World's Fair; but, in the editor's opinion, Midnapore (with population of twelve at that time) was more suitable, being ten miles handier for members of the House of Lords who would come by Calgary, and closer for the Indians on the Sarcee Reserve who would be the principal patrons. At least one traveller from England, detraining at Calgary, enquired in the best of faith how to get to Okotoks for the purpose of attending the World's Fair.

As Okotoks people wondered what would come next, they read: "The astronomers have discovered a peculiar 'spot' on Saturn and are greatly excited about it. Yet there are plenty of peculiar spots, no farther away than Okotoks and Claresholm." (18 July 1903) The next issue reported: "We understand from latest advices that croquet is regarded as a very swift game in Okotoks." (25 July 1903) Two weeks later, the comment was that "Billy Cochrane of High River has introduced the first automobile into Alberta. High River is the pioneer of progress. Okotoks still clings to the Red River cart." (8 August 1903) And as a feature of the Calgary Fair of 1904, "an exhibit of seedless prunes," raised at Okotoks. (30 April 1904)

What Okotoks residents resented most was the report of an alleged conversation when a stranger seeking a business location visited the town and interviewed the Board of Trade. "I have looked over your town," he said, "and have practically decided to locate here. Having studied the life of Okotoks pretty thoroughly within the last week, I am confident I can do well here and shall send for my family at once."

"What business are you in?" an Okotoks member asked hopefully; and the reply was, "The embalming business." (8 August 1903)

Calgary, Edmonton, and Winnipeg were frequently under editorial fire; and, of course, the fabulous Town of Hootch. No doubt Edwards knew the exact location of Hootch, but for the reading public it was just, "a thriving burg along the branch running out of Calgary . . . the centre of the great drinking industry of Alberta . . . Situated near the foothills of the Rockies, whose majestic peaks are visible from the town, fanned by gentle blizzards in winter and swept by cooling hail in summer, Hootch has become a favourite resort for those contemplating suicide." (16 September 1916)

Bob Edwards wrote many columns about Hootch and its people. Nobody knew how much truth there was in his report about going there to spend a Thanksgiving Day and finding all his friends in the town jail. As it happened, however, the jail-keeper had to make a trip to Youngstown for the day and named Bob to the office of deputy jail-keeper. With the jail-keeper absent, the deputy released everybody after getting a promise that all would be back by midnight. At midnight, two hours before the senior officer returned, the prisoners were back and locked up and everything was in good order. It was a great Thanksgiving Day at Hootch.

Travelling Hootchward

Guessing the real name of that town was a popular pastime in High River and later in Calgary, but the exact identity was one secret on which Bob Edwards never made a disclosure. Some readers believed it was Drumheller; but wherever it was, "Billy Sunday decided not to attempt to save it. Too far gone." (17 March 1917)

No editor loses local favour by merely humiliating neighbouring towns and villages; and no writer should be condemned for discussing his own follies. Bob Edwards was never known to try to divert the public gaze away from his own mistakes and failings. And High River enjoyed his account of a near-fatal mistake with a corrosive sublimate pill, taken by mistake for a sleeping tablet. Suspecting the error very quickly, he called the doctor; and the dialogue, as the *Eye Opener* recorded it, was like this:

> "What did I take, Doc? Anything dangerous?"
> "Oh no, only corrosive sublimate . . . They kill rats with that."
> "Then I suppose I'll be pushing clouds in about ten minutes."
> "Oh dear no! Not that soon."
> "How much of it kills a man?"
> "One grain according to medical experience."
> "And how much did I take?"
> "Seven."

"Well," the editor added in relating it, "we hung in the balance for a couple of hours. It is a curious fact, but the actual fight with Death, when he is liable to give you the half-Nelson and throw you any minute, does not produce fear. When there is but the twinkle of a star between you and the boneyard, your mind becomes very cold and collected. It is not half so fearsome as it is cracked up to be, especially to one who has lived so virtuous, noble and exemplary a life as we have. The fight was hammer and tongs while it lasted but having a good second in Doc, we won out. Had we lost, it would have been a case of the *Eye Opener* suiciding sure. We know how dearly we are loved by some people here." (5 September 1903)

The medical man in the dialogue, as identified by himself many years later, was Dr. G. D. Stanley, who could recall other trials in the High River life of the editor.[1] One of the first major conflicts involving Bob Edwards and a section of the town population occurred after a new minister arrived. Until more suitable accommodation could be secured, the churchman occupied a room at the Astoria Hotel. There he was made as comfortable as possible, but on the very first Sunday he denounced most scathingly the hotel life of High River. Springing to the defence of his hotel-keeper friend, Jerry Boyce, the editor referred to the complainant as a "cad." At once an indignation meeting was called in the Methodist Church, "it being the largest building in the burg." Dr. Stanley was asked to be chairman and then to assume the unpleasant task of communicating a formal protest to the editor. Bob replied to the doctor by letter, regretting that a friendship he esteemed so highly was in danger of being broken: "Nevertheless," he concluded, "when I need you, I shall still send for you and I know you'll come."

[1] Presumably this disclosure, and others like it throughout *Eye Opener Bob* that can't be found in print sources, were recorded by MacEwan in personal interviews.

Happily, the friendship was not broken; rather, it became richer as the years passed.

In covering the High River news, there were items that Bob Edwards insisted upon reporting with absolute accuracy, while other stories invited pardonable embellishment. There are times, he conceded, when it is a mistake to "spoil a good story by sticking to the facts." When Cowboy "Dogie" Wilder had an unusual accident, the editor may have seen it as a time to exercise his license to improve the story:

> "Dogie" Wilder who works on a ranch, south-west of town, [was attacked] by a skunk while lying asleep out in the yard one warm night and had his nose bitten off before he could wake up and scare the disagreeable animal away. However, he picked up the piece, stuck it on again and secured it firmly with a handkerchief bound round his head. The handkerchief was removed for the first time last Friday in the presence of an anxious group of cow punchers. It was found that the piece had slipped and grown on his face an inch to the left of the proper position. This awkward bit of surgery has left him with one nostril in its right place and the other growing out of his cheek. (18 July 1903)

But to "Dogie" Wilder, distinctiveness held its own charm, and the transformation made him laugh "immoderately every time he looked at himself in a glass."

"Dogie" Wilder was just one of a host of High River and community characters who seemed to inspire Bob's way of writing. Jack Rivett, better known as "Sir John," "Coyote Charlie," "Nigger John," "Slippery Bill," and "Undertaker Rheinhart" were the perfect subjects for an Edwards.

Because of the importance of his occupation, Rheinhart may have received a larger than average share of editorial attention. In habits, speech, and dress, he was everything that should not be found in an undertaker. His "parlor" consisted of a second-floor room which could be reached only by ladder. When his services were required—which wasn't often in a community where nearly everybody was youthful—the town knew about it.

Death overtook a rancher from west of town just when Rheinhart, as secretary of the Turf Club, was preparing for a race meet. For the benefit of the cowboys who climbed the ladder to look for the last time upon the face of the deceased, the inspired undertaker delivered an oration on which there was the following Edwardian report:

> Gentlemen, this here is a corpse which I am about to plant. Deceased has his sorrel entered for one of the races but I guess she'll be withdrawn now. You will understand it is highly inconvenient for me to have a corpse bedded in my parlors on the eve of the race-meet. But, as secretary of the Turf Association, I mention that the pony dash is half a mile, not a quarter as some imagine.
>
> Our genial corpse, poor fellow, had actually entered the mile and one-eighth. But I don't think [the sorrel] had a chance. Her distance is really three-quarters of a mile. My line of coffins is unexcelled. This one on display is a ten-dollar proposition but I can get dandies for $12.50. The bucking contest comes on about 4 o'clock so be on hand.
>
> In bidding farewell to our dear departed, we hope he is going to a happier land and before I close the lid on this handsome coffin which is really cheaper than they are selling in Calgary, I think we may tender congratulations to the dear departed for missing the humiliating defeat of his sorrel. The sorrel mare will be raffled tonight to defray funeral expenses. I really should have charged $15 for this coffin; it's worth every cent.
>
> In bidding farewell to our friend I also announce that there will be an Indian Ghost Dance in front of the hotel. You are all cordially invited. The sorrel's entrance fee of $5 has been paid and will be used to drink to the memory of the dear departed. We may attend to this feature of the obsequies at once. (20 July 1904)

And so, one and all, they clambered down the rickety ladder and moved slowly over to the hotel, "pondering the mystery of death."

For a time, Bob Edwards adhered nobly to the promised policy of "pleasantness and peace." But he was a bold and fearless writer and such policy was trying. When he came face to face with dishonesty in any of its forms, the self-imposed restraints had to break. He censured the Mounted Police for arresting boys who were playing with a toy pistol on a Sunday, and he criticized Rev. Mr. Campbell for threatening to lay a charge against those seeking Sunday relaxation by playing polo. (8 August 1903) The result was a mounting resentment in some High River circles.

The cattlemen accepted his sarcasm about their failure to eradicate the mange, but the Methodists and Presbyterians didn't take his innuendos so well. "Strange man, this Edwards," some citizens said. "He's on good terms with every poor family in town, yet he makes no effort to cultivate High River's 'best people.'" The critics could not understand a man who could quote Shakespeare and captivate the people around him, and yet ignore many of the people with the best Sunday clothes in High River.

For the best part of a year the Presbyterians and Methodists carried their church notices at the top of the *Eye Opener*'s "Local Column." But in August of 1903 the editor acknowledged that things must be pretty bad when the church people were requesting withdrawal of the weekly notices being furnished without cost to them. The rift widened with passing weeks. As the editor became bolder in his denunciation of anything smacking of sham and hypocrisy, churchmen spoke more loudly of a "menacing influence." For frequenting the High River bars, a man might have been forgiven by the moral guardians of the community, and Edwards's cynical references to socially prominent citizens might have been overlooked. But when he was blamed for the humiliating anti-climax to a Sunday demonstration of "canned music" in the Methodist church, they couldn't forgive.

Frank Brazil, who ranched to the southwest, was at church on that Sunday when the "canned music" program created a sensation, and he was present with Bob Edwards on another Sunday when the pomposity of a certain conceited newcomer was immersed in the mire at Dan Riley's corral. The immersion took place when many of the townsfolk were at the barn and corral to see some broncos which Jack Matheson had brought in from the hills west of Okotoks. The noisiest person present was a young immigrant who boasted of having ridden in the Grand National, and he didn't think it was much of a trick to stick in a Canadian stock saddle. Nearly every district, it seemed, had one of these blustering fellows, and too often his braggadocio went unchecked.

On this occasion, Bob Edwards whispered something to Brazil—something about conceit being an evil disease and hard to cure. There were some bad horses in the corral. One of the equine outlaws was promptly roped and saddled at the corral fence; and just as expected, the young boaster volunteered quite eagerly to demonstrate his skill on a horse. With the young fellow in the saddle and still talking about his Grand National triumphs, the untamed bronco was released in the sea of mud and manure, made knee-deep by weeks of rain. Spectators did not have long to wait for the shock treatment which had been prescribed. The bronc pitched, kicked, jack-knifed, and parted company with its rider somewhere well above the level of the corral fence. The fellow's descent was anything but graceful as he landed in the mire. At least the softness of the water-soaked ground made injury unlikely, but nice clothes and a clean face were so covered with mud and filth that neither remained recognizable.

Men waded into the mire to help extricate the embarrassed jockey, and then there was the problem of cleaning him up. But everybody was co-operative, and the bedraggled victim was held below the spout of Dan Riley's pump while Bob Edwards worked the handle. With minutes of pumping, enough of the mud washed away to reveal the man's features; and, spectators hoped, some of the offensive conceit dissolved away also. Edwards had a few words of advice—friendly advice—for the fellow, and relationships were better thereafter.

And so it was not totally strange that eyes should be turned toward Bob Edwards when the Sunday evening service seemed to backfire in the face of those who planned it. It all started when a salesman for religious music on phonograph records arrived in High River and set about to sell the merits of his wares to the Methodist minister. His technique was subtle enough; most church troubles stem from the choir, he reasoned. There had been cases of ministers eloping with choir leaders, and often enough a minister's first critics were the choristers. Then the clever promoter pointed to the moral hazards attending the custom of Thursday evening choir practice, as young people, male and female, journeyed homeward in the hours of darkness after the meeting; temptations were inevitable, and no understanding minister could sit idly by without fear of consequences.

The solution to the problem, argued the slinky traveller, lay in the installation of a Gramophone Choir with a good stock of sacred music on records. The orthodox choir could be discharged and the moral pitfalls that accompany mid-week practice would disappear. The minister's peace of mind would be restored. It was very simple.

The minister was impressed. He had heard that certain young couples weren't going straight home from choir practice. He agreed to a demonstration at evening service on the very next Sunday.

The salesman, arrogant and confident, made some appropriate selections from his recorded music and placed them in proper order for the church service. He then repaired to the bar at Jerry's hotel and spent Saturday evening in relaxed and reckless celebration. That someone might tamper with the gramophone records in his leather case did not occur to him, nor that his bombastic manner at the bar was making him very unpopular.

What happened from there on is best told by Bob Edwards, who was sitting in a back pew on that memorable Sunday evening, but who kept most of the details to himself for a number of years:

> When Sunday morning dawned, the professor was in horrible shape for lack of sleep and too much of Jerry's Finest Old Glenhorrors. Anyway, when Sunday evening came and the fateful hour arrived, he had a hang-over and was very nervous.

All High River was at church to hear the Gramophone Choir. "The gang" was thickly bunched in the back pews. Sure enough, there was the instrument perched on a little table, with the professor capering about arranging records.

"Hymn number 471," announced the preacher. "'Hark the Herald Angels Sing,' hymn number 471, omitting the third stanza."

"See here," interrupted the professor, "this here choir omits nothing. I can shut 'er off at the end of the third and omit the fourth, if you like, but no hops and skips in the middle."

"Proceed, sir."

"All right, let 'er go! 'Hark the Herald Angels Sing' by the Edison quartette."

As the notes of the beautiful hymn wafted through the church, the professor stood beaming at the congregation, as much as to say, "Got 'em faded!" The people were evidently charmed and the minister looked gratified, the latter afterwards adding a few appropriate words on the marvelous advances in science and the many wonderous inventions and discoveries vouchsafed to us by the Almighty through the medium of human genius.

The next hymn announced in the course of the usual service was "Nearer My God to Thee," and the congregation bent forward expectantly. The professor took a fresh record from the pile and wound her up. The preliminary coughing and shuffling into comfortable positions drowned the announcement from the gramophone itself, but it was not long before it dawned upon the congregation that the new choir was singing, "Just Because She Made Them Goo-goo Eyes." The professor hastily stopped the machine and started to put on another record but the minister stopped him with the remark:

"The resignation of the Gramophone Choir is accepted. Let us pray."

Next morning a scrubby-looking individual with large satchel, immense horn and tremendous jag, might have been seen wending his way over to the depot, bound for Macleod. The professor's idea was all right but poorly executed. It called for at least a small modicum of sobriety. His records must have got mixed on the Saturday night. (21 September 1918)

Bob Edwards's long silence added to the suspicion that he knew quite a bit about the affair.[2] Whether he was guilty or not, church opinion was welling against him and more people were ready to accept a midsummer evaluation by himself: "The unco' guid of High River must envy us our shady character in this hot weather." (25 July 1903)

High River was being difficult—like a jealous husband. The fact was that the town's two personalities were very clear. One, with the sparkle of good champagne, recognized real worth in the man who had been guilty of creating a certain amount of social turmoil; the other, serious and humorless, seemed to resent anything that was unconventional.

As Bob Edwards made his way along the street he heard female whispers: "There he is. He's sober today." It hurt—hurt like the thrust of a rusty nail. He could see it now; too many people were unfriendly. That was the reason *Eye Opener* support was declining. Perhaps High River, like Wetaskiwin and Leduc, was the wrong place. Perhaps he had been there too long. Or was it that he had too many drinking friends? It could be. "It was all we could do," he wrote, "to get out a paper between drinks."

But before giving up at High River, there was some special writing he wanted to do—an experiment in frontier fiction, some sort of serial. It may have been prompted by an evening with Charlie Russell, when that western artist was visiting rancher Phil Weinard. Bob and Charlie had many of the same tastes and follies and there was mutual admiration. There is reason to believe that Russell challenged the editor to give his readers some Bob Edwards fiction about cow punchers or bartenders or remittance men. Bob promised, and a new storybook character was created.

[2] According to Hugh Dempsey in *The Best of Bob Edwards*, the incident was reported in the next issue of the *Eye Opener* (16 January 1903). Regardless, it's hard not to surmise that Edwards was behind the switcheroo.

CHAPTER FOUR
The Adventures of Bertie

> "A little learning is a dangerous thing but a lot of ignorance is just as bad."
>
> (20 August 1921)

> "With a certain class of high-bred Englishmen there is only the twinkle of a star between the glory of a well-wined mess . . . and a shack on a western ranch."
>
> "A good man who goes wrong is just a bad man who has been found out."
>
> (22 September 1917)

IT WAS WHILE HIGH RIVER was becoming uncomfortable for Bob Edwards that *Eye Opener* readers made the acquaintance of Bertie, whose fame throughout the Chinook Belt mounted like the price of wheat when farmers have none to sell. Bertie was a young Englishman, of a particular variety well-known on the frontier. He was a remittance man, a second or third son whose well-to-do family found it more convenient to ship him to some remote place in the colonies and maintain him there than attempt to curb his perverse ways at home.

High River with its cow-country traditions seemed to attract remittance men, and some prize specimens stopped at the Astoria Hotel in Bob Edwards's time. A certain type of problem son would arrive with an impressive wardrobe, a well-polished gun, a taste for liquor, and some ill-defined ideas about becoming a "rawncher." With money lavishly sent from home, the better ones did establish themselves; while the others, like our Bertie, lived wastefully for a time and disappeared.

Many of them were likeable chaps with an advanced education which did nothing to increase their usefulness. Bob Edwards argued his support for classical education; but at the same time, he wanted a school system which would make people useful as well as pleasant and ornamental. The schools and blue-blood society of which these remittance men were products turned out thousands of:

> . . . politely-ignorant youth, gentlemanly fellows with charming sisters, used to the best of everything . . . and totally dependent on the pater for clothes, money and general guidance. . . . What can you expect of young men brought up in a fox-hunting and pheasant-

shooting atmosphere? It is heresy to say anything against the noble spirit of chasing a lone fox and seeing it rended to pieces by a pack of hounds, for fox-hunting is part of the British constitution and consequently sacred; but we [must] expose our contempt for their fashionable pastime of pheasant shooting as being nothing more than a ridiculous and perverted form of alleged sport, sanctified by the traditions of generations of country gentlemen and their city imitators. (2 December 1905)

That fox-hunting and pheasant-shooting society! Class distinction! Privilege! They rankled because Bob Edwards believed passionately in equality of opportunity. He didn't entirely blame the remittance men—rather something behind them. It was simply that he had small patience with aristocracy and inherited advantage. Having a rich father didn't bestow any special congenital rights to torture foxes or destroy pheasants. Bob Edwards admired the resourcefulness of most young people on the frontier and would do anything to help newsboys and their kind, but he could not hide his contempt for anyone who showed no will to be useful.

Well, Bertie, to be sure, was one of those likeable but unfortunate remittance men. To give him his full name, he was Albert Buzzard-Cholomondeley of Skookingham, Leicestershire, England. The fact of Bertie being nothing more than a Bob Edwards brainchild, and the letters fiction, didn't lessen public interest in either. In the young man's letters to his aristocratic sire, almost always inspired by the need for more money, Bob Edwards's originality mingled with wit and mischief to remind readers of what the editor of the *Eye Opener* might have done in the field of creative writing. The Edwards imagination was unfailing, and with his scholarly vocabulary the man might have been the novelist for whom the new country was waiting.

The *Eye Opener* carried the Bertie epistles, described as "letters from a badly made son to his father in England," during late 1903 and early 1904, to give the alleged sender about as much local fame as that enjoyed by the celebrated Li'l Abner in later years. In the abridged letters[1] following, the noble blunderer may speak for himself and prove to exasperated fathers and mothers everywhere that they have not yet experienced the worst in parental anguish.

Peace River, NWT
The Fall, 1902.
Dear Father:
I often think of dear old Skookingham Hall and the splendid shooting. How I should enjoy one of our good old grouse drives again. The only shooting I have done out here of late years has been at craps, a different species of game from grouse or partridge.

About things in this country. The few thousand pounds you gave me to start farming with in Manitoba were duly invested in a farm. In my labors I had several assistants, Hi Walker, Joe Seagram, Johnny Dewar, Benny Dikteen, men of exceptional strength and fiery temperament and in place of serving me as their master, soon became my masters. So it was not long before I had no farm. I then went tending bar for a hotel keeper in the neighboring village whose prosperity seems to have dated from the hour of my arrival in the country.

The love of liquor which I must have inherited either from yourself or my grandfather, made me a failure as a bartender and I soon got the bounce. So I packed my things in a large envelope and hit the blind baggage for the West where I went cow punching. Worked during the summer till the beef gather and lost all my wages in one disastrous night at poker. After a long hard winter as cookee in a lumber camp I struck for Peace River country where I am now.

I am married to a half-breed and have three ornery-looking, copper-colored brats. We are all coming over to visit you at Christmas when you will be having the usual big house party at Skookingham Hall. I shall so like to see the dear place again and my wife is most anxious to become acquainted with her darling husband's people and obtain a glimpse of English society. The Hall will be quite a change for her from the log shacks and teepees she has been used to all her life.

If I only had about a thousand pounds just now with which to start afresh, I would invest it in cattle right away, settle down to business and

[1] MacEwan's abridgements have here been further condensed to allow room for more supplementary material. Please consult *Irresponsible Freaks*, etc. for the complete texts of all seven extant Buzz letters.

forego the pleasure of a trip home and remain right here. But I do not know where to lay my hands on that amount. With love and kisses to mother and the girls, believe me, dear old Dad.
Your affectionate son, Albert Buzzard-Cholomondeley

(24 October 1903)

Bertie received the thousand pounds, well in advance of Christmas sailings to be sure, and Skookingham Hall did not have him and his half-breed family at the festive season. In his next letter, written from Edmonton, he acknowledged receipt of the money, mentioned his wife's illness and announced intention of becoming a business man. The idea was to start a newspaper at Leduc, "an alleged town twenty miles south of Edmonton." In this business, he explained to his father, one has to move around a good deal. "After busting in one town, all you have to do is start up in another," always receiving the whole-souled welcome such as is accorded a new preacher, until the editor starts collecting. "The moment he evinces a longing to be paid for his ads, his finish is in sight. It is time to start moving the plant."

But life in the Territories was uncertain and Bertie found himself in trouble beyond anything he had ever known. The lofty thought about journalism had to be abandoned and nothing could show reasons more convincing than his letter written from Fort Saskatchewan on 3 November 1903.

Dear Father:
When you open this letter at the breakfast table do not read it aloud to mother and the girls. Am at present in the direst distress and have had to postpone indefinitely my newspaper venture at Leduc.

You remember me writing to you that my half-breed wife was very ill and was being attended by an Indian medicine man who beat a tom-tom by her bedside to drive away the evil one. Well, she's dead. Her untimely death affected me deeply. So enraged did I become, often brooding over the maladroit practices of the tawny Aesculapius that I determined to kill him. Before doing anything rash, however, I consulted a friend, one of the most distinguished bartenders in Edmonton, who promptly offered me his profound sympathy and a small flask. His advice seemed reasonable enough. He said: "Shoot him by all means but do as the gamekeepers in the Old Country do with boys bird-nesting. Don't use shot. Put salt in your shells and you will thus both scare and hurt the brute without getting yourself into trouble."

Returning to camp I loaded up a couple of shells with salt as per advice. I also put the little old flask out of business before I mustered up courage enough to pepper the gentleman with the salt. Then I let him have it with both barrels at a range of about three feet. He dropped like a log and never came back. He was stone dead.

Then began my troubles. The coroner examined the body carefully and the jury returned a verdict of wilful murder. I explained that I had only used salt, not wishing to do other than nip him a little. "Yes," said the coroner, "that may be so, but unfortunately you used rock salt." As a matter of fact, I didn't have any table salt.

I am now incarcerated in Fort Saskatchewan awaiting trial. Dad, I must have a thousand dollars immediately to secure the services of a competent lawyer from Calgary. There is a famous criminal lawyer down there by the name of P. J. Nolan whom I should like to get. All the best murderers of the West employ him. There is no doubt but what Mr. Nolan would accept a fee of $1000 if I can give him reasonable assurance that it is all I've got.

Should I hang, the papers will bristle with lurid descriptions of the execution and shocking headlines, all of which will be copied into English papers.

"Buzzard-Cholomondeley, son of old man Cholomondeley hanged today! Painful scenes on the scaffold!"

"The Gates of Hell ajar! Buzzard-Cholomondeley strung up for foul murder! Says he had no table salt."

"Buzzard-Cholomondeley, the assassin, in dying speech attributes his fate to refusal of father to provide funds for lawyer. Sympathy felt for doomed and indignation expressed towards unnatural parent!"

"Scion of old English family sent to Kingdom Come for Brutal Murder! Death Instantaneous!"

Cable over the money at once. Sending by mail means disastrous delay. If I can secure P. J. Nolan I am saved. If not, I am a gonner. They say he won't save a man's neck on jawbone.

Your wretched son, Albert Buzzard-Cholomondeley.

(2 January 1904)[2]

[2] To give some idea of the many difficulties in sifting through Edwards's literary legacy, this issue was erroneously dated 2 January 1903.

However concerned the elder Buzzard-Cholomondeley in England may have been about the outcome of the wayward son's newest misfortune, certainly the people at High River and back in the foothills waited anxiously and not too patiently for the next report. They couldn't bear to think of Bertie being hanged. Bungler and fool though he was, Bertie seemed to belong to High River. Periodically the people on the street revived speculation about the identity of some local character who had been Bob Edwards's inspiration. This was one of the times. Some folk supposed Jack Rivett was the man—the town's "astronomer," who discovered the "fourth star" on Hennessey's Three Star Brandy. Dr. G. D. Stanley, who gave many faithful years of horse-and-buggy medical service after going there in 1901 with "tuberculosis and a year to live," believed the man to impart the Bertie idea to Bob Edwards was the local personality known as "Lord Dutton." The said "Lord" was known to have employed some novel devices to get money "from home;" and when all the old ruses were failing, he had one of the boys on the High River lacrosse team cable a message to England reporting the remittance man's death and estimating funeral expenses at $250. There was an immediate reply furnishing instructions about burial and the much-needed $250. For "Lord Dutton" and his High River friends, his "funeral" was a joyful affair, but thereafter the perpetually thirsty "Lord" found it almost impossible to obtain money from overseas.

Anyway, when the *Eye Openers* carrying the crucial instalment were delivered from the Calgary printers on that January day in 1904, the proudest man in High River was "Lord Dutton." Jerry Boyce furnished free copies for reading at the bar; and that good woman, Mrs. Stanley, a bride of a few months and still waiting for her busy doctor husband to find time for a honeymoon at Banff, let the supper burn while she read the latest news about Bertie. Even the Methodist minister fabricated an excuse to borrow a copy of the *Eye Opener.*

And Bertie did not disappoint; though he had shown himself to be a squanderer, he possessed a hitherto undiscovered resourcefulness—one at its best when Bertie was in trouble. And, quite clearly, one thing remained unchanged—Bertie needed money. The letter was written from Calgary:

Dear Father:

Your cable to the bank at Edmonton for one thousand dollars has saved my bacon and the honor of the Buzzard-Cholomondeleys.

Mr. Nolan, after looking me over carefully and talking with me on general subjects, entered a plea of insanity. The fact of my being a bloody Englishman made the task an easy one for my learned saviour. On the morning of the trial he came to my cell with a pair of very baggy pants for me to put on, also a pair of leggings and a remarkably high white collar which made my ears stick out at right angles like the topsails of a ship in distress. They decided I had a violent form of dementia and that the asylum for the insane at Brandon was my proper sphere.

The following day, in the charge of a North West Mounted Policeman, I started for Brandon asylum, with the machinery in my idea-box turned on at full pressure. While waiting for the midnight flyer going east, the policeman and I strolled leisurely up and down the platform. The butt of his revolver protruded temptingly from his pocket. There was no one on the platform at that late hour and everything was quiet. We were just turning around close by the fence of the CPR gardens when, quick as thought, I whipped out his gun from his pocket and told him there was the twinkle of a star between him and his finish. Me to the bug house? "Na, na my bonny Jean."

Swiftly I steered him into a labyrinth of boxcars and made him peel off his clothes and hand over his uniform, boots, hat and overcoat. At the same time I took off my own togs and ordered him to put them on. Thus we exchanged raiment. I was the policeman, he the lunatic.

In the pockets of my new clothes I found railroad tickets, money, warrant for my, or rather his, incarceration in the bug house, and a set of shackles. I lost no golden moments shackling my man to the seat. Of course he kicked up a tremendous row and appealed for help to the conductor and passengers—knowing I wouldn't decently shoot him in a car—but ha, ha, my dear old dad, I was a Mounted Policeman and he was an insane prisoner. The brakeman even suggested knocking him over the koko with a coupling pin to keep him quiet.

I turned over my unfortunate victim to the asylum authorities at Brandon, explaining to them his pitiful hallucinations about being a policeman and got a receipt in full for the delivery of "Albert Buzzard-Cholomondeley."

Having the policeman's return ticket and his little wad of money, I thought I might as well return to Calgary where no one knows me. It did not take me long to rustle a suit of civilian clothes on my arrival there.

Now look here, dad. Although I may not be dead, I am dead broke. The trick I have played is sure to come out sooner or later and I must get out of here. I cannot get out without money. Cable over another hundred pounds to take me home. I shall come alone, my two children being still [out] on shares at Lesser Slave Lake. Cable on receipt of this letter and I shall start right away.

Love to mother and the girls.

Your affectionate son, Bertie.

(9 January 1904)

Like the editor of the *Eye Opener*, Bertie had his ups and downs. Now there was something better in store, a real Calgary bonanza. Without looking for it, he found the work for which he seemed to be created, and the monetary reward would allow him to return "to dear old Skookingham next year, a comparatively rich man." That prospect, however, did not stop him from inviting further contributions from the family exchequer.

After thanking Father for the last hundred pounds cabled over, Bertie explained that for the first weeks after getting back from Brandon where he had left the policeman a prisoner in the "daffy house," he had had to lie very low to allow his whiskers to grow. By way of further disguise he then went to a haberdasher and got himself dressed up in "a harmonious arrangement" of baggy pants, yellow leggings and a blue tie with little dots. He then ventured forth as "J. Montmorency Curzon, fresh out from Cheltenham, England. Crossed over on the Campania—they do you very well on that boat, you know."

With this attire, Bertie found it easy to gain entrée to the best circles at the Ranchmen's Club and the Alberta Hotel. By good fortune he learned that a great project was being planned for Calgary—a Dipsomaniac Asylum. The shareholders were looking for a manager and Bertie was their man. They hired him to take office forthwith; and in the celebration which followed, the new manager placed himself in position to become the first patient at the institution to be known as Tanglefoot Hall. But Tanglefoot promised to become well patronized, and the considerate son concluded the communication under review by reminding his father that, "If you would like to buy a few shares in Tanglefoot Hall Co., Limited, send me a couple of hundred pounds and I will get you in on the ground floor."

There came a day, strange to tell, when Bertie's thoughts were directed at nobler things; and if he wanted money from home, he wasn't saying so. Of course, he had started a distillery and sold it for cash, and now his yen was to do something for humanity; what could be more natural when he felt "torn with anxiety for the moral welfare of mankind?" But it was a familiar pattern: first the struggle for survival, then the desire for wealth, and finally this urge to serve one's country as a politician. But as his next letter shows, he was the same Bertie for whom High River people had to admit a growing affection. That next letter was dated Calgary, 17 March 1904:

> My Dear Dad:
> When last I wrote you I was running the Black Cobra Distillery full blast in conjunction with my friend Courttenay. Since then I have sold out my interest and am at present worth all of $50,000. In consequence of this pleasant accession of wealth I am resolved to branch out and return on a visit to the ancestral home in England, crowned with laurels and with honours thick upon me. With this laudable aim in view it is my intention to enter the Dominion Parliament, running on the Prohibition ticket. Money being plentiful, my chances are excellent.
>
> As soon as the committees of the two great parties learned that I was willing to spend $20,000 on getting elected, they besought me with tears in their eyes to run on their respective sides.
>
> The Prohibition ticket I am running on is pretty sure to be a winner as the liquid I propose prohibiting in this case is water. The hotels will pull for me as one man and the local sports have promised to stand by. My committee is a singularly influential one, being composed of all the bartenders in town, with Fred Adams as chairman. Every man who steps into a hotel for a shot is presented with a quart of Black Cobra with "Vote for Buzzard-Cholomondeley" blown in the bottle, together with a little circular containing my electoral address. This latter effusion runs as follows:
>
> "Fellow citizens: In soliciting your suffrages I beg to state that my

attitude on all public matters will be one of unswerving adherence to my own political interests. I believe in a public man getting out of it all there is in it. Let us be honest in our villainy. What is the use of me telling you that I will only stand for clean government when you know and I know that if the opportunity presents itself for making a stake at the expense of the people, I will drop on it like a bee on a posy? As a good straightforward grafter I expect to make my mark in the House. I shall always be on the side of the Government so that if any horrible scandal should arise, a carefully selected commission of enquiry will whitewash me and make me clean. You will lose nothing and I shall be having my treasure on earth that neither moths nor flies will corrupt.

"I am a Prohibitionist. What I propose to prohibit is the reckless use of water. Its effect on health, habits and moral character of the community is disastrous. Look at the interminable series of typhoid cases with which our hospitals are filled from month to month, people dying who never died before, young men and maidens who have not reached the middle arch of life passing away down to a watery grave. It is sad to contemplate the distressing results of the steady tippling of germ-laden water. Every sample of the horrid stuff shows the presence of colon bacilli and an excessive number of other bacteria including pollywogs. If men would only confine themselves to a good stiff rasping old whiskey like Old Cobra, Calgary would be happier and better today. Any germ that can live after a gulp of Black Cobra has struck it, must be a corker.

"I propose erecting a beer fountain at my own expense in the CPR gardens and having it playing there all the time instead of the band. Although my business connection with Black Cobra has been severed, I can still recommend it as a means of grace and as a hope of glory. It touches the spot.

"On this platform I appeal for your support. If I prove recreant to my trust and false to my promises by becoming too darned immaculate, I shall be willing to resign. But there is no danger. I leave myself in your hands. Call at the committee rooms and get a bottle of Black Cobra.

"Respectfully, A.B.C."

Perhaps, father, you think I am crazy to issue a brutally frank address such as this, but believe me the rank and file of the voting public in Canada have reached such a pitch of exasperation toward the smooth flannel-mouths who pose as saints on the hustings and turn out to be nothing more than common-place sinners when in office, that they are ready to welcome with open arms a man who is honest enough to announce beforehand that he is not seeking their suffrages for his health.

Money talks without stammering in this country. . . . Graft is the rule. Boodle is the stake. Were I to tell the people that I disapproved of that sort of thing and would not tolerate it in others, they would instinctively distrust me. So my Bismarkian tactics of artless frankness will win me the day.

That beer fountain at the CPR park I shall open just one week before election day and give the people to understand that I am presenting it to the city by way of perpetuating my memory, keeping it green and so forth. They will think the fountain is to go on forever, like the brook, but the morning after the election, no more beer will be forthcoming.

So, father, you may expect a visit from me some time in the fall when you can introduce me to all your friends as the Member for Calgary. Love to Mother and the girls.
Your affectionate son, Bertie.

(30 April 1904)

The next instalment would have revealed the outcome of the election. But there was that incident of the gramophone choir at the High River church, and there was disapproval from a town group of which Bob Edwards was becoming more conscious. Moreover, Jerry Boyce was leaving. Bob was now thinking of quitting High River too. Consequently, the next chapter was never written. Nobody ever knew if Bertie was elected. It almost seemed that the plunge into politics had finished Bertie as it had finished some other men. But it hadn't entirely. It takes more than that to keep a good man down; and after a long absence from the columns of the *Eye Opener*, the familiar name appeared again when "Mr. Buzzard-Cholomondeley" attended a Rotary Convention in Calgary. He had just received some money from home and was staying at the Palliser Hotel where there was "lots of marmalade on hand" for guests with his taste, and where he found a salesman prepared to sell him a gold-mine on Snake Creek, just south of Calgary.

Presumably Bertie remarried, because the *Eye Opener* of 5 September 1912, reported that "Mrs. Buzzard-Cholomondeley astonished her friends last week by giving birth to quadruplets. The attending physician said it reminded him of shelling peas. Mother and offspring doing well."[3]

The folk at High River, where memories were good, reminded themselves that Bertie was never a man to do things in moderation and quadruplets were no surprise.

But in the High River of 1904, not even the popularity of the unpredictable Bertie could restore Bob Edwards to the position an editor should enjoy. Declining *Eye Opener* revenue was a symptom of something more serious; more than once in those last months at High River the editor wished that he, like Bertie, had a rich father to whom he could appeal for a thousand pounds with some hope of receiving it.

[3] Not exactly. MacEwan omits an initial that stands in the way of his good story. The original entry reads: "Mrs. P. Buzzard-Cholomondeley, of Eighteenth Avenue, astonished her friends . . ." Perhaps a close relative?

CHAPTER FIVE
Calgary Next

"Picturesquely situated so as to be within easy reach of the brewery, Calgary extends right and left, north and south, up and down, in and out, expanding as she goes, swelling in her pride, puffing in her might, blowing in her majesty and revolving in eccentric orbits round a couple of dozen large bars which close promptly at 11:30 right or wrong."

"A man may be too old to enlist but his age never keeps him from going to the front at the Grand Theatre when there is a leg-show on."

(9 March 1918)

"Although the citizens of Calgary are not what you would call violently insane, they still indulge in picnics to an alarming extent, eating sand and ants and doing other things which we admit are mildly idiotic."

(12 April 1913)

"YOU'D BE BETTER in a city; you come to Calgary," Paddy Nolan said to Bob Edwards when on one of his High River trips to defend a cattle rustler. Edwards was attracted by the heavyset lawyer whose nationality was as obvious as the peaks of the Rockies and whose wit was as sharp as an Irishman's peat-axe.

A few months later, while the cloud of righteous indignation from certain incidents remained over him, Bob Edwards made the decision, confessing publicly to understandable discouragement: "These small towns are awful. Wetaskiwin threw us down. Leduc threw us down. Strathcona, being dead anyway, shook its shrivelled finger at us. High River is passing us up. Ye Gods! That we should have lived in such places."

Calgary would be different. But would Calgary be better?

For Methodist ministers and transient editors there was special advantage in being mobile. With no printing plant, no office, and no professional equipment, Publisher Edwards could pack his belongings and make himself ready for moving while a liveryman was hitching to drive him away. Leaving High River, all his worldly belongings except his precious books were packed in one of those accordion-type valises which could expand like a snake that had swallowed a cat.

Departure made him sad. Jerry Boyce had already left to operate a hotel at

Gleichen, but there were various other loyal people to whom he was obliged to say "farewell": sporting Billy Cochrane, who owned the first automobile in the Alberta country; Dan Riley (later Senator Riley), whose wealth was ten dollars tucked in a shirt pocket when he walked to the foothills in 1883, and who then lost the ten dollars when he washed the shirt in the Bow River; Phil Weinard, the German-born rancher and friend of Artist Charlie Russell; Dr. G. D. Stanley, who saved the editor's life a few times; the devil-may-care Shorty McLaughlin, and others. Nor could he get it out of his mind that he was writing "Failure" on another chapter in his life.

Calgary loomed as the next experiment—Calgary, which had begun when the North West Mounted Police built an outpost at the junction of the Elbow and Bow rivers twenty-nine years before, and which now seemed to be the real beating heart of the West. Calgary's three-man police force counted a population of 9,554. According to Bob Edwards there were just two classes in local society: "those who sent their washing out and those who took it in." Stephen (8th) Avenue was the business lifeline. Most of the hotels, including the Alberta, Royal, and Queens, were on the south side of the avenue, and "ladies" chose to walk on the north side. There was this about it, that an editor who became incapacitated by drink now and then wouldn't be conspicuous, and half the people on the avenue wouldn't be making it their business to know how he was spending his evenings.

Arrival in Calgary was without fanfare. The fire department's brass band, led by proud Crispin Smith in Prince Albert coat and bearskin busby hat, was on the street—but it wasn't for Bob Edwards. He went to the Alberta Hotel, took a one-dollar room, shut the door with a slam and threw himself on the bed to think about his next move in a city in which his acquaintances were few. His paper in Calgary would be his fifth publishing venture in the Territories and he had no capital. He might have had a few dollars, but there had been some debts to meet before leaving High River, and he had given the clerk at the trading company thirty dollars to provide groceries for the wife and children of an improvident fellow who deserted in the night. Bob was practically destitute and his "banker," Jerry, was far away. Moreover, kind-hearted Jerry had troubles of his own and probably couldn't help anyway.

It was too bad about Jerry; just to think that he had had to face the court on a charge of being an accomplice in connection with a mail robbery. Late in 1903, ten thousand dollars were stolen from the mail between Calgary and Winnipeg, and Jerry, in the course of raising a loan with which to buy a property in British Columbia, had the misfortune to get some of the hunted money and was caught with it. Before the court finished with the case, a mail clerk was convicted and sentenced to seven years in penitentiary, while a Calgary lawyer was sentenced to

Patrick James "Paddy" Nolan

eighteen months for complicity, and Jerry Boyce had to do some explaining to clear himself.

Gripped by a hitherto unexperienced feeling of loneliness and failure, Bob's inclination was to go to the bar—that bar for which the Alberta Hotel was famous. But he knew that if he went while feeling depressed, he'd stay too long and bedevil more than ever his entry into Calgary business.

While the conflict between a yearning and a conviction continued, there were heavy footsteps in the hall and a knock at the door. This was no ordinary gentle knock, but a pounding that might be from the fist of a giant. Before Bob could call, "Come in," the hinges squeaked and the broad frame of Paddy Nolan filled the doorway: black-moustached Paddy, greatest lawyer in the Territories, whose cultured Irish accent and incomparable humour drew men to him like syrup draws flies. Paddy Nolan was exactly what Bob Edwards needed at that moment as on many subsequent occasions.

"The clerk downstairs told me he had just registered an honest Scotsman and I wanted to see with my own eyes," the lawyer began. "Sure, and it's welcome to Calgary, me man."

Bob seized the big outstretched hand and felt a charge of reassurance from it. "Paddy Nolan!" he exclaimed. "The Irish are not all knaves, or they hide their guilt damned well. It's months since I saw you. Tell me, why have you not been High River way these last months?"

"The Cashel case," Nolan replied. "Trying to save an accused murderer from the gallows can take a lot of time, you'll understand. We almost did it, but—poor Ernest—after all my effort to prove his innocence, he confessed the shooting to Dr. Kerby on the eve of his hanging."

Before there was any talk about Bob's business problems, Paddy Nolan related the Cashel story—one that had filled the newspapers and excited the people of all Canada for months. In October, 1902, Cashel, wanted for forgery, was in the Red Deer district, ostensibly to secure cattle with which to stock his ranch. Ellsworth was the name he was using. After staying at the shack of Isaac Rufus Belt, it was noted by friends that both men had disappeared. Police searched along the Red Deer River but found nothing to support their suspicions. Cashel was found and arrested on a charge of forgery; but before the police got him to Calgary, he jumped to freedom from the washroom window of a fast-moving train. Next, Cashel stole a horse and was arrested again. But in the meantime, the decomposed body of Belt was discovered at the mouth of Trail Creek on the Red Deer. Cashel was charged with murder and Paddy Nolan was retained for defence. Tried before Chief Justice Sifton, the slippery Cashel was convicted and sentenced to hang on 15 December 1903.

Earnest Cashel, c. 1903

Cashel was still hard to hold. Following a visit from the condemned man's brother, John Cashel, the convict confronted his guards with two revolvers, herded them into his cell for safekeeping and walked calmly out into the night and disappeared. Paddy Nolan, by this time, was in Ottawa seeking a new trial. As he talked with the Minister of Justice on 10 December, the Minister was handed a telegram. After reading it, the government man turned to Nolan and announced, "Your man has escaped." Nolan is reported to have replied: "Thank you sir; goodbye."

A mighty manhunt followed. It was the hunt for a ruthless man, and everybody knew it. Actually, he never left the Calgary district. He was in hiding just about seven miles east of the city, spending part of his time in an abandoned shack and sleeping in a den he had hollowed out of a haystack. When finally located, he was ready to shoot it out with the police, until straw around his shack was set afire. Only then did he throw down his guns and surrender. Ernest Cashel did not escape again, but paid with his life on 2 February 1904.

"Poor Ernest!" said Paddy Nolan. "Fascinating fellow and smart; but a damned fool, of course."

Bob and Paddy dined together that night and communed understandingly. A friendship which had begun feebly at High River was now being reinforced by shafts of intellectual agreement. Both men loved humour and humility and both hated sham, a form of dishonesty. Together the two men walked on Atlantic (9th) and Stephen (8th) Avenues to consider locations which might be suitable for an editor's office and residence; and together they visited the Alberta bar to drink the success of the *Calgary Eye Opener*.

Bob Edwards knew very well that Paddy Nolan was not only a good companion but a good guide in and about Calgary. This brilliant man with Limerick, Ireland, for a birthplace, 17 March for a birthday (1864), and an honours degree in classics from Trinity College in Dublin, had been in Calgary since stepping off the train as a total stranger in 1889. In his first year in the country he was admitted to the bar of the North West Territories and now, as he counselled Bob Edwards, he was regarded as the best defence lawyer and the finest orator in the country. Before leaving High River, Bob Edwards acknowledged that "all the best criminals go to Paddy Nolan."

Before long Bob Edwards was moving to quarters on the second floor of the Cameron Block at the corner of Stephen Avenue and Osler Street (8th Ave. and lst St. E.). There, a bedroom and double office comprised living and business premises.

News travelled quickly on Stephen Avenue and everybody knew the *Eye Opener* had a new home. The only really public announcements, however, were indirect ones from the editor's own pen; first, that a weekly paper was about to start in Calgary under the "absurd title of *Eye Opener*. It is said that the editor has never drawn a sober breath in his life . . . His rag will probably go bust inside six months." Then there appeared an item telling readers that the local brewery planned an addition but, "this has no special significance in connection with our coming to locate in Calgary; they were going to put it up anyway." (2 January 1904)

Actually, Bob Edwards was no stranger in the Calgary of 1904. He had a speaking acquaintance with many local people, and while at High River he had editorialized playfully about the city which was now "the logical leader in all that is fashionable, immoral, gay and joyous in the Territories." On various occasions he had managed to ruffle the composure of the City Fathers and members of the Ministerial Association. Now, as a resident of Calgary, he would chastise the members of the City Council more than ever when they showed weakness; more than ever he would "roast" those smug city-dwellers who were inclined to parade their wealth and their righteousness.

His intentions were good. He realized that this was a fresh start, and again he declared a policy for himself and his paper. The paper would "appear, henceforth, with unfailing regularity." Instead of following Horace's dictum to "mingle a little folly with your wisdom," he proposed trying the converse as an experiment. "If you get your paper regularly, you will know it is working all right."

But in spite of good intentions, the *Eye Opener* continued on its irregular course, appearing when the one-man staff had it ready and mirroring the everyday life of

Calgary and Alberta. Local politics received constant attention; the humbug in society was exposed; booze was accepted philosophically, and details were provided regularly about horse races and prize fights. The *Eye Opener* became Calgary's top entertainment and readers accepted irregularity with resignation.

Calgary streets seemed to generate new life and interest. One pioneer said, "We didn't realize how much fun had gone unnoticed until we began reading the *Calgary Eye Opener*." What prompted the remark was Bob Edwards's account of a Stephen Avenue incident, the adventure of a man who had remained too long at the bar. It was near dusk as the subject of the story made his way along the Avenue, opposite the Post Office.

> Passing Shaver and Graham's undertaking rooms, he espied the hearse standing outside all ready hitched up, the end doors open where you shove in the coffin. He began to wonder what it felt like to be a corpse in a hearse. The driver being in the office, he seized the favourable opportunity to find out what the sensation was like and crawled inside, slamming the end doors after him. Hearing the doors slam, the horses thought the funeral had started and promptly ran off down the Avenue. The gentleman rattled around inside like a pea and from the way the handles were fixed, could not open the door from the inside. Away down near Fourth Street a couple of new NWMP recruits were walking up from the barracks and saw the hearse coming tearing down the street. Here, thought they, was the time to make a rep. and get in line for promotion. Stepping out in the middle of the road they succeeded in stopping the runaways, which they tied to a post pending developments. They thought they had better see if there was a corpse inside and, if so, if it was all safe. Opening the end doors and peering in, they saw a dilapidated form creeping gingerly towards them. With a yell they took to their heels and made for the barracks on the dead run, looking back fearfully over their shoulders as they ran. The man himself got sobered up with the jolting and, mounting the seat drove the hearse back to the infuriated proprietors. As for the policemen, all the satisfaction they got when they related the gruesome story was a lecture from the Sergeant-Major on the dangers of going up against Calgary whiskey. He advised them to cut it out. (30 April 1904)

There was a sporting spirit about that Calgary to which Bob Edwards went in

1904; a good horse-race would empty the offices on Stephen Avenue any afternoon, and a boxing match would leave most Calgary women sitting alone at home for an evening. Much of the credit for outdoor sports and games belonged with the two-fisted fire chief, James "Cappie" Smart, of whom Bob Edwards saw much in after years. Cappie was the official starter for all road races and administered justice at hockey and boxing matches. Bob Edwards knew more than he would tell about a Calgary-Edmonton hockey match played on the Elbow River with ten players on each side, and ending in a free-for-all with both Referee Cappie Smart and his chunky pal, Bob Edwards, in the midst of it.

What a man was Calgary's Cappie who occupied the office of fire chief for thirty-five years after 1898! Arriving from his native Scotland in 1883, he did some carpentry work in Calgary and then tried undertaking; but it was at a fire or a fight that he was at his commanding best. It was Cappie Smart more than any other factor that caused Calgary boys to resolve to be firemen—perhaps to reach the eminence of chief and stand conspicuously beside a burning building, megaphone in hand, and roar commands to his men. There was one embarrassment about Cappie's thunderous performance at a fire; smoke, he explained, made him swear, and sometimes his language was as scorching as the flames he was fighting.

James "Cappie" Smart, 1914

The fire chief knew nothing about writing editorials, and Bob Edwards knew nothing about fighting fires, but in other respects there was striking similarity. Cappie was just a year younger than Bob; both were Scots; both departed from the ways of sobriety too often; and both were extremely fond of horses. Indeed, Cappie Smart's fire horses were the pride of all Calgary. When a visitor to the city was considered sufficiently distinguished, he rated a demonstration run by the fire rigs—usually in the direction of the brewery. White Wings, an old grey mare whose job was to pull the two-wheeled chemical cart, was a special favourite. It happened once that the fireman fell off the cart as it drew away from the fire hall, but the old mare dashed away as usual and didn't stop until she reached the scene of the fire.

One of the grandstand attractions at the Dominion Exhibition at Calgary in

1908 was a demonstration by two horses from the local fire hall. It was Calgary's biggest exhibition effort up to that time, with top features like daily flights by "Strobel's airship," and the *Eye Opener* issuing a clarion call: "All the inhabitants of the earth, civilized and uncivilized, rich and poor, honest and from Ottawa, are cordially invited to the Dominon Fair, June 29 to July 9 . . . " Cappie's two fine horses were released on the infield in front of the grandstand and a fire-wagon was placed on the track with harness suspended in front of it. An alarm bell was sounded, and the horses abandoned their grass and freedom and bounded at what they recognized as the call of duty to stand in front of the wagon long enough for the harness to be dropped and fastened. Then away they went at a gallop to round the track for a madly cheering crowd. Bob Edwards, who was a frequent visitor at the horse stalls in the fire hall, was just as proud of the performance as though he had trained the horses himself.

Another quality Bob and Cappie had in common was generosity; and there is the testimony of an early resident who knew both, that when Christmas was passed, "Cappie Smart and Bob Edwards were always broke," having spent as lavishly as their resources would allow on Christmas charity for needy folk in the city.

Actually, the fire brigade—many of whose members began as volunteers with a reward of seventy-five cents for each fire attended—was a dominant force in the social life of Calgary. Cappie's firefighters had the best brass band; they staged the annual 24 May sports program; and they sponsored the leading social event of the year, the St. Patrick's Day Ball. There at the Ball, held in the Hull Opera House on the corner of Angus Avenue and McTavish (6th Ave. and Centre St.), Calgary's most stylish clothes were displayed. Still, nobody stayed away because he or she did not have fine things to wear. Even Mary Fulham, early Calgary's celebrated keeper of pigs and disturber of the peace, would be present, dressed in paddy-green to guard against any possible doubt about her nationality.

Soon after Bob Edwards arrived in Calgary, Paddy Nolan saw to it that he met Mrs. Fulham, best known as "Mother" Fulham, whose residence and piggery were on Angus Avenue. Of medium height, plump, and scandalously dressed, Irish Mother Fulham could neither read nor write. But that did not stop her from speaking loudly and often, as she did when there seemed the slightest provocation. She considered herself to be the highest authority on pigs. To feed her herd she gathered garbage from various hotels: the Alberta, the Royal, the Queens, the Windsor; and from some restaurants.

On 17 March she went to the Ball and on the 12 July she again dressed in green and hurled defiance at the marching Orangemen. Now and then she celebrated too freely; and when she had to be taken to police headquarters, it was a task calling for the entire police force—Chief English and his two constables. Even on court appearance, whether plaintiff or defendant, Mary Fulham did not hesitate to speak for herself, but Paddy Nolan usually acted for her. And when the Fulham-Nolan combination was to appear in court, all Calgary, it seemed, wanted to be present. Bob Edwards found Calgary people still talking about a case of a few years before, when the courtroom had been too small.

It was like this: driving her spotted pony and democrat, Mary Fulham had arrived at the back of the Alberta Hotel just in time to observe a Chinese employee from the hotel bent over the barrel of garbage, presumably stealing pig feed. There was an altercation, with resulting bruises and black eyes. The magistrate couldn't satisfy himself about who did most of the hitting; and so, after prolonging the case a reasonable time for purposes of public entertainment, he dismissed it.

Cleanliness was not one of the lady's virtues; and as Bob Edwards soon learned, Dr. H. G. Mackid had shocking demonstration of the fact. Meeting the doctor on Stephen Avenue, she reported a sore foot. The kindly pioneer doctor, who had practiced in Calgary from the time of his arrival in 1889, said, "Come in to Templeton's Drug Store and I'll look at it." Together they entered the store, and promptly the woman took off a stocking. Glancing with some horror at the bare leg, Dr. Mackid exclaimed: "By George, I'd bet a dollar that's the dirtiest leg in Calgary."

Mother Fulham's Irish responded quickly. "Put up your money, Doctor; I'm betting it's not and here's my dollar."

With that, she pulled off her other stocking and exposed another leg that was quite obviously, just as dirty. The doctor paid his bet.

Mary Fulham, who was an ideal subject for a newspaper man like Bob Edwards, became well known beyond Calgary; and even Sir William Van Horne, when president of the CPR, had her company forced upon him. Her cow, Nellie, wandered on to the right-of-way and was killed by a train. For a long time the settlement which the woman expected did not come, and when she learned that the president was in the city, she presented herself at his private car and blamed him for the cow's death. Sir William, in defence, is reported to have said: "Your cow shouldn't have been on the tracks, you know; we have signs forbidding entrance to the right-of-way."

"Ye poor damn fool," she replied with an expression of sympathy, "and what makes ye think me pore old cow could read?"

The president weakened and promised her another cow, but still she wasn't satisfied that the CPR could get another cow "as good as my old Nellie."

Bob Edwards, one may be sure, gave Mother Fulham every chance to express her Irish views about Calgary society. He would laugh at her—making his typical belly-giggles—as she expounded about the pink teas, but he was inclined to agree with her. He became her friend and won her trust.

With people like Paddy and Cappie and Mary and others with strong individualism about him, the Calgary days were not likely to be dull. As time passed, Bob was seeing more and more of Paddy Nolan. It was becoming clear that they were good for each other. They had the same sense of humour and both enjoyed the kind of mischief in which no undeserving person was hurt. "It becomes immoral when somebody suffers by it," was their reasoning.

Innocent pranks which added interest to living and sometimes carried a lesson were hard to resist. Bob Edwards could call the Scottish proprietor of one of the "better" restaurants on Stephen Avenue and remark: "I must congratulate you on the skill of your employees, one in particular."

Swelling with pride, the businessman enquired as to which of his helpers had reached such a pinnacle of proficiency, and the reply was: "That son of a gun who skims the milk for you. I've never seen it done so well."

And Paddy could mislead a visiting Mounted Policeman and make him enjoy it, as on the night of a "swell ball" at Hull's Opera House. The Mountie, according to Bob's telling, was:

> Inspector Donnie Howard . . . who came down from Edmonton for the affair. Along about 2 AM, Donnie felt pretty dry and asked Paddy Nolan if there was any chance of hustling a drink anywhere. Paddy explained that the bars were all closed but he knew of a quiet blind pig close by, to which he had the key. A few of the best of them, he said, kept this blind pig for their own use when the Ranchmen's Club was too distant.
>
> So Paddy led the inspector a short distance up Sixth Avenue, just a few doors West, in fact, and after looking cautiously around to make sure there were no spotters following, walked up to the door of a dwelling and produced a key, unlocked the door and stepped inside.
>
> "Don't make a noise," whispered Paddy. "Wait here in the passage and I'll bring it to you. No, that's all right—this is on me."
>
> After a lot of tiptoeing about in the dark he returned with two horrible snorts of Scotch, which they downed. Paddy listened attentively at the door for a minute or two before venturing to open it again. Satisfied that all was safe, they tiptoed out and returned to the Opera House.
>
> Next day Inspector Howard happened to be passing along Sixth

> Avenue with a friend when he espied familiar surroundings.
>
> "Say," said he, confidentially, "do you see that house with all the trees in front? Looks mighty innocent, doesn't it? Well, it's a blind pig."
>
> "That house over there?" exclaimed the other. "Why, you damfool, that's P. J. Nolan's residence." (19 October 1918)[1]

Almost immediately after arrival in Calgary, Bob Edwards set himself up as a critic of civic administration. An opposition, he noted, has an important role in democratic government; and he could see himself doing a service, with that "most popular, semi-occasional, bi-monthly, catch-as catch-can newspaper west of Winnipeg," as the mouthpiece, keeping Mayor Ramsay's city administration in a state of agitated alert. Local governments were far from being models of decorum and efficiency, and even Calgary's City Fathers left themselves open to criticism. According to the story reaching Bob's ears, when city police made whiskey seizures, the Mayor and Aldermen found it necessary, sometimes, to satisfy themselves that the stuff really was whiskey, and on occasions felt obliged to retire to a closed meeting and try it over and over again for proof.

Whether that report was correct or not, City Council was to learn that to relax in the discharge of duty was to invite *Eye Opener* onslaught. "Instead of another license inspector," the editor proposed after a series of public charges, "the Council should appoint a civic laundryman to handle the dirty linen."

It is a matter of record, however, that Bob Edwards had some genuinely progressive ideas for the future of his recently adopted city. As time was to show, he was right in believing the community was not doing enough by way of planning. He was anxious that Calgary take the lead in preserving the spirit of the Old West; he would have promoted more of industry even at that early period and he was the most ardent booster for the annual Exhibition in the years before the Stampede events became features.

But while he claimed a right to criticize his city, criticism from outside, especially Edmonton, would bring the *Eye Opener* to the defence. Perhaps the editor went looking for an excuse to give his views about Edmonton. It suited Calgary people, anyway, to read that:

> Like Hootch and other unspeakable prairie burgs, Edmonton has been having trouble with its fire brigade. Edmonton, after all, is still the same dear old frontier town. Subjection to municipal discipline is

[1] Edwards concluded this anecdote by playing parenthetical tour-guide: "(The house here referred to is 113 Sixth Avenue West and is now occupied by Cappie Smart.)"

abhorrent to its soul. It is still in the reeve stage, with town marshall and calaboose, barber who organizes the local band and the inevitable enthusiastic hook and ladder company to give the burg something to be proud of. They are still advertising, "Good opening in Edmonton for a blacksmith shop." (9 March 1918)

Taken altogether, life in his adopted city suited Bob Edwards pretty well. Life was simple but rich—uncomplicated by oil promotion, parking problems, and a superabundance of bylaws of which most people knew little. His summary, written years later, suggests rather general approval:

> The Royal Hotel was at its zenith.
> Most young men had livery bills.
> You never heard of a "tin Lizzie."
> Doctors wanted to see your tongue.
> Nobody started the day without a Collins.
> Advertisers seldom told the truth.
> Farmers came to town looking frowsy.
> The hired girl drew twelve dollars a month.
> The butcher "threw in" a chunk of liver.

Nobody "listened in" on a telephone.
There was no telephone.
The men did all the drinking.
You stuck tubes in your ears to hear a phonograph.
People thought politicians were statesmen.
The Alberta Hotel was considered a Waldorf-Astoria.
We were all broke and happy."

(9 March 1918)[2]

Poverty, as the editor reminded his readers, was not uncommon. There were those whose niggardliness in sharing with needy people drew Bob Edwards's ire; but to be fair to the young and relatively carefree city, there was an over-riding kindliness—a sense of fellow-feeling which evidently reached even to the magistrate. Bob Edwards took satisfaction in telling about the Calgary magistrate, Tom Burns, before whom one of his friends was brought on the familiar charge of drunkenness:

Said Magistrate Burns, "I'll have to fine you seven dollars and costs."
"Can't pay it," replied the prisoner.
"How about five dollars—can you pay that?"
"No, your honour."
"I'll make the fine two and a half then," said Mr. Burns.
"Your Honour, I'm broke," confessed the unfortunate fellow.
"And dry too, no doubt," the magistrate added.
"Yes, your Honour."
"Well," said the man on the bench, "get the hell out of here—and here's two bits for a wee snifter!"

Nor was the Calgary bailiff any more conventional than the magistrate. According to Bob's reporting, that worthy officer went to seize the contents of a house in posh Mount Royal district. The inventory, as the bailiff took it down, began in the attic: "One sideboard, oak. One dining room table, oak. One set of chairs, (6) oak. Two bottles of whiskey, full."

Then the word "full" was stricken out and replaced by "empty," and the inven-

[2] Either as a concession to outmoded vernacular, or out of concern the phrase be misread as sordid, MacEwan changed "plunks" to "dollars." He excised the lines "Nobody wore white shoes," "Jules Verne was the only convert to the submarine," and "Mayor Costello and Everett Marshall were linotype operators on the *Herald*, and the editor of this paper was a bull on the whiskey market somewhere in Alberta." He also monkeyed with the rhythm of the final line: "We were all broke and happy—only twenty years ago."

tory was continued in a hand that straggled and lurched diagonally across the page until it ended with, "One revolving door mat." (9 March 1918)

It was one of the tragedies of Edwards's life that drink, of which he wrote so freely and flippantly, got the better of him now and then and he would be taken to Holy Cross Hospital for a period of recovery. Sad as was his condition when he came for a five- or six-day stay, he was always reserved and careful in his speech. Never did he leave the hospital without arranging for a gift for his nurses.

Not even in the hospital did he lose his originality. It happened that he and one of his drinking companions were in Holy Cross Hospital at the same time, receiving delirium tremens treatment in which the purgative calomel was prescribed. Bob and friend, clothed in dressing gowns, met in the hospital corridor while on the way to the bathroom at the end of the hall. Now largely recovered from their illness, they greeted each other enthusiastically and proceeded together, arm in arm. At that moment, the Mother Superior appeared and with some justifiable astonishment asked, "What's all this?"

While convalescent, the editor composed merry quips and jests for his paper.

With the characteristic boyish twinkle returning to Bob's eyes, he replied in song: "Tis the march of the Calomel Men."

It wasn't surprising that Calgary and the *Eye Opener* became almost synonymous in the years ahead. It happened that a well-known Albertan, when driving in Southern California, answered an enquiry by stating that he came from Calgary. To this, the owner of the service station at which the conversation took place responded: "Is that the name of a town? I thought it was just the name of a paper—*Calgary Eye Opener.*"

CHAPTER SIX
The Alberta Hotel

"There isn't a woman living so bad in arithmetic that she cannot calculate how much her husband would save if he didn't smoke."

(20 July 1918)

"Prosperity never spoils men that adversity cannot crush."

(24 November 1917)

"Isn't it queer that only sensible people agree with you."

(5 October 1912)

SEVENTY-FIVE THOUSAND DOLLARS for a hotel! It did seem fantastic, yet that was what Norman Jackson paid for the Alberta just at the time Bob Edwards moved to Calgary. But the buyer got more than a fourteen-year-old structure; he got traditions, memories, and sentiment, because no building in Calgary had such a story as the old sandstone hotel, started in 1888 and opened for business in 1890.

It was the crossroads at which businessmen, cattlemen, and salty characters met; and for Bob Edwards it exerted a magnetic pull soon after he took up residence on Stephen Avenue. If a person looking for the editor didn't find him in his Cameron Block offices the place to look was the smoke-filled rotunda, the noisy bar, or the excellent dining room, just two blocks to the West. There at the hotel much of the copy for the *Eye Opener* pages was written.

The Alberta bar was the longest between Winnipeg and Vancouver, and the most famous; its hours were 7:00 AM to 11:30 PM and drinks were two for a quarter. Behind the 125-foot-long bar were ten busy men, among them well-known early Calgarians like Fred Adams, Tom Pierce, and George Rutley, who became about as much a part of the place as the swinging doors. Fred Adams, "the eminent mixologist," was Bob Edwards's nomination for the office of committee chairman to see the fictional Bertie Buzzard-Cholomondeley elected to the House of Commons for Calgary constituency. And when Pierce retired, his total dispensations, according to Bob Edwards, were enough liquid to fill all the horse troughs in the province and sufficient left over to float the two boats which made up the Canadian navy.

Everything, it seemed, started at the Alberta Hotel: business deals, fights, and fun—even gunplay now and then. With Mother Fulham calling daily for garbage, things could be lively at the back of the hotel as well as the front. Calgary's A. A. Gray, who came to the city in the same year as Bob Edwards, could recall one of those occasions when the back of the hotel became a centre of interest. At that time he had a job painting the hotel rooms at a dollar a day. As usual, Mother Fulham tied her horse in the lane and entered the hotel kitchen, hoping to qualify for a piece of leftover pie or a cookie. Gray's painting partner whispered to the chef to detain the lady with an extra morsel of food while he attended to a self-assigned task. He slipped out, unhitched Fulham's pony, shoved the shafts of the democrat through the CPR wire fence and re-hitched with democrat on one side of the fence and horse on the other.

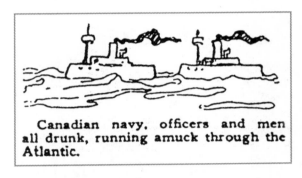

Canadian navy, officers and men all drunk, running amuck through the Atlantic.

In her own good time Mother Fulham left the kitchen, and like a princess ascending a throne, mounted her democrat without suspecting any felonious act. She hesitated, took the old clay pipe from her mouth, and ran her grimy fingers through her hair, wondering momentarily if she was really sober. Then it dawned upon her that she was the victim of a vile Protestant trick. By this time she had an audience and shouted her curses, making it very clear what she would do if she could get her powerful hands on the responsible miscreant.

And gunplay? The Alberta didn't escape. Tom Pierce was the hero in humbling one gunman at the bar. When Pierce wasn't pouring, he was polishing glassware or something else, a habit ingrained by years of practice. Bob Edwards always regretted being absent that day when a stranger with a criminal glint in his eye stepped up to the bar as Pierce was polishing. The man took a revolver from his hip pocket and placed it on the counter-top with the muzzle only inches from the bartender's navel. Pierce, however, had not tended bar all those years without developing a certain callousness. He continued to polish the soda siphon in his hands but raised it slightly until the nozzle was in line with the gunman's face; then he pumped a big charge of fluid into the bad man's eyes, and casually picked up the gun.

E. A. Shelley, night clerk when Bob Edwards first stopped there, recalled that guns went off rather frequently around the hotel. As one who started as a twelve-year-old bellboy the very day the hotel opened and finished as manager when it closed its doors in the face of prohibition twenty-six years later, he should know. Vivid in his memory was the day when the barroom seemed to be full of bullets. Into the bar rode an Englishman on his black horse. Without dismounting, he began shooting wildly. Customers and workers ducked and cleared out, but the shooting continued until every mirror and most of the bottles were shattered. Next day, when confronted with a bill for damages amounting to $2800, the gunman settled cheerfully by writing a cheque, then went away searching for some new form of amusement.

Lobby of Alberta Hotel, with E. A. Shelley at desk, c. 1900.

Of course, the fellow was one of those remittance men with lots of money for a few days each month. The Alberta Hotel had a special attraction for them, and for other Old Country travellers who came to launch a hunting expedition into the mountains. They admired the stuffed heads of bighorn sheep and bears in store windows, bought the best guns and often did not get nearer the mountains than the end of Stephen Avenue.

But striking as were the long bar and the amusing fellows with money and monocles, the Alberta had something far more unique—a collection of acclimatized foothills personalities giving patronage to one part or another of the hotel. Here was a personality cross-section without parallel.

Bob Edwards could enjoy unusual outdoor people like the volatile firefighter, Cappie Smart, and the unschooled garbage queen, Mother Fulham; but for steady fare he needed more men like Paddy Nolan with whom he could engage in relaxed and varied conversation. Indeed, it was one of life's sweetest prizes—conversation. More and more he was becoming conscious of a need for that mental exercise afforded by discussion and intelligent repartee. At Wetaskiwin he had tried to starve the intellectual part of himself, and at High River to feed it with half rations. Now, in the associations of the old Alberta Hotel, Bob Edwards found something for which his need was increasingly clear—men with ideas and the capacity and will to share them. Here was a community within a community, one made attractive by brilliant individuality. More and more he was drawn into that labyrinth of Alberta Hotel life, surroundings from which he gained many of his richest experiences.

Of the friends he made around the hotel, many will be forever nameless; but now and then one springs from obscurity to say, "Dear old Bob—many were the snorts and the good hours I had at the Alberta with him." At the same time, a most significant percentage of the Makers of Southern Alberta were thereabout. Ramrod-straight Col. James Walker might be found there at almost any time—the old Colonel who was a member of the first troop of Mounted Police that trekked across the plains to build Fort Macleod, chairman of Calgary's first administrative committee, president of the Agricultural Society when the first Calgary fair was held, and a man who, according to General Sir Arthur Currie, "breaks out every fifty years and goes to war." Fred Stimson, first manager of the Bar U Ranch, kept a room there for years; and so did cattle kings Pat Burns and George Lane. R. B. Bennett lived there for a while and made his noon meal at the Alberta a long-time practice.

Here were the aristocrats of the new country, and Bob Edwards's delight at the end of a day was to draw a chair close to one of them and talk through a cloud of smoke from cigars "made in Calgary." George Lane, whose cowboy frame suggested that it might have been pieced together by a committee, could tell about long cattle drives, rustling and bad winters—hardships to discourage all but the stout of spirit. And yet he could say that since coming to the Foothills as a "mail order" cowhand at thirty-five dollars a month in 1884, the good years which followed bad ones invariably wiped out losses. Now his biggest worry was settlers and their damnable barbed wire. More feathers would be ruffled before this mounting conflict between ranchers and grain growers would be settled.

But George Lane was cheerful. His last trainload of steers had sold at Winnipeg to net him close to four cents a pound. Why, "this very day" he had seen John Ware, that massive Negro rancher with massive heart, driving out of Calgary with a brand new buggy. And markets couldn't be very bad when George Emerson, who released the first cattle west of High River in 1879, could lose a Gordon, Ironside and Fares cheque in payment for steers sold in the previous year and not even miss it until Billy Fares enquired why it had never been cashed.

"Yes sir, Fares sent his son-in-law out to Emerson's ranch to find out why that cheque issued ten months before had never gone through the bank in the customary way. Old George couldn't recall what had happened to it, supposing only that it was deposited to his account. He said he would look in his pockets, however, and sure enough, in an old vest hanging abandoned in the woodshed, he found the cheque where he had stuffed it away months before."

For Bob Edwards, no lobby party was complete until his kindred spirit, Paddy Nolan, joined it; and then it was perfect only if it did not exceed a total of three or four people at a time. In one respect, Bob and his incisive friend were not alike; a large audience inspired Paddy's natural gifts of oratory but tended to silence the relatively bashful Edwards. And so it was at a lunch table, or where a few chairs were pushed together in a cluster, that Bob was at his best. Then he would lead with bold verbal thrusts to invite equal boldness from the big and affable lawyer.

Bar of Alberta Hotel. Bartenders, George Claire, left, and Fred Adams.

Paddy's appearance there would make Rancher George Lane wish again that the man had not quit a special assignment from the Western Stock Growers' Association to assist with the prosecutions of all suspected cattle rustlers. Nolan could be pardoned for favouring defence, in which his success was phenomenal; but when he was arguing for alleged cattle thieves, ranchers found it doubly difficult to get the convictions necessary to stamp out the menace of rustling. Bob recounted that after one of Paddy's clients was cleared of a charge of horse stealing, the lawyer asked: "Honour bright, now, Bill, you did steal that horse, didn't you?"

"Now look here, Mr. Nolan," was the reply, "I always did think I stole that horse, but since I heard your speech to that 'ere jury, I'll be doggoned if I ain't got my doubts about it."

For others, Paddy's arrival would suggest some recent gossip—perhaps the lawyer's proposal to change the name of his law firm from Nolan and Eaton to the more meaningful one of "Drinkin' and Eaton;" or it might be the story Bob published about his friend's misfortune on a trip to Fort Macleod to defend a case when the journey had to be made by stage coach. When fording the river close to the Fort, the stage upset and the passengers received a ducking. The town had no dry clothes big enough for Paddy and the court wouldn't wait for wet clothes to dry.

The anxious client bought a Hudson Bay blanket, the biggest one in the stores, wrapped it around the unclothed frame, and made sure his high-priced advocate was present for the moment of his great need. The spectacle was one never before seen in court, with the lawyer assuring the judge, quite cheerfully, that everything was all right; "I'm here, Your Lordship, to present the naked truth."

Paddy protested that the story as it came out of the South was exaggerated, and added the comment that "Fort Macleod is an outlying district and the men I've met down there can outlie any encountered this side of Edmonton."

With Paddy drawing a chair into the little circle, the stage was being set for repartee. Bob could be expected to offer a learned question about Ancient Greece or Canadian law; or it might be pure mirth—a definition of a lawyer, for example.

"A lawyer," said Bob, pointing to the recognized wellspring of Irish humour, "is a man who induces two others to remove their coats for a fight and then runs away with the coats."

"Yes," responded Paddy, "but if he stole an editor's coat, he wouldn't get much—some buttons and a corkscrew from the pockets."

"Never mind, Paddy," Bob would reply. "You with your big income and me with my buttons and booze bills, we'll all be on the same dead level a hundred years from now. But tell me, Paddy—you should have the answer for this—do you know how to weigh a pig, in the absence of a scale?"

Paddy had to confess he didn't know, although, to be sure, it was a reflection upon the Irish who were supposed to know all about pigs.

"Well, I'll tell you. You first balance a strong plank across a sawhorse. On one end of the plank you place the pig, and on the other end place a stone that is exactly the right weight to counterbalance the pig. Now, with the pig and the stone in perfect balance, all you have to do is guess the weight of the stone; and if you guess close enough, you will have the weight of the pig."

"That I shall remember," Paddy would promise, while making abdominal chuckles which seemed, almost, to vibrate the picture of the pacing champion, Dan Patch, where it hung on the wall.

To Paddy, still chuckling, it suggested something: "Last night as I was walking home, I heard sharp squeals coming from the direction of the river. Somebody said it was 'Scotty' Johnny Fraser breaking in a new set of bagpipes; but now that you've expounded your formula, I'm damned if I don't think it was old Mary Fulham weighing her swine."

"Ah Paddy, I always feared that good music was wasted on you. If I thought there was even a remote chance of you going to Heaven, I'd feel constrained to tell you that if the angels are really such superior creatures, they'll not be playing harps; they'll stop at nothing less than bagpipes, you may be sure."

"Is it true, Bob, that the 'oatmeal savages' from which you spring adopted kilts because they couldn't get their big feet into trousers?"

"Well," replied Bob, "if you expect an answer, I must inform you of what you might never learn at Dublin University: that the kilt has utility and beauty and is thus the peer among good clothes. You will concede, won't you, that the Scot in Highland uniform is the world's best-dressed man?"[1]

Others with names to become famous in western story were coming, going and pausing to pick up some gems of humour in that particular hotel thoroughfare. From an outside point it could be Dan Riley from High River, or Story-teller Dave McDougall from Morley, or Rancher Douglas Hardwick from Snake Valley. Pat Burns might stop briefly to have Bob or Paddy confirm his uncertain arithmetic ere he closed a cattle deal; he was always in a hurry. Cappie Smart couldn't linger because he'd have a game to referee somewhere. But Col. G. C. Porter, editor of the *Calgary Herald* between 1904 and 1906, would come purposely to join the little group; so would W. R. Hull, a founder of the livestock and meat industry in British Columbia and Alberta; and, until his death in 1906, D. H. Andrews, who supervised the biggest farming and ranching spread Canada had known up to that time.

Men of experience—every one. And what experience! This Andrews had moved from Wyoming to the North West Territories to manage Sir John Lister Kaye's chain of ranches—"76 Ranches" as they were known—where 30,000 sheep grazed, and around 10,000 cattle. And when Sir John's company was failing, Andrews went to England, reorganized and returned to continue managing the far-flung outfit.

And W. R. Hull, or "White Man" Hull as he was known? That 225-pound, distinguished-appearing Englishman with magnificent whiskers and a story about

[1] These chestnuts were drawn from various issues of the *Eye Opener,* as well as "the common wellspring."

adventure, couldn't stay away when he knew Paddy and Bob were ensconced in Alberta Hotel chairs. He could contribute something about the toughest trails in the western world, having walked across the Isthmus of Panama after crossing the Atlantic, walked inland from the mouth of the Fraser River to ranch and build a meat trade in the British Columbia Interior, and driven 1200 half-wild horses from the Kamloops area over mountains and through the passes to sell them in Calgary in 1883. Liking Calgary, he located there the next year and directed his ranching and meat trade from the new base.

Hull might have had reason to be displeased with Nolan. He wasn't, however. At a recent court sitting he had been the object of some Nolan fun, but even that did not blight his admiration for the lawyer nor his desire for the Nolan-Edwards company. Paddy was defending a chap charged with stealing cattle from Mr. Hull, and it was the lawyer's right and duty to cross-examine hull about identification of a certain steer alleged to have been stolen.

"Mr. Hull," Paddy began, "you are one of Alberta's biggest ranchers?"

Hull nodded agreement.

"And you have a lot of cattle around Claresholm, Mr. Hull?"

Again Hull's answer was "Yes."

"Where are your headquarters, Mr. Hull?"

"My headquarters are in Calgary," the cattleman replied.

"Your headquarters are at Calgary. Then where would you say your hindquarters were located?"

Thoughtlessly, the honest and friendly Hull said, "Claresholm."

"Well, well," said Nolan, "with your headquarters at Calgary and hindquarters at Claresholm, you are indeed the biggest rancher I've seen."

It was during one of those lobby sessions at which Colonel Porter was present that Western Canada heard the first proposal for a pipeline to carry anything except water. Alberta's oil resources were still among nature's most closely guarded secrets, but with thirsty people in the *Herald* building directly across the avenue from the Alberta Hotel, Bob Edwards proposed: "A pipe-line across the street and under the roadway to accommodate the staff and save their valuable time. Mr. Perley, proprietor of the Alberta, was willing to lay a half-inch pipe to convey whiskey across to the office but Mr. Young (managing director of the *Daily Herald*) insisted upon an additional two-inch pipe for beer. The negotiations fell through." (12 May 1919)

Even stockily built Jimmy Reilly, former mayor of Calgary, would come over to the Alberta when he had time to leave his own Royal Hotel, hoping to find Bob and Paddy occupying their big chairs near the entrance to the bar. And Calgary's archi-

COL. G. C. PORTER
Conservative Candidate for Hootch

tect, "Deafie" J. J. Wilson, often joined the group though he missed all parts of the conversation except the periodic suggestions about visits to the bar. To all questions directed at "Deafie," his answer was the same: "Don't mind if I do."

Clearly, the Edwards–Nolan combination was giving both the Alberta rotunda and the City of Calgary a bit of special lustre at that time. "Old Man" Simpson, editor of the *Cranbrook Herald*, said: "The three sights of the place are Paddy Nolan, Bob Edwards and the City Hall." (*Calgary Herald*, 10 February 1905) He was reporting on the Western Newspapermen's Convention at Calgary in January 1905, at which Nolan gave a paper on the Law of Libel. Continuing with Simpson's report: "Those who have not met either of the gentlemen named have lived in vain. The Lord never created a better entertainer than Paddy Nolan. As an after dinner speaker he is par excellence and compared with him, Chauncey Depew looks like a newspaperman's promise to pay a note of a million dollars. It is said that for years when a man contemplated the act of appropriating another man's steer or horse, he first retained the services of Paddy Nolan. Bob Edwards is a modest individual who is editing a Sunday School publication known as the *Eye Opener* with the laudable ambition of bringing the recreant souls of Calgary to their milk."

Indeed, most men thereabout who knew the Edwards–Nolan team made no attempt to resist the attraction. There was just one notable exception. Thirty-five-year-old R. B. Bennett, with an expression of grave responsibility, would leave the Alberta dining room where he took meals quite regularly, and walk briskly past the lighthearted group in which Bob Edwards sat, without either pause or recognition.

Bob had his enemies—many of them; but in that colourful Alberta Hotel community there was only this one man with whom he was not on friendly terms. For that there was a reason, however; perhaps a chain of reasons.

And so an evening would wear on. As their friends retired, Bob and Paddy would be left alone. Both were nighthawks. But they liked each other's company at any time and liked to have a while alone, not to rib each other but to talk quietly, philosophically, about their friends and themselves.

"Some great friends we've got, Bob," Paddy observed on one of these late nights. "They're people who have found their joy in their tasks. Do you ever feel that you want to ask the people around you where they find or hope to find their greatest satisfaction?"

Bob's eyes twinkled at the challenge. "I suppose Cappie Smart would be happiest refereeing a big boxing battle at Madison Square Garden; and Chief Cuddy would dream of a land where the wicked cease to make trouble; Commissioner Samis would hang the editor of the *Eye Opener* and Bennett would wind up his estate."

"All right Bob. Without any levity, tell me where you find the best satisfactions. I know you don't expect such a question but I'm serious."

"Come, Paddy, do you expect me to have the answer ready? Well, these hours with you and George Lane and Colonel Porter and the others are priceless, and writing copy for the old paper is one of my pleasures; but what a question to ask a man when he's sitting a few feet from a barroom door! Hang it, Paddy; I guess the Saturday morning hour when I meet the boys who sell the paper and pass out their copies for street trade is the best one in my week."

"Tell me this, then: how many kids get papers without payment?"

Bob looked puzzled. "Why do you ask that? I've never discussed it . . . The mothers of three of those lads are widows, you know, and another . . . "

"That's what I thought."

"There are other things too, Paddy. I live with a sort of secret hope that between drunks I'm doing something to give this new West an individuality—social and political individuality."

"And give its people reason to be proud they turned their backs on the security and comforts of the old communities in the East and elsewhere?"

"Yes."

"And make the CPR and Bennett rue their mistakes?"

"Yes."

CHAPTER SEVEN
The Bennett Table

> "It is not strictly true that Bennett invented oratory but doubtless he would have done so had he been there at the time."
>
> (23 March 1912)

> "Mrs. Fulham gave one of her delightful musicales on Wednesday afternoon."
>
> "The statement attributed to Mr. W. R. Hull in a recent interview that he intended purchasing the late pontiff's herd of papal bulls to put on range adjacent to the New Oxley Ranche for the purpose of improving the breed is entirely without foundation. Mr. Hull has no such intentions."
>
> (8 August 1903)

> "Zinn's dancing girls who occupied the boards of the Lyric all last week did big business . . . Although the wages of Zinn is death, many of the girls with this company seem to be laying up treasure in their stockings where neither moths nor flies do corrupt."
>
> (24 November 1906)

BOB EDWARDS, EDITOR, and R. B. Bennett, lawyer destined to be a Canadian Prime Minister, were personality opposites. Paddy Nolan recognized it and asked: "How could such people understand each other?"

Bennett had a faculty for amassing wealth, while Edwards was perpetually poor. The lawyer opened his office punctually and worked systematically, while the editor was hopelessly irregular. Bennett was a teetotaller and a devoted churchman; Bob was neither. Good Methodist that Bennett was, he couldn't possibly approve of all that Edwards said and did. He wouldn't even indulge in frivolous conversation in the rotunda of the Alberta Hotel. The two men seemed to be a world apart, and for two years they didn't speak to each other.

They called him Richard "Bonfire" Bennett around the Legislature of the North West Territories where he sat as Calgary's representative for seven years prior to 1905. Across the prairie country, the name of this son of Hopewell Cape on the New Brunswick side of the Bay of Fundy was winning attention; and within the city of Calgary, to which he went in 1897 to be a junior law partner with Senator James

Lougheed, he was a growing force. Calgary bad been his new home for a mere matter of weeks when he and the Senator attended a political meeting called to accommodate Frank Oliver of Edmonton as the speaker. Bennett, with an inborn confidence sharpened at Dalhousie Law School, arose to ask a question. Before the meeting ended, this young Conservative was on the Liberal platform answering his own questions and causing Calgarians to enquire: "Where did this orator come from?"

Bennett possessed a natural fondness for the smoke of political battle, and after just one year in Calgary he accepted the Conservative nomination and was elected to the Territorial Legislature which met at Regina. There he sat with Premier Frederick Haultain, the frontier statesman who knew, better than anyone else, what should be done to give provincial status to the country between Manitoba and the Rocky Mountains.

Of Bennett's impact upon the community there could be no doubt. He could make a speech about nearly anything; stimulate political fervour; and excite the mothers of unmarried daughters, who saw him as an eligible bachelor, immaculately dressed and promising as a lawyer. Still, the man was something of an oddity on Calgary streets. He was an intellectual, with no interest in horse racing or boxing—couldn't even saddle a pony. But was not this unusual fellow the first person with the courage to appear on Calgary's Stephen Avenue wearing a Prince Albert coat and top hat?

For several years after Bob Edwards began living in Calgary, he saw Bennett nearly every day; saw him at the Alberta Hotel where he had his lunch regularly at a special table. "The Bennett Table," set for six, was at the back of the dining room, and there the proud and proper politician presided during every noon hour, surrounded by the more or less scholarly men of his own choosing. It wasn't a noisy table—not by any means. There sat William Georgeson, a fine-looking man in the wholesale grocery business; John Kenny, a retired mail clerk who lived at the Alberta Hotel; George Peet, an Irishman who had opened a coal business in 1897; and Charles Taprell, after he became manager of the hotel. Others like Rev. George Kerby were guests now and then.

When Bob Edwards and Paddy Nolan lunched at the Alberta, they sat on the opposite side of the dining room; at least, that's the way it was for three years after Bob went to live in the city. Everybody knew about the *Eye Opener* campaign of criticism against the CPR, for which company Bennett was solicitor, and about the growing bitterness between solicitor and editor. Bennett took everything Edwards said and wrote about the railroad in a personal way, and in his anger vowed he would "run the editor of the *Eye Opener* out of town." (25 November 1905)

Railroad policy in Canada was wrong, Bob Edwards editorialized. Land grants and cash subsidies to the railroads were unjustifiably generous; the CPR was unpardonably monopolistic; and finally, as plain as the mischievous twinkle in Paddy Nolan's eyes, there was the railroad's failure to install adequate safeguards at crossings. At the Calgary crossings on Osler Street (1st E.) and Scarth Street (1st W.), accidents had occurred altogether too often.

At its September meetings in 1904, Calgary City council considered the need for safer crossings, but deferred action "until the solicitor [Bennett] of the CPR returns to the city." For the next year and a half, with the *Eye Opener* leading the campaign to save lives at crossings, Bennett was caught in the centre of the disputes. The railroad company, presumably on Bennett's advice, barred the *Eye Opener* from its trains. That hurt a good deal, but the editor struck back with blows which proved even more painful. He began reporting all CPR accidents across the country, doing so in the greatest and most embarrassing detail. Readers could almost see the dead bodies of men and horses strewn across the tracks. Needless to say, it was the sort of publicity the railroad management would have preferred to suppress.

Either 1905 was a year with unusually many rail accidents or it just seemed an unlucky year. Even Bennett had an accident, but fortunately for him it was not at a crossing. He bought one of the first automobiles in Calgary, and on the evening of 19 April 1905, while out for a drive on Stephen Avenue, he swerved to miss a youth on a bicycle; his car mounted the pavement and struck the wall of the Imperial Bank, wrecking the majestic one-cylinder vehicle and ending forever Bennett's desire to be his own chauffeur.

The rail crossings at Calgary's busiest intersections were not receiving the attention demanded and accidents were recurring. Each time something happened, Bob Edwards gave readers a full account. When there was no accident during a week, the *Eye Opener* report was scarcely less humiliating to rail officials: "Not a life was lost or a buggy smashed at the CPR crossing last week." (24 March 1906) When there was no accident for two weeks, readers learned that "Calgary luck is still on the ascendant. No tragedy at the crossing. This is fool's luck." (7 April 1906)

The rail officials, including the solicitor, could be forgiven for their growing fear and hatred; but Bob Edwards refused to be silenced—not until he won his objective of safe crossings, anyway. Bennett's advice to his railroad associates was not brilliant; he underestimated Edwards's determination and advised the company to ignore the *Eye Opener*. But the pages of the paper carried more and more accounts of accidents to humans and livestock and more pictures and cartoons. The company withdrew the rail pass normally granted to an editor; but the *Eye Opener* went on its merry way, and the issue of 7 April 1906 featured on its front page three pictures showing "Recent CPR Wrecks in Alberta." Then, on an inside page appeared a big picture of R. B. Bennett, with the caption: "Another CPR Wreck."

Another C.P.R. Wreck.

In that same issue, however, the editor reviewed all that had taken place and proposed a settlement. He explained the company's action in forbidding sale of the *Eye Opener* on trains, told about the forfeiture of the transportation pass, and then laid down conditions for an end to hostilities. If the company would just fix up the perilous crossing at Scarth Street in Calgary, so that lives of pedestrians and drivers of street vehicles "will not be needlessly endangered," the *Eye Opener* would end its campaign of "ridicule and awkward truth," which, otherwise, was just starting. "If they will make the crossing safe . . . we will forgive everybody connected with the CPR—except Bennett, of course."

In the issue that followed, (21 April 1906) pictures of wrecks were omitted to give the railroad company a chance to meet the editor's terms, but there was a note of reminder: "No, gentle reader, we shall not bore you with any CPR wrecks this issue—not but what we've got 'em."

The rift between Bennett and Edwards had its ramifications. *Eye Opener* opposition may have cost Bennett his election to the first Provincial Legislature of Alberta, when he lost to Liberal W. H. Cushing by twenty-nine votes. It was a humiliating defeat for the man recently named as leader of the Conservative Party in the new province.

In time the crossings were made safer and the *Eye Opener*'s campaign of "awkward truth" ended. But there were those other differences between Bennett and Edwards. The "straight-laced" Bennett was repeatedly held up as an example by those who criticized the editor. There was the matter of liquor. Bennett had such strong views that when guests at a Calgary reception for a member of the Royal Family were instructed to charge their glasses and drink to the health of His Royal Highness, "R. B." alone drank with water. And in an election campaign when told by workers that unless liquor were provided, a certain block of votes would be lost, Bennett replied: "Then they'll have to be lost."

The rift between the two men placed Paddy Nolan in an awkward position. Paddy was loyal to Bob; and as for his fellow jurist, he was anxious to preserve a professional friendliness, and, perchance, a relationship which would allow a degree of teasing. Practically every person in the legal fraternity could expect to be the victim of Paddy's ribbing at some time. One may attempt to picture a certain court scene: A Calgary judge, listening to a case in which a widow is being charged with the conduct of a lottery, recalls to his consternation that only the day before he had allowed the lawyer for the defence to sell him two of the illegal tickets because the help would go to a "needy widow."

Bennett may have known more about the theory of law, but Nolan knew more about human nature and had the advantage of the superior sense of humour. Meeting about the city, the two men showed proper respect for each other; but there were times when Bennett's parade of dignity made the big Irish lawyer want to humble him, as on the day when Nolan and Bennett appeared on opposite sides in a certain court case. Bennett, as usual, was laden with imposing legal references, and turning to his assistant, said, "Boy, give me Phipson on Evidence." A few minutes later, another order: "Boy, give me Kenny on Crimes." Nolan must have considered the show as having gone far enough because, when he arose, his first utterance was: "Boy, get me Bennett on Bologna."

Moreover, though Bennett was acknowledged to be a great orator, he was quite overshadowed by Nolan as an after-dinner speaker; and this may have bothered the perfection-loving Bennett. Paddy could always find the right humorous note, especially if his pal Bob Edwards was present to inspire him. Calgarians remembered the dinner arranged by Pat Burns, a sumptuous meal, after which a world traveller told about a tour through Europe with stops in Austria-Hungary. Edwards nudged Nolan to get to his feet and propose the vote of thanks to the host of the evening. Paddy, in discharging the pleasant duty, noted that a traveller might go "through Europe and Austria-Hungary, but Pat Burns would never let anybody pass through Calgary hungry."

But the hostility between two of his notable friends bothered Nolan a good deal, and there is reason to believe that he hinted to both that they should forget their differences and their dislikes.

Then there was an unexpected meeting between the two antagonists. Even the setting seemed beyond belief. It was a Sunday morning and Bob Edwards was seated in a back row at the Salvation Army citadel. A man was ushered to the seat beside him. The man was R. B. Bennett. Both spent an uncomfortable hour, both wishing for an excuse to escape.

Neither was more than a casual visitor at the Army Church. Bob, who had small regard for sectarianism, liked to attend a church service occasionally but chose to be a denominational transient. Bennett, in his immaculate Sunday attire, was a faithful attendant at the new Central Methodist Church, where dynamic Dr. George Kerby preached until he resigned to become the first principal of Mount Royal College. Why Bennett was not in his accustomed pew on that particular morning was known to himself only.

But there they were, Bennett and Edwards, men who hadn't spoken to each other in more than two years, sitting side by side at a Salvation Army service. At the instant the church hour ended, the uncompromising Edwards was ready to leave quickly, but the other was too fast for him; the Bennett hand was out and the man behind it, making a valiant effort to appear friendly, said, "Good morning, Mr. Edwards. Glad to see you here. The Army does magnificent work."

Bob Edwards, acting like a nervous school boy, accepted Bennett's hand, said, "Good morning," and nothing more. To have forced an appearance of congeniality at that moment would have been dishonest, because Bob Edwards was not one to believe in concealing feelings or compromising principles.

He withdrew, quite puzzled about Bennett's behaviour, marvelling at the skilful manner in which that man met the situation. Was it just an accepted church gesture on Bennett's part, or was he really extending an invitation to friendliness? Bob reported to Paddy and was told to give Bennett every chance to demonstrate the quality of his overture.

A short time later, Bennett was giving a banquet for his political friends at the Alberta Hotel. Strange as it seemed to Bob Edwards, he was invited, and Paddy's advice was to accept. Bob was not sure that Mr. Bennett had a high motive in this bid for a friendlier relationship; it could be that he was simply seeking the political advantage of *Eye Opener* endorsation. He is an adroit politician, Bob reasoned. He knows now that he can't run the editor out of town as he once said he would do. Probably he has concluded that if he must live in the same city and frequent the same hotel, there would be practical advantages in peace.

Anyway, Bob told Paddy he would go to Bennett's banquet, but not to repudiate his former ideas about the CPR or its solicitor—not yet at any rate. Nobody would get the chance to use Bob Edwards as a mere political tool. He was supposed to be a Conservative; but in most respects he was an independent—one who would not bend to anything in which he did not believe.

Bennett's new wish to cultivate Edwards was quite obvious; and as the guests were called to take places at the banquet table, Mr. Bennett, as host and master of ceremonies, called upon Bob Edwards to say grace. There was an awkward moment of silence—one that seemed more like an hour—and then Bob spoke: "If you don't mind, Mr. Chairman, I'd prefer that the good Lord didn't know I was here."

Bennett's patience at that period was commendable. Quite clearly he was in earnest. Bob was like a girl willing to be wooed, but not before seeing the proof of good intentions. There followed, however, an invitation to Edwards and Nolan to sit at the Bennett table at lunch times, and while Bob was consulting his conscience and his Scottish independence, Paddy was accepting on behalf of both.

On the first visit to the Bennett table, Bob was quiet and everybody except Paddy seemed uneasy. Gradually, however, the evidence of reserve disappeared and an entirely new mood pervaded the table's company. There was more laughter, more good-natured banter, and even Bennett found new enjoyment. He forgot his usual and dignified formality as he laughed at the trouble which George Peet, sitting opposite him, was having with city officials. Bachelor Peet believed in cleanliness and had a big metal bathtub in the centre of his one-room quarters over Hall's Hardware. There came an inspector to explain that a city bylaw forbade bathrooms in bedrooms. George Peet, his anger aroused, replied loudly: "Well, there's no bylaw that says I can't have a bed in my bathroom. Now, get out, you fool!"

For the first time, Bennett was displaying unreserved pleasure in relating stories about Paddy. Bob would come to the table enquiring if there were any choice bits for the pages of the "Great Moral Weekly." Bennett might reply: "Can't think of anything breezy enough for that, but did you ever tell your readers the one about Paddy Nolan and Shorty McLaughlin of High River? The CPR train hit five of Shorty's cayuses and killed them. He wanted Paddy to act for him in suing for damages. Paddy listened to Shorty's account of the horses straying and getting in the way of the Calgary–Fort Macleod train. Paddy asked again if the CPR train actually ran these horses down, and when Shorty confirmed that it did, Paddy said, 'Well, I'm sorry, Shorty, but I can't take that case. Any horses that can't outrun a CPR train are better dead. You're lucky to be rid of them.'"

Bob was pleasantly surprised; Bennett was not only in a joking mood, but he was finding enjoyment in a story that touched lightly upon the proud railroad company for which he was solicitor. Bob found himself admiring the man. Things appeared different. In his earlier views, he had been prejudiced—and unfair. He confessed to Paddy that he had been all wrong in assessing Bennett. "That man would annoy a saint at times," Bob said to Paddy, "especially when in one of his sanctimonious or irritable moods; but he has a fine intellect, and, I must admit, I'm fascinated."

"Yes," Paddy agreed, "he was going to run you out of town once. And today he isn't happy unless you're sitting next to him at his table. Quite a remarkable fellow—could have a great future. He'll bear watching in politics. He protests that he has no intention of running in the next Federal election, but he has ambitions and he'll be in it. Mark my words; if he gets half a chance, the same Bennett will be Prime Minister of Canada some fine day."

Bob Edwards was nodding agreement. "In some ways he makes me think of a young fellow in England who has striking promise—Winston Churchill. Both can make pretty speeches and both love to do it. When I read Churchill's recent speech in the British House of Commons, my thoughts turned to Bennett: 'Take away that control from the House of Commons, and they pull away the lynch pin from the coach of freedom.' Sounds like Bennett, doesn't it?"

"There's just one thing that would worry me about Bennett's political future," Bob added. "For one who so dearly loves to make speeches, our Richard is liable to talk too often and too long for his own good—talked five hours without a break in the Legislature recently. His secret hope, I suspect, is to occupy a platform seat in Heaven, with the privilege of addressing the angels from the throne."

It was Paddy Nolan's thought that "Whatever one may say about Bennett, the vitality of that New Brunswick ambition is wonderful. It's damned refreshing to encounter a man with such determined goals: they tell that when he was still in school he declared his intention to be a lawyer, a millionaire, and a Prime Minister. If he becomes a candidate for the post of Prime Minister, Bob, I hope you and I are still around to give him our support."

"Yes," Bob Edwards agreed, "and what a pair of drinking men like ourselves should recognize, Paddy, is that he's a good advertisement for prohibition. I only hope that his abstention doesn't take him to an early grave. Did you ever notice that the germ diseases seldom if ever strike the boozers? It is doubtless due to the inability of the germs to live in the whiskey belt and withstand the poison. This shows what rotten stuff whiskey must be made of. Microbes seem to have sense enough to pass up both tobacco and whiskey. You and I may be knocked out occasionally by the bottled stuff, Paddy, but never by the microbes." (22 April 1905)

By 1909 Bob Edwards was unreservedly on Bennett's side and helped elect him to the Provincial Legislature in that year. Bob's allegiance was not something to be turned on and off like a water tap; once won, it would flow constantly. The editor helped to elect Bennett to the House of Commons in 1911; friendship and admiration were strengthening with the years—even to the point of Conservative Mr. Bennett giving public endorsation to Independent Candidate Edwards when the latter ran in the provincial election.

Looking back on his Calgary years, Bob Edwards would count among his closest friends Paddy Nolan (my Minister of Defence); W. M. Davidson, editor of the *Albertan* (my Minister of Understanding); Rev. Robert Pearson (my Minister of Eternal Affairs); and Hon. R. B. Bennett, (my Minister Never Without His Portfolio).

CHAPTER EIGHT
The McGonigle Affair

"Some men spoil a good story by sticking to the facts."
(25 January 1919)

"The public will pay more for laughing than for any other privilege."
(11 May 1918)

"Gallons of trouble can come out of a pint flask."
(22 May 1915)

AS BERTIE BUZZARD-CHOLOMONDELEY carried the name of Bob Edwards across foothills and prairies, so Peter J. McGonigle took it beyond the Atlantic Ocean where it almost precipitated an intra-empire crisis. Fantastic as that international trouble might seem to strangers, those people knowing Bob Edwards and Peter McGonigle would not be surprised at anything of their doing.

McGonigle was a man of many parts, having indulged dangerously in publishing, bootlegging, ranching, and horse stealing. Frequently he was drunk; sometimes he went to jail; but to give him his dues, always he was cheerful. If Western Canada was naming a "Man of the Year" in 1906, Peter McGonigle would have been a candidate. His following was one of which a movie star might be proud. Nearly everybody had some knowledge of him; men who congregated at village livery stables, while wives shopped for groceries, talked about Peter McGonigle and followed the fortunes and misfortunes of his stormy career with nearly as much interest as that with which the community people of a later decade followed their favourite hockey teams. The fact that his conduct was not always exemplary didn't, somehow, injure his popularity.

But Peter McGonigle was no ordinary mortal. A few pictures of the bewhiskered fellow appeared on the pages of the *Eye Opener*, but nobody actually saw the great Peter in the flesh; he was another mythical character created by Bob Edwards to entertain his readers and carry the jibes intended for public figures, especially those who were inclined to take themselves too seriously. But readers following the tribulations which made the poor fellow famous seemed satisfied to forget that he wasn't real.

The reasons for the McGonigle name have been debated. Edwards may have been inspired by his knowledge of William McGonagall of Edinburgh whose so-called poetry was so lacking in measure that it brought him fame. More likely, however, it

"I wonder who this man McGonigle is!"

was from Clay McGonagill, noted American cowboy and rope artist, that the Bob Edwards hero of many a fictional adventure took his name.

For those interested in family history, Bob Edwards explained that Peter inherited many of his characteristics from his father, Old Man McGonigle, whose health finally gave way because of "his inordinate love of Burke's Beer and he passed away full of years and tumors in '98, leaving a large family, of which Peter J. is the eldest, to mourn his loss. His further family history may be found in Burke's Beerage." (19 September 1908)

The name of Peter McGonigle appeared for the first time on 22 August 1903, when the *Eye Opener* was carrying a High River dateline.[1] For the next seventeen years, few names in the West enjoyed higher news value; Peter became almost as well-known as his celebrated creator. And with some of the same weaknesses as his creator, it is not surprising that McGonigle tried his hand at journalism. His prominence blossomed when from the pages of the *Eye Opener*, admirers read: "A newspaper has been started at the flourishing town of Midnapore, nine miles south of Calgary. It is called the *Midnapore Gazette* and it is edited by a gentleman whose writings will never be mistaken for those of Mr. Goldwin Smith." (18 August 1906)

Nobody ever saw a copy of the *Midnapore Gazette*;[2] but if a person could judge from the items about the calf branding, local romances, and family squabbles for which the *Eye Opener* gave credit to the *Gazette*, the editor had a pretty good nose for news. And evidently the *Gazette*'s editor placed more than news in his paper. On a Wednesday evening as the boys were lined up at a Calgary bar, Editor McGonigle "annexed a bottle of rye" and hurriedly wrapped it in newspaper and was on the way out when Bartender Fred Adams saw what was happening. Called on to put the bottle back, McGonigle denied having it.

"But I see the bottle in the paper right now," said Adams.

Said McGonigle, as he continued his leisurely walk toward the door: "My friend,

[1] Yes and no. The issue in question carried an item about "the eminent cowman 'old man McGonigle'" and his daughter Imogene. "Peter J. McGonigle, editor of the *Midnapore Gazette*," as such, does not appear until 12 January 1906. Even then, however, Edwards's most famous creation was still somewhat embryonic: 1906 also saw notices concerning the decidedly McGoniglesque misadventures of Peter Bendigo (8 September) and J. B. Johnson (10 November), each listed as "editor of the *Midnapore Gazette*." Bendigo was an alleged horse-thief, Johnson an unlucky adulterer. Neither was heard from again.

[2] Not McGonigle's, anyhow. See next chapter.

you mustn't believe all you see in the newspapers." (18 July 1908)

Poor Peter, he just couldn't keep out of trouble, or so it seemed. But to be fair to him, he carried the blame for more than his own transgressions; he would lend his name when it was charitable to hide the identity of the real character in any good local story. Often, however, it wasn't difficult to identify the person for whom the willing Peter carried a story. So it was when one of Peter's romances went wrong:

> P. J. McGonigle, the Midnapore journalist, is the most unfortunate of men. It appears that during the despondent stage following hard upon his last drunk, Mr. McGonigle got religion and joined the church. Having a voice far louder and more raucous than any of Mr. Brodeur's St. Lawrence River fog-horns, they put him in the choir and he distinguished himself the very first Sunday by nearly shattering the Rock of Ages into a thousand fragments. The trustees asked him to draw it mild but as he has since been fired out of the church altogether, this makes no material difference.
>
> There happened to be a pretty widow who sang contralto in the choir and Peter warmed up to her in great shape. They sang out of the same hymn-book and all that sort of thing. The other fellows naturally grew a bit jealous although they did not seriously think that an ornery-looking fellow like McGonigle would have much chance with the merry widow. However, the hot running made by the celebrated editor made them not a little uneasy.
>
> Now it must be explained that on Mondays, Tuesdays and Wednesdays, when he didn't have to write stuff for the *Gazette*, Mr. McGonigle turned an honest penny by selling sewing machines. He bethought him one evening that to try and sell a sewing machine to the widow would be an excellent excuse for calling. So between eight and nine o'clock, accompanied by his faithful dog, he knocked at the front door of the lady's residence, and on being admitted, ordered the little dog to lie down on the porch outside and wait for him.
>
> While he was inside doing the polite, the dog sprang down from the porch to run after a passing rig, and during the five minutes that the dog was absent, Mr. McGonigle rose to say good-bye. He meandered down to the hotel to get a drink before the bar closed and then went to bed, wondering hazily what had become of the dog.
>
> It seems that the dog, after chasing the rig for quite a distance

down the road, returned to the porch of the widow's cottage and lay down to wait for his master. He was a very faithful animal. Between five and six o'clock the next morning some Midnaporeites who had to get up early to do their chores espied McGonigle's dog lying asleep at the widow's front door and drew their own conclusions.

Before ten o'clock it was the scandal of the town. In vain did McGonigle try to explain. In vain did the poor widow try to make the women-folk believe in her innocence. The Minister called at the *Gazette* office and cancelled the editor's membership in the church. McGonigle threatened to write the whole lot of them up but inadvertently got drunk instead. In point of fact, there was no issue last week and it is not likely there will be another for a month, as this drunk looks as if it's going to be a prolonged one. The widow has gone east to visit friends and the confounded little dog may be seen at any hour of the day lying outside the bar-room of the Nevermore Hotel waiting for his master. McGonigle threatens to move his plant to Okotoks. (2 May 1908)

But nothing in the McGonigle career brought more notoriety to himself and Bob Edwards than the account of the Calgary banquet tendered to McGonigle on the occasion of his release from penitentiary where he had been serving a sentence for horse stealing. Though the celebration as reported was nothing more than a figment of Bob Edwards's imagination, the echoes from it were heard around the world.

It started with the story in the *Eye Opener* on 6 October 1906. Calgary had experienced a succession of banquets with monotonous similarity; the next would be for McGonigle, and it would be different. It was different. The menu included *Herald* and *Albertan* Roasts; Commission Style Calf's Head Without Brains; Muttonhead Cutlets à la City Council; and Boiled Owl, Aldermanic Variety. According to the *Eye Opener*:

The banquet tendered by the Calgary Board of Trade to Mr. Peter McGonigle on the occasion of his release from Edmonton penitentiary, where he had spent some time trying to live down a conviction of horse stealing, proved a great success. Quite a number of prominent citizens were present and, with Mayor Emerson in the chair, the songs, toasts and speeches passed off with all the eclat available at such short notice.

Letters of regret were read from Lord Strathcona, Earl Grey,

Premier Rutherford, Charlie Wagner, Joseph Seagram, Josh Calloway, W. Callahan, Col. G. C. Porter, W. F. Maclean, Joseph Fahy, Rev. John A. McDougall, Con. Leary and others.

Lord Strathcona's letter reads as follows:

"John Emerson, Esq., Mayor, Calgary—

"Dear Jack; You don't mind me calling you Jack, do you old cock? I regret exceedingly that I shall be unable to attend the McGonigle banquet at Calgary, but believe me, my sympathies go out to your honored guest. The name of Peter McGonigle will ever stand high in the roll of eminent confiscators. Once, long ago, I myself came near achieving distinction in this direction when I performed some dexterous financing with the Bank of Montreal's funds. In consequence, however; of CPR stocks going up instead of down, I wound up in the House of Lords instead of Stoney Mountain.

"Believe me, dear Jack.

"Yours truly,

"Strathcona."

Mr. McGonigle then proceeded to thank all present for their cordial greetings, stating that he was willing to let the dead past bury its dead. The horse in question had died shortly after he was parted from it. As a matter of fact, he had been working for a dead horse for a number of years. (Applause.) Had it not been for the ignorance of his lawyer he might have been acquitted, for the horse he stole was not a horse at all, but a mare. This point was entirely overlooked at the trial. It was a horse on him. (6 October 1906)

People on Calgary's 8th Avenue read the story, chuckled, and thought no more about it. They knew Bob Edwards and supposed they understood Mr. McGonigle. They were not even surprised that Earl Grey, Lord Strathcona, Premier Rutherford, and Joe Seagram were drawn into this bit of fiction.

Farther from home, however, such a story could be misconstrued; and sure enough it was. To the desk of John Willison, editor of the *Toronto Evening News*, came a copy of the *Eye Opener*, and, knowing nothing of the background, this gentleman was filled with amazement. At once he sensed news of an international interest in the account of this strange banquet, with Lord Strathcona and Earl Grey paying tribute to a notorious horse thief. Being the Canadian correspondent of a daily paper published in London, England, he at once prepared a story about the banquet and Lord Strathcona's interest in the guest of honour and cabled it to London.

Reading his morning paper over a pleasant cup of tea, Lord Strathcona's eyes fell upon the story from Canada, and to his horror noted that he was quoted as praising the ex-convict, McGonigle. At once, this serious-minded man phoned the editor of the London paper demanding an explanation. The editor, no less puzzled about it all, cabled Sir John Willison, and the latter wired the Mayor of Calgary for some clarification of the strange affair.

Calgary's mayor reported that it was just a hoax, that McGonigle was purely mythical, that Edwards was a humorist editor, and the best thing for all concerned would be to forget it. Not satisfied to await an explanation, however, the enraged Strathcona cabled to his lawyer friend, Senator Lougheed of Calgary, instructing him to take legal action against the author of this infamous libel.

Senator Lougheed, along with other Calgarians, had read the story in the *Eye Opener* and laughed at it; but to explain to an infuriated Lord beyond the Atlantic that it was only a joke, was, at first, impossible. To Strathcona, who had missed the fun of knowing Bob Edwards and reading about McGonigle, it was a serious matter—certainly not one to be pushed aside by calling it a joke.

"Is there no justice out there in Western Canada?" Strathcona boomed. His associations with the frontier in earlier years should have furnished the answer, but it didn't. "Somebody must pay for this impertinence."

He was not one to be repressed easily; but through the perseverance of Senator Lougheed, the noble Lord was at length persuaded to withdraw from legal action and forget the incident over which most of the people in Alberta and the rest of the West were having a prolonged laugh.

The inimitable McGonigle, however, was not one to be discouraged easily. He would not surrender his place in the columns of the *Eye Opener* just because his indiscretions happened to produce a threat to intercontinental calm. He would go forward to other tasks awaiting him—worrying men in high places, entertaining a host of admiring readers, and surviving the mishaps which seemed to plague his existence.

Along in 1911, however, there was reason to believe that McGonigle's end had come. It was a sad day when they buried the great editor in the garden patch behind the *Gazette* office at Midnapore. Death can be cruel, but nobody would expect it to strike McGonigle in any average sort of way. For some months after the funeral, the sorrowing widow was possessed with the thought that her Peter was not really dead when they buried him. "Mrs. McGonigle, for a squaw, was a widely read woman, having educated herself by constant perusal of the lurid columns of the *Gazette.*" She had read stories about people being buried when in a state of catalepsy, which outwardly resembles death. It became an obsession that Peter, buried alive, might even after the lapse of months, be alive.

Bob Edwards reported what happened:[3]

> Obtaining an order from a judge of the Supreme Court Mrs. McGonigle communicated with several well known doctors and made arrangements for the coffin to be dug up from the vegetable patch . . . Some cabbage and lettuce had been planted over the grave but the bereft woman was ready for any kind of sacrifice to have her dear departed back.
>
> It took fully an hour before the spades struck the lid of the coffin. The excitement ran high. Mrs. McGonigle had to be restrained by physical force from jumping into the grave. One of the diggers rapped loudly on the coffin and cried, "Pete, ho Pete! Are you there?"
>
> In a few minutes the coffin was gently raised to the surface and reverently borne into the old home. Jimmy, the grizzled bar veteran, held the crowd back and prevented all but the physicians from entering the house. Whereupon followed a general stampede back to the garden, there still being about half of the keg left.
>
> The coffin having been placed on the kitchen table, it was the work of only a few minutes to pry open the lid. There, cold and pallid, lay the great editor.
>
> Mrs. McGonigle peered into the face of her beloved Peter and allowed a tear to fall on his rugged features.
>
> "He looks so natural," she sobbed. "He hasn't changed a bit. I'll bet a cookie he's alive and in a trance."
>
> "We'll soon see," said one of the doctors, as he removed his coat and turned up his sleeves as if about to dress a hog. Bending over the coffin, he took hold of the corpse's nose between thumb and finger and gave it a violent twist.
>
> "What do you think about it, doc?" asked the poor woman anxiously.
>
> "Well, he looks to be as dead as a door mat but after all he may be in a condition of flexibilitas cerea. How long has he been dead?"

[3] What follows is abridged. The complete text of the episode can be found in *Irresponsible Freaks, etc* .

"About six months."

"Oh, well, there's no particular hurry. I should like to hold a professional consultation with my fellow-physicians over at the Nevermore House. We won't be over ten minutes."

The physicians then put on their hats and hied over to the Nevermore House for their consultation, promising to call in before returning to town in their motor.

Left alone, Mrs. McGonigle looked curiously into her husband's face and then began hunting for a corkscrew. This found, she quickly opened the bottle and sat down beside the coffin. With great deliberation she filled a tumbler to the brim and held it beneath the nostrils of her Peter. Nothing happened for several minutes, while the woman could hear her own heart thumping. Then a faint, almost imperceptible flicker of the eyelids appeared. The glass almost slipped from the devoted woman's hand. The next perceptible movement was of the lips, which seemed to twitch slightly. Then the mouth slowly opened. Mrs. McGonigle inverted the glass, allowing half of it to trickle down his throat. A slight shudder and a faint exclamation which sounded not unlike, "Wow!" and Mr. Peter J. McGonigle opened wide his eyes.

"Where am I?" asked Peter, staring in a dazed way at the ceiling.

"Never mind where you are, Pete. You're all right at home with me. I've a whole bottle of whiskey for you and I'm going to give you a drink right now."

"But say, look here—my but I feel weak; I thought you hated to see me drink whiskey."

"Well, Pete, this is your birthday and I want you to drink it."

"All right my dear, let's have the hooker. Say, Great Scott! What in thunder am I doing lying in a box? Has somebody been putting up a job? I wonder how I feel so weak: I never felt so queer before."

"Here, Pete, after you down this I'll tell you all about it." Peter downed it and lay back to listen to the tale. Instead of being awed by his narrow escape from a frightful death, struggling for life in a coffin six feet underground, the great editor grinned broadly. "You can't keep a good man down," said he, "and how is Jimmy?" (20 May 1911)

And so Peter J. McGonigle was back with the readers of the *Eye Opener* for some more years. Everybody was pleased. As a matter of fact, Bob Edwards had several other character-heroes. Of course, as we have already recounted, there was the celebrated Bertie Buzzard-Cholomondeley, who had quite a run; and Peter J. Puddicum, who had been a premature baby born "in a captive balloon which escaped from its moorings at a county fair in Donegal" (14 July 1906), had a spell of popularity; but it was Peter McGonigle who became the favourite across the West. Many people thought he was real and wrote to commend or condemn his conduct. The editor of the *London* (England) *Morning Leader* wrote a column of criticism, contending that Mr. McGonigle deserved a better treatment than he was receiving from the *Eye Opener*, adding that the brutal frankness with which a brother journalist was treated was shameful and "this sort of thing would not be tolerated in England for a moment." (21 December 1912)

But whether the prairie people understood all about McGonigle or not, they were generally on his side. Although time might level people down to make them uniformly nice and dull, frontier admiration for robust individualism was as plain as the brand on a bronco. McGonigle was frequently a matter of convenience in relating news stories; but just as often, he was a Bob Edwards protest directed at custom and convention.

But even McGonigle couldn't escape death indefinitely. In dodging it he had been singularly skilful or fortunate, and was one of the few mortals who could look back upon the year of his first funeral. By 1920, however, his luck seemed to be exhausted, and tragedy brought his eventful career to a close. Bob Edwards didn't fail to chronicle the last sad hours:

> While Peter McGonigle was examining an ivory-handled revolver which the bartender of the Nevermore House accepted from a stranger in lieu of payment for a two-day drunk, the weapon unexpectedly went off, and lodged a bullet in McGonigle's abdomen. A physician was hastily summoned from Calgary.
>
> In the meanwhile, Jimmy the barkeep summoned help from round about, and had his old friend raised from the floor and stretched on the bar with his head resting comfortably on the slot machine. Mr. McGonigle retained consciousness, but complained of great pain. A tumbler of brandy eased his sufferings somewhat but he whispered to Jimmy that he feared he had been sent for at last. . . .
>
> An auto suddenly pulled up in front of the Nevermore House and out jumped the doctor with his small black case. He ordered Mr.

McGonigle removed to Calgary for the expert attention that only Calgary could give.

Two days later word was brought to Midnapore that Peter J. had breathed his last on the operating table. The operation was said to have been highly successful but Mr. McGonigle's heart, storm-beaten as it was by many a howling gale, failed to rise to the supreme call. The physicians were of the opinion that the rather unfortunate circumstances of his heart stopping had more than a little to do with his death.

Before being taken to the operating room, Mr. McGonigle made a will. He directed that the printing plant of the *Gazette*, upon which he had made two payments, be shipped back to the Toronto Type Foundry. The bunch of mares which he had been accused of stealing from the Bar U were directed to be sold for the benefit of his wife.

The will, which was quite brief, ended with the earnest wish that if the worst happened, Jimmy the barkeep should marry the widow, Janet McGonigle, after a decent period of mourning—say a week.

Thus passed a great spirit. The body was shipped back to Midnapore and interred in the little garden back of the printing office.[4]

McGonigle of Midnapore! No history of the West will be complete without some reference to him, and no Board of Trade could have done as much to publicize the district.

Thirty years after the McGonigle death was reported, an eastern tourist stopped at the little village on the Macleod Highway, about eight miles south of Calgary, and enquired: "Any members of the McGonigle family still living around here?"

[4] This is, in fact, the 15 October 1910 account of McGonigle's first death. It does appear, however, that Edwards re-killed off the long-suffering editor at some point between Fall 1910 and Spring 1915 (the 3 April 1915 *Eye Opener* reports a bartender's "touching reference to the late Peter J. McGonigle"), but the relevant number of the *Eye Opener* is lost. Arthur R. Ford (*As the World Wags On*, Toronto: Ryerson Press, 1950) offers a second-hand recounting of McGonigle's later passing: "Amid blazing guns six Mounties arrested him when he became drunk, took him to jail and confiscated his weapons. He was so humiliated that he allowed himself to be arrested by a mere force of six Mounties that he cut his throat with a rusty butcher knife he found in the rubbish in his cell." The article allegedly accompanied a photo of Edwards's friend Colonel Garnet Clay Porter, captioned "Poor Garnet Clay Peter McGonigle." Ford admits to not knowing which issue contained this second passing.

CHAPTER NINE

"Why Did Peter Have to Die?"

"...IT IS APPOINTED UNTO MEN ONCE TO DIE," according to scripture (Hebrews 9:27) but why was Peter McGonigle obliged to face the ordeal twice? His sorrowing fans and followers across the West did not understand, although they should have realized that Peter was no ordinary mortal and might have been expected to suffer double portions of misfortune.

What the reading public did not know about Peter's first confrontation with death was the reason behind Bob Edwards's decision to terminate the *Midnapore Gazette* and end the life of its illustrious editor. Much as Edwards regretted the necessity of destroying an old friend and popular hero, the circumstances left him with no reasonable alternative.

Normally frank and honest, Edwards was not given to keeping secrets from his readers, but his reason for McGonigle's premature death was an exception; he did not disclose it publicly, but close friends were aware of the circumstances, among them Mrs. Ethel Davidson, whose husband, W. M. Davidson, had been a long-time editor of the *Albertan* and a friend of Edwards. As Mrs. Davidson related the details in a letter to the author (27 March 1958), the widespread interest shown in the fictitious *Midnapore Gazette* and Peter McGonigle brought a vision of fortune to a local reporter with the *News-Telegram*, Bill Degraves. He was sure that a real newspaper carrying the *Midnapore Gazette* name would be greeted with general interest and assured of profitable sales. What would stop such a scheme? There being neither copyright, registration, nor incorporation in connection with the *Gazette*, there was no apparent obstacle to the adoption of the name, even without Bob Edwards's permission.

It was part of the reporter's plan to have the initial issue of his *Gazette* coming from the press in time for street sales during the week of the Calgary Exhibition, when many farmers and visitors would be in the city. All the McGonigle fans—meaning all the readers of the *Eye Opener*—would want to buy copies.

Sure enough, the paper—the first issue of the *Midnapore Gazette* to appear in the clear light of reality—reached the streets as planned, and thousands of Calgary residents and guests lining the Exhibition parade route were startled by the rush of newsboys selling the *Midnapore Gazette*, printed on pink paper and presented with

THE MIDNAPORE GAZETTE

THE PAPER THAT TELLS ALL — THE TRUTH ALL THE TI[ME]

Number 7 — MIDNAPORE, ALBERTA, SATURDAY, DECEMBER 10, 1910 — Five Cents

SHOW SHOP NOTES

(By Neal Anderson)

[illegible]

THE GAZETTE'S MUNICIPAL SLATE

YOU'RE GOING TO VOTE for somebody to represent you in the next City Council; somebody who will represent the business and commercial development of this city of Calgary.

But who's the real fellow back of the somebody?

It's YOU—isn't it?

Isn't it YOU!

After all's said and done, don't most of us do for ourselves—for our own interests—for our own pocketbooks?

And can they blame you for doing it on Monday next?

Is blind partisanship or hero-worship for [illegible] going to woo you into voting for men who have in the past proved themselves traitors to the [illegible] and to the interests of the citizens. Remember, it was your interests that Mayor Jamieson tried to [illegible] over to the Canadian Northern. It was your interests that he betrayed, when with Ald. Egbert he favored the giving away of a power site that will mean much money to this city in the years to come.

And remember, there's a secret ballot. No threat can be made good when the other fellow doesn't know.

No, Mr. Calgarian, the real ticket is: Vote for yourself.

And you do vote for yourself when you vote for men on the slate we have outlined. These men are for the things that you, as a good citizen of Calgary, are for the things that count—good government for all; a healthy development of the whole city, and a determined attempt to make Calgary a happy and prosperous city, and its citizens a happy and prosperous people.

This slate is the workers' slate; the business men's slate; the professional man's slate, of this civic campaign. It is the only slate there is, outside the corporation slate of Mayor Jamieson and Ald. Egbert, and the citizens of Calgary do not want that slate.

The men on this slate stand for—

Municipal Ownership of all utilities.

A vigorous publicity campaign for Calgary.

Encouragement of all industries of a permanent nature, but with no exemptions granted.

A policy of parks and park improvements in all parts of the city.

Commission form of Municipal Government.

Calgary first, last and all the time.

This, Mr. Newcomer, as well as Old-timer, is our only real platform—the way things are going and the way you want them to go.

So, vote for YOURSELF on Monday next.

And VOTE FOR THIS TICKET.

And VOTE EARLY.

FOR MAYOR
JOHN W. MITCHELL

FOR COMMISSIONER
S. J. CLARKE

FOR ALDERMEN

Ward One	Ward Two
Magnus Brown	W. T. D. Lathwell
John L. Gibson	Daniel McDonald
Chas. Pohl	Fred Currie

Ward Three	Ward Four
R. A. Brocklebank	Clifford T. Jones
Jas. A. Hornby	C. B. Riley
S. B. Ramsey	J. G. Watson

VOTE FOR CHAS. POHL

CANDIDATE FOR ALDERMEN IN WARD 1.

A vote for CHAS. POHL, the Peoples' Candidate, is a vote for the protection of the Citizens, for Public Ownership, and for the best interests of Calgary.

WARD 1.

Election for Aldermen.

MAGNUS BROWN	
A. B. CUSHING	
JOHN L. GIBSON	
THOMAS HART	
ROBERT B. HUNT	
CHARLES POHL	X
A. J. SAMIS	

[illegible]

Can't Come Back Club

MUNICIPAL COMMENTS

We have been following the municipal election meetings held all over the city during the past two weeks very closely, and after thinking the whole thing over have come to the conclusion that there is only one issue involved. This one issue is whether the citizens of Calgary believe in municipal ownership being PREACHED or PRACTICED. If they believe in the former only, then Ald. Egbert will be elected mayor, and Mayor Jamieson will be elected commissioner. If they believe in the latter, then Ald. Mitchell will be elected mayor, and Commissioner Clarke will be re-elected to the position he has filled so trustworthy since the commission form of government was first introduced into Calgary.

That is the sum and substance of the whole affair as it appeals to us. To those who have watched things from the beginning, it is amusing to see the present mayor preaching municipal ownership, and the policy of Calgary first, Calgary last, and Calgary all the time, now that he is up against an election, and then to sit back and compare his preaching with his practicing when the interests of Calgary were concerned and he was in a position to act, in the past. For two years he has been mayor of Calgary, but he has not shown up as a municipal ownership man.

Where was his present policy when he tried to bind the city hand and foot, to the Canadian Northern Railway? Where was he then with his Calgary first, Calgary last, and Calgary all the time? Surely he did not have the interests of Calgary at heart when he sat in the office of the manager of the Canadian Bank of Commerce, and, with a few jelly fish aldermen proposed to let the Canadian Northern enter Calgary just in the manner that railroad wanted to enter it and to close up every avenue and street that railroad wanted to close up. Was it the interests of the Canadian Northern that he had at heart then, or was it the interests of Calgary? What excuse has the mayor offered since that time to explain his attitude on this important question? We can [illegible] for one.

Then take the more recent matter of the power site. When he advocated the city of Calgary giving up a power site that may mean millions of dollars to Calgary in the years to come, did he think of the city then? Was it Calgary first, Calgary last, and Calgary all the time when he wanted to see a private corporation get that power site, and advocated this both in and out of the council? Where were his municipal ownership ideas at that time? We hear a lot of them now, but now he is before the electors, and he knows what the electors want, so he promises it to them. He gave similar promises before. He prated of municipal ownership before, but when the chance was given to prove that at heart he was a municipal ownership man, he failed to make good. Instead he proved himself what he is a corporation man pure and simple.

The Gazette has no idea what Mayor Jamieson hoped to gain by giving this power site to a corporation. We know that the real estate firm with which he is connected, namely, Joe, Ltd, had the selling of nine townsites along the line of the Canadian Northern coming into Calgary? Perhaps that accounts for the stand he took in dealing with the Canadian Northern, but is there anything to account for the stand he took on the power question?

Then take his attitude towards any of the ratepayers who have been forced to call upon him during his term as mayor. Did he listen to them and give their grievances proper consideration? If they were of a certain class he did, but if they happened to be working people, or people without influence, what was the treatment they received. In open meeting he has been charged with snubbing them; with dealing with them in an impudent, autocratic way. In fact with intimating to them that he was Reuben Rupert Jamieson, mayor of Calgary; that they were only ratepayers who did not know what they wanted and who would have to take what he chose to give them?

This is the attitude of all corporation men toward the great mass of the general public. Mayor Jamieson spent many years with the C.P.R. He was a tried and trust servant of that corporation. This is no disgrace. It showed that he must have had ability along certain lines, but those lines must have been corporation lines. He must have been able to squeeze men. To sap the life blood out of towns and cities at the command of the corporations.

Such a man, with such a training, cannot hope to delude the people into believing that he is a municipal ownership man; that he is a man of the people, and has only the welfare of the people at heart. He showed this when he kowtowed to the Canadian Northern, and when he bowed the knee to a power corporation that was desirous of getting a hammerlock on this city, and in later years squeezing the citizens to its heart's content.

Against this we have the record of Commissioner S. J. Clarke, who is opposing him. A scant two years

(Continued on Page Four)

a format resembling that of the *Calgary Eye Opener*. The demand was instantaneous, just as the reporter had expected it would be. Thousands of people who knew McGonigle's *Gazette* by reputation, but had never seen a copy, were now eager to buy. As Mrs. Davidson recalled, "the sensation distracted hundreds of people from the parade and the *Gazette* sold so furiously that both sides of the street soon blazed like ribbons of prairie sunset, quite outshining the Indians and colorful acts staged by the Exhibition, as people spread out the pink sheets to make hasty examinations of what they had bought."

Where was Bob Edwards when this was happening? Fortunately or unfortunately, he was out of the city and totally unaware of the infringement. Repeating a course he had followed too frequently, he was hospitalized at Banff, being rehabilitated after a heavy spell of drinking.[1] What he would have done to stop the intrusion or what he could have done—if anything—is impossible to say. At his return to Calgary in due course he heard about the publication and sale of a *Midnapore Gazette* and was very much upset. No doubt he consulted with Paddy Nolan about the possibility of legal action but presumably it was concluded that he had no hopeful recourse. Edwards had never established a formal claim to the name of the nonexistent *Midnapore Gazette* or to that of its equally nonexistent editor.

Some people supposed that reporter Degraves embarked upon the enterprise for strictly financial reasons, but there is doubt, or he would have taken advantage of the instant success and been anxious to continue publication. Requests and orders for his paper were coming from greater and greater distances. It could only help the *Gazette's* sales when readers far and near supposed that the paper's publication was a gag contrived by Edwards himself; the bawdy contents helped to support this theory. Anyway, Degraves found himself with more orders than he could fill. Rumour had it that the *Gazette* was outselling the *Eye Opener*. Certainly the publisher of the *Gazette* could not overlook the possibility of profitable competition with the *Eye Opener* and a new and challenging career for himself.

But instead of going his own way and continuing to publish his instantly popular paper, Degraves resolved to pay a visit to Edwards while the latter's anger continued to burn furiously. Exactly how the discussion turned will never be known, but Mrs. Davidson believed that Degraves "lost some of his nerve at this time and tried to persuade Edwards that it had been just a joke." Apparently, Edwards, who could see nothing funny in the events, proved most persuasive and "Degraves

[1] If the first issue of the *Gazette* appeared in the summer of 1910, Edwards was actually in Winnipeg (see Chapter 11). That even Edwards's friend perpetuated the jagcureatorium story is a testament to the enduring myth of Boozological Bob.

emerged from the interview committed never to repeat the experiment.[2]

"With that settled, Edwards cooled down and assumed a good natured attitude and professed to his friends to see the same humour in the episode that other people saw. But he immediately went to work to put out another *Eye Opener* in which he killed off McGonigle . . . One reason for the fantastic extravagance of that fiction was to present McGonigle as indubitably fictitious, beyond the credulity of the most obtuse. He made no reference whatever to the pink *Gazette,* nor to its authors. Many readers continued to think it had been his own invention."

From the columns of the *Eye Opener,* everybody now knew that Peter McGonigle was dead. With the editor having passed from the earthly scene, the *Midnapore Gazette* had to die also. Neither Degraves nor any other person could hope to publish a paper in the name of a dead editor. Western people forgot about the pink sheet and Degraves and his friends left the city. For Bob Edwards, all danger of a serious plagiarism seemed to have passed, and he began to feel lonely for the imaginary companion of many years. His decision was to resurrect the great Peter. It required imagination and ingenuity to make the resurrection convincing, but a whiff of whisky produced the miracle and Bob Edwards was happy to have his old friend back with him, to serve as a "straw man" and bring fresh reasons for laughing to Western Canadian people.

[2] Dempsey reports that the *Midnapore Gazette* "did not die so easily. It continued to struggle along spasmodically until February 1911, when its editor and owner were charged with criminal libel and sued for $30,000 after the paper had attacked Calgary detective W. A. Grimsdall. As the case lingered before the courts, the *Gazette* finally came to an inglorious end."

CHAPTER TEN
Edwards vs. McGillicuddy

"Forgive your enemies, but if you have no enemies, forgive a few of your friends."

(20 April 1918)

"When a man is driven to drink, he usually has to walk back."

(4 August 1906)

"It is well that there is no one without a fault for he would not have a friend in the world."

(11 December 1915)

BOB EDWARDS WAS A SCOT, a Conservative of sorts and a drinking man. Daniel McGillicuddy, who came to Calgary from the East to publish the *Calgary Daily News*, was none of these. The only thing they had in common was journalism and their ideas were so completely different that it only added irritation. The newcomer wrote a lot about sin and gave the impression he had come to reform Calgary. Between the two editors, mistrust was mutual from the moment of meeting, about the time the first issue of the *News* was printed on 28 March 1907.

In the initial issue the editor declared that, in coming before the public, the *News* was "wearing no party collar, and would print all the news that's fit to print." But while he denied political affiliations, most observers concluded that the *News* editor had a pretty definite political mission.

Eye Opener politics were generally independent, but it was easy for its editor to become violently anti-Liberal, especially when certain prominent party men were concerned. Edwards disliked Sir Clifford Sifton and his policies, and he did not hesitate to give his criticism a sting. It was rumoured that Sir Clifford, having grown tired of *Eye Opener* insults, had encouraged or backed McGillicuddy to start the new paper. If such were so, one of the purposes behind the News was to counteract the Bob Edwards influence. On the very day the famous libel case came to court, a *News* editorial confessed: "It is the intention to put it [the *Eye Opener*] out of business." That, however, wasn't easy to do; especially when the *News* circulation, after a year in Calgary, was still less than 3,000, while the *Eye Opener* was at nearly 12,000.

When Sifton support became fairly evident the journalistic sniping increased, and Edwards, with his peculiar skill in mixing condemnation and humour, held an

A youthful Edwards (l) and Hoary Old McGillicudy (r), 1908.

advantage. This must have been the main reason for the vicious editorial attack upon the character of the *Eye Opener*'s editor. It was one of the most savage in the history of journalism, and all Alberta reeled from its impact.

The libellous letter appeared in the *News* on 6 October 1908, less than three weeks before a federal election about which there was a lot of local feeling. The *Eye Opener* had reported some derogatory stories about Frederick Borden, and it was hinted that it had some equally unfavourable stories about Sir Clifford. The *Daily News* admitted it was in "possession of information with regard to a conspiracy—by which it is designed to publish an election issue of the *Eye Opener*. . . ." The "letter," therefore, may have been the outburst of an editor who could no longer control his dislike for Bob Edwards and J. J. Young of the *Calgary Herald*, in whose plant the *Eye Opener* was being printed; or it could have been an attempt to silence the *Eye Opener* and thwart its publication of more political missives. It was the view of *The Edmonton Journal* that *Eye Opener* "warfare upon Fred Borden and Clifford Sifton" was the chief reason.

At any rate, the libel case which followed was Calgary's Event of the Year. In a strictly legal sense, the judgment was a victory for Plaintiff Bob Edwards; but, at the same time, it was the most bitter experience in his professional career, and even in victory there was humiliation for both *Eye Opener* and editor.

When Bob Edwards bought his copy of the *Daily News* on that October day, 1908, his eyes fell at once upon a letter to the editor, carried two columns in width and the full depth of the front page, and over the name "Nemesis." The doughty Edwards was not easily shaken; he could give and take with the best editorial fighters and do it with a smile, but here was something he had never encountered before—a writer lashing out savagely and unjustly. Such invective hurt terribly. Recovering from the first shock, he read the letter again. The shock was no less severe the second time. He wondered if he was sober and reading correctly. But there it was for the gaze of the world:[1]

> To the Editor of the *Daily News*; Sir,—For years this City of Calgary and the Province of Alberta have been cursed with a make-believe journalist in the person of one Robert C. Edwards, who has brought disgrace upon both city and province by bringing out semi-occasionally, a disreputable sheet, the mission of which has been blackmail and the contents of which were slander and smut.
>
> During a number of these years I have waited to see some action taken by the authorities to suppress this Journalistic hermaphrodite and his infamous sheet but I have waited in vain. The authorities are afraid to move because some of their own skirts are not clean and they fear the vengeance of the journalistic bully; the Citizens' League is a "false alarm" when real work for moral renovation is required; and the Ministerial Association has been too busy dealing with the Organic Union of the Churches and such like complex questions to give time to the squelching of a moral leper and the eradication of a vile publication that has done more harm to the moral uplift of the community and brought more disgrace upon the fair name of the City of Calgary than all the other vile agencies in the city combined.
>
> It is only a week or ten days ago since a couple of ordinary blackguards were fined severely by the police magistrate for peddling obscene literature in Calgary. Why are not the police and the magistrate equally strict with the output of the putrid brain of Bob Edwards and the printshop of J. J. Young—for my information is that the *Eye Opener* is printed and mailed from the *Herald* job room.
>
> I know that during the past few days copies of that filthy sheet

[1] MacEwan has abridged the Nemesis letter. For the full text, consult—what else—*Irresponsible Freaks, etc.*

have been hawked about not only by boys on the street but by men who have been looked upon as reputable citizens, and even members of the executive of one of the political parties of the city. Yet no effort has been put forward to put the dirty sheet under the ban and to fine the blackguards who are responsible for its production, as was done to the fellows who peddled the obscene literature in Calgary a week or ten days ago. It seems to me that this question is up to the morality department, the Citizens' League, the Ministerial Association and Magistrate Crispin Smith.

From my long experience, however, I know that nothing will be done by any of these agencies and I have determined to take hold of the matter myself by going after the figurehead whose name adorns the publication column of the *Eye Opener*. I know that skinning a skunk is not a very pleasing occupation, but I know also, that it is a very necessary one at times and that profit to the public results from the operation.

Now I should like to know by what law, divine or man-made, does this ruffian Edwards constitute himself the keeper of the morals of not only Calgary, but Alberta and Canada at large? What is it that the people should take his ipse dixit on matters of moral and political rectitude? What are his antecedents or other qualifications to give him the right to sit in judgment upon others? These are questions that will occur to every right thinking man who looks upon the subject and after they have done so I am willing to ask each and every one of them whether or not they approve the publication of a filthy sheet such as the *Eye Opener* undoubtedly is by a creature whose literary fulminations cannot but create the impression that he was born in a brothel and bred on a dungpile.

Who is this terrible giant who would give the impression that he possesses the power to frighten the people by bellowing Beware, Beware? His alias is R. C. Edwards and his reputation was on the black list in the United States long before he saw the Province of Alberta.

With his upbringing from the slums or his antecedents from fleeing from Spokane I will not at present speak. I will deal with him since he came to Alberta and trace his career at Strathcona, Wetaskiwin, High River and down to the present time when—miserable wreck of a depraved existence that he is—he seeks to make a living by scribbling rubbish that would turn the stomach of a professional refuse handler. As this will be merely the opening article of a series dealing with the record of this dealer in literary carrion, I will only touch upon a few of the topics that I intend going into at length later on.

First I want it to be known that Robert C. Edwards is a "four-flusher," a "tin-horn" and a "Welcher" where poker debts are concerned. I will give the dope in full later on.

Second—He is an ingrate and when I give the readers of the *Daily News* the story of his treatment of Jerry Boyce, they will see that the dunghill breed sticks out of him on every side.

I intend to show that he is a libeller, a character thief, a coward, a liar, a drunkard, a dope-fiend and a degenerate, and I hold the cards to play the game.

That he is a degenerate no one who has the slightest opportunity of seeing him can doubt, and the way in which he divides his time between the Jap-houses and the hospital admits of no doubt. In Paris it is well known that there are two kinds of degenerates. The "Apachees" are the thugs who rifle, rob and plunder the community in the criminal portions of the city. They resemble the Hooligans who infest Whitechapel in London. Edwards, if he were in London or Paris, would not be able to enroll in either the "Hooligans" or the "Apachees." He is a physical coward and could not qualify for a position where nerve was required. Why someone has not batted his block before now is one of the things I don't understand for while he goes up and down with what he considers to be the swagger of the Bowery tough he is a physical coward of the meanest type and a ten-year-old boy, possessed with the courage of a jack-rabbit could spit in his eye with impunity and Edwards would sprint in the opposite direction.

.... More anon.

Nemesis.

Bob Edwards, as editor of the *Eye Opener*, had employed strong and searing criticism lots of times; but never had he resorted to such editorial brutality, such gross inaccuracies as in this. He was stunned. If half of it were true, he should do nothing less than proceed to Centre Street Bridge and jump off. What were the alternatives? He could search out McGillicuddy and show him who the coward was; he could submerge his troubles in alcohol; he could admit he was beaten. But these thoughts left him as quickly as they entered his mind and he turned, almost instinctively, to locate his ever-staunch friend, Paddy Nolan.

When the famous lawyer read the article, he was no less shaken than was Edwards. His Irish temper burned to think that anybody would use such malicious terms about his brilliant companion, Bob Edwards.

"We can't let McGillicuddy get away with that," said Nolan. "We'll charge libel, Bob; I'll handle the case and McGillicuddy'll have a summons before noon tomorrow."

Bob felt better—some better. He needed to be assured by Paddy that the charges were really fake. Paddy could impart new strength at any time. That had been proven before.

First thing next morning a charge of defamatory libel was sworn out before Police Magistrate Crispin Smith,[2] and the case in its preliminary stage came to court on 8 October. Bob Edwards was absent, he was in hospital. But the case was adjourned and then set over to the fall assizes. In the meantime, the *Daily News* repeated many of the charges contained in the letter attributed to "Nemesis," even reprinting a large portion of the letter. The editor promised to follow with the remaining letters in the series. Reporting gleefully that, "R. C. Edwards is at present confined to the Holy Cross Hospital, a fact which like charity, covers a multitude of sins," the editor of the *News* was sure he was going to destroy the *Eye Opener*—remove "that wart on the journalistic body."

It was the legal battle of the year. It was the leading topic of conversation about the hotel lobbies and up and down Stephen Avenue. Quite a few Canadian newspapers gave it their biggest headlines. To match the able Paddy Nolan, the defence brought E. P. Davis from Vancouver, and both lawyers directed their parts with skill. But both Davis and Kilgour, who was Sifton's lawyer from Brandon, seemed bewildered by the evident lack of concrete evidence with which to support the editorial accusations from the *News*.

In presenting the case for the defence, Davis relied almost entirely upon copies of the *Eye Opener*, sifting from them, here and there, extracts that might be regarded as objectionable. "What the defence charges," he said, "is that this man is a moral degenerate. . . . If shown that he was a moral degenerate, it would be in the public interest that the paper be squelched. . . . The writings of this man Edwards reeked with filth and corruption. One issue of this paper, reaching about 10,000 readers, would do more harm than all the Sodomites that ever lived."

The first issue of the *Eye Opener* from which the defending lawyer quoted was

[2] McGillicuddy's own paper reported his arrest at 2:45 PM on 7 October 1908.

that of 27 June 1908, in which he sought to reveal the disgraceful "creed" of Editor Edwards. Here, he contended, was condemning evidence of degeneracy:

> What is a child? A nuisance.
> What is good? Hypocrisy.
> What is evil? Detection.
> What is friendship? Humbug.
> What is money? Everything.
> What is everything? Nothing.
> Were we not happier when we were monkeys?[3]

Then, attempting to magnify the seriousness of these remarks which produced only a smile on the faces of people who knew Bob Edwards and the cynical ways he had of trying to make people think deeply, the lawyer said: "No words are strong enough to characterize such a man. Scoundrel! Skunk! I say we want a new language to describe such a man."

Paddy Nolan accused the defence of imputing a distorted and evil interpretation to Bob Edwards's writing, dragging red herrings, and "smelly ones at that," across the legal path. And Dr. Mason, Bob's medical man, testified that apart from getting drunk now and then, he believed that none of the charges against the man could be sustained.

The six-man jury, after being out five hours on 11 November 1908, returned to report: "We find accused guilty of libel. We find the plea of justification not sustained."

In the rider that accompanied the jury's verdict, however, was an expression of disapproval about some articles and stories which had appeared on *Eye Opener* pages, and a recommendation to the judge to caution the paper's editor about this.

Mr. Justice Beck imposed a nominal fine of $100 without costs upon McGillicuddy; and in line with the jury's suggestion, offered a strong rebuke to Edwards, using words like "debasing and demoralizing" as he referred to certain material which had been published.

In view of the nominal nature of the fine, McGillicuddy tried to interpret the outcome as a moral victory, and had the temerity to publish the second letter in the

[3] The catechism, in its entirety, reads: "What is creation? A failure. What is life? A bore. What is man? A fraud. What is woman? Both a fraud and a bore. What is beauty? A deception. What is love? A disease. What is marriage? A mistake. What is a wife? A trial. What is a child? A nuisance. What is a devil? A fable. What is good? Hypocrisy. What is evil? Detection. What is wisdom? Selfishness. What is happiness? A delusion. What is friendship? Humbug. What is generosity? Imbecility. What is money? Everything. And what is everything? Nothing. Were we not happier when we were monkeys?"

proposed series intended to ruin the *Eye Opener*. That, along with the judicial reprimand, would surely silence his political and journalistic rival. Bob Edwards was embarrassed—and worried, almost to the point of being sick. The thing that saved him from utter despondency at that time was the loyalty of friends; they were standing by him and some who occupied editorial posts paid timely compliments. In the words of a Winnipeg editor:

"The only thing of a personal nature that could be said against Mr. Edwards was that he occasionally drinks too much—a failing that he has never even attempted to deny—a failing concerning which he frequently ridicules himself in the columns of his paper—a failing that is not confined to any class of society. . . . Mr. Edwards has rendered more real public service through exposing iniquity and depravity in public life than has any cheap editor who fears to compromise himself by defending him."

The *Lethbridge News* was another paper that sprang to the support of Edwards, stating boldly:

> We beg to repeat for the particular information of the old hypocrite who runs the *Calgary News* that . . . if there were more papers and editors in Canada with the independence and fearlessness of the *Eye Opener* and Mr. Edwards, and fewer prostituted journalists like the editor of the *Calgary Daily News*, the country would be infinitely better off. . . . If it takes a man 'born in a brothel and bred on a dunghill' and all the rest of it to produce the *Calgary Eye Opener*, what kind of a mind must that be which is capable of producing such an article as that signed by 'Nemesis' himself. Also, what brief does a man hold, writing under a nom de plume, to call a 'coward of the meanest type,' a man who, whatever comment he ever made, has always made it frankly under his own name. (*Lethbridge News*, 16 October 1908)

Public opinion was split at the very middle. As clear as the cleavage between Liberals who trusted Frank Oliver and Conservatives who followed R. B. Bennett, was the split that divided those who believed Bob Edwards to be a good man and the ones who were sure he was a sinner. As for the man who had won a doubtful victory in the courts, he was most unhappy. He was forced to admit indiscretions in some of his writing. To realize for the first time that some of the material appearing in the *Eye Opener* had bothered quite a few earnest and honest readers, upset him. He was worried, but with Paddy Nolan's encouragement he was not beaten. Paddy reminded him he still had his independence and must continue to write with courage and frankness.

On 21 November, after an absence of seven weeks, the *Eye Opener* appeared again. There was an apology to readers for having skipped a few issues, and an explanation that the "editor was not much in the mood to get out a paper while the celebrated libel suit was pending."

The editor in characteristic fashion, proceeded to bring *Eye Opener* readers up to date on the case. He quoted Judge Beck as saying at the end of the trial that counsel for the accused asserted it was not the intention of the "letter" to charge Mr. Edwards with the abominable crimes suggested in it. In the same report, Edwards conceded certain mistakes in his journalistic policies and promised to correct them; but to relax in his fight against what he considered to be wrong? Never, as long as he was publishing.

> The editor of the *Eye Opener* is not going to allow himself to be bulldozed or intimidated by any meticulous group of bum politicians back east. That paper will be run henceforth on strictly legitimate lines, with risque or objectionable matter entirely eliminated. This we do in deference to the criticism handed down by the judge in the recent trial. This criticism we recognize as sound and there will be no cause for complaint in the future. In other respects, the *Eye Opener* will be run along the same old lines, commending here and censuring there, giving grafters on the public purse all that is coming to them, and clamoring for . . . at least average decency in the private lives of public men. (21 November 1908)

In references to the trial Edwards was sarcastic, but he was not as guilty as McGillicuddy in continuing to feed the flames of hate. Bob was willing to close the discussion, while the other insisted upon prolonging it. When the editor of the *News* was reported to be ill, Bob extended what was at least half-hearted sympathy, hoping to see "the old chap" on the streets again, "shaking hands with his numerous creditors."

Whatever may have been the reasons, *Eye Opener* circulation rose steadily while the *Daily News* suffered some decline. Less than six months after the famous case had been settled in court, McGillicuddy's *Daily News* was sold and came out on 26 March 1909, as the *Calgary News Telegram.*

But not even rising circulation and the report about the sale of the *Daily News* meant that Bob Edwards was contented. He wasn't, in spite of efforts to convince his readers and himself that all was well again. The fact was that the McGillicuddy affair

IN DARKEST CALGARY

was like a bad dream he couldn't forget. More and more he was resorting to drink. The situation was not good.

If the haunting thoughts about those brutal charges contained in the "letter" did not leave him, he would be compelled to turn his back upon the scenes suggesting them. But where would he go? No place was as attractive to him as Calgary. Friends counselled patience—that after a few months the old sense of contentment would return. But what if it didn't?

CHAPTER ELEVEN
The East and Back

"By the time the average man is old enough to gratify his tastes, he hasn't any."

"The way of the transgressor is very popular."

(8 May 1915)

"Neighborly sympathy often turns out to be nine-tenths curiosity."

(11 January 1919)

"To do right is easy when sin ceases to be a pleasure."

(21 February 1920)

IT WAS DISCOURAGING that after nearly five years in Calgary, Bob felt very much as he had during the last months at High River. The McGillicuddy trial was a bad experience any way one looked at it. Others might forget about it but Bob couldn't.

He didn't want to leave Alberta; but how else was he to get away from the thought of that terrible "letter," the humiliating days of the trial, and the public rebuke from the judge? Even the memory of his own conduct during that period disappointed him—yielding to a siege of drunkenness as soon as Paddy had taken charge of the case and allowing nearly two months to pass without an issue of the *Eye Opener.*

When trouble had accumulated at High River, he had torn himself away and made a fresh start. He resolved to do it again; and sorrowfully, Paddy Nolan agreed that he should go. But where would he go? He didn't wish to move back to a small town, and Edmonton was too close; Winnipeg's handicap was that he had worked there before. Perhaps the East and Toronto were not as bad as people said of them. Toronto it would be, for better or for worse. There was one thing about it—except for the player piano and his library of books, all his worldly possessions would go in one trunk and moving was a small problem.

When it was known that Bob Edwards was leaving Calgary, the public reaction was quite mixed. A Winnipeg paper insinuated that, at last, he and the *Eye Opener* were being run out of the foothills city. No doubt some people were pleased to think that such was the case, but far more striking were the genuine expressions of regret and wishes for a speedy return which marked his departure. Daniel McGillicuddy must have found it disconcerting to read the *Albertan*'s tribute on the eve of leaving, that, "Mr. Edwards is a quiet and retiring person . . . cultured, widely read, well-educated and a very likable young man." It didn't sound like the same person of whom "Nemesis" had written only a few months before.

From friends in and about the newspaper offices in Calgary came a gold watch as a parting gift. Of the presentation, the *Calgary Herald* reported:

> By some skillful manoeuvring, R. C. Edwards was lured into the *Herald* office last evening and before he had time to realize that there was an ulterior motive in getting him there, he was presented by W. H. Davidson of the *Albertan*, on behalf of newspaper men of both offices with a watch, chain and charm, the latter bearing the inscription, "To R. C. Edwards, from Calgary Scribes." In a brief presentation speech Mr. Davidson spoke of Mr. Edwards's popularity among the fraternity in the city and in fact the whole province, and predicted prosperity in Toronto for which point he left last night.[1]

As the day of departure had drawn near, Bob would willingly have reversed his plans and remained in Calgary. It was just the fact of those well-meaning farewells which prevented him changing his mind. And as always, Paddy Nolan had the appropriate counsel: "Leave your piano and books here; you'll be back after a while." That was the way it would be; and on 27 April 1909, with the Rockies displaying a sparkling clearness against the western horizon, Bob Edwards boarded the east-bound train—the words of Paddy Nolan ringing in his ears: "You'll find Toronto a nice old aunt but don't feel you must marry her."

The Toronto experience was in the nature of an experiment. Bob admitted that. As things turned out, however, there was incompatability from the day of arrival, and the experiment was a short one. Bob couldn't understand the Toronto he had hoped might accept him, and apart from the few who were *Eye Opener* customers through the years, Torontonians were inclined to look upon this new citizen from Calgary as a barbarian threat to their comfortable composure.[2]

[1] The *Albertan* (April 27, 1909) reiterated the *Herald*'s backhanded praise, agreeing that the *Eye Opener* "possessed a cleverness and breeziness unique among Canadian newspapers and has expressed independent opinions in a clever and unusual way" despite having "some features to which objection has properly been taken."

[2] Typically, there's a bit of mystery surrounding Edwards's brief Toronto sojourn. On 14 April 1909, the *Calgary Herald* reported: "It looks as though the negotiations that have been pending for several months for the transfer of the *Eye Opener* to Toronto would go through. The offer was originally made early last fall by a group of business men in that city for the incorporation of the property into a joint stock company, with R. C. Edwards, the present owner, in control." The article went on to claim that the paper would "become more national and less local in its tone," necessitating relocation to Toronto. This supposed development is at odds with the content Edwards published in Ontario, suggesting the deal—if, indeed, it existed—soon fell through.

Nothing was right in Toronto. "The Reform League was here, there and everywhere." The sky was overcast with "Don'ts," and even the birds in the trees along the avenues seemed to be warbling threats: "Pro-secute you . . . Pro-secute you. . . ."

Toronto offered much about which to write, and Bob waxed more cynical than ever. He saw women in fine clothes walking on Yonge Street as though they resented the necessity of sharing a sidewalk with women in shawls. And well-to-do males in plug hats tried not to see the squalor beside the routes over which they went to church on Sunday mornings. Bob Edwards couldn't refrain from striking at social wrongs wherever he encountered them. Many Torontonians didn't like it and were shocked, as he expected them to be, at some of the material he wrote for his pages. Of course the Reform League would object to candid comment such as that appearing under "Answers To Correspondents":

> Sport, Edmonton: Record for high jumping is 1,000 feet, made from the top of Eiffel Tower, Paris, by a genial suicide.
>
> Anxious Mother: Name of lady in your village who gave birth to triplets eight years ago was Mrs. J. B. Prewen. It was her husband who got off the sparkling jest about her being full of prewens.
>
> Constant Reader: You lose. Shakespeare was not a Scotchman, although his talents would justify the supposition. He was an Englishman.
>
> Phil Weinard, High River: You lose, Rainbow and Niobe [the two ships in the Canadian Navy] were not won by the late Sir Wilfrid Laurier in a raffle. They were purchased from England many years ago.
>
> Petronius, Moose Jaw: The solar plexus blow was invented by Fitzsimmons. Some one has been stringing you. A left hook is not a demi-mondaine who has missed her train.

Prudish and pious people should be shocked. Some Toronto trends were dangerous. "The churches are ultrafashionable;" and what good can come from that? Sunday was the day when nobody dared to laugh aloud. "Compared with a Toronto Sunday, the Scottish Sabbath is a French ball." The intolerant Reform League was practically telling other people they were not entitled to have independent views. It was depressing, Bob wrote, and he wasn't even surprised that a good portion of the population "seemed to put in their time committing suicide off the Rosedale Bridge."

However much Bob may have been guilty of exaggerating the Toronto situation, he quickly concluded that it was not the place for him. After a few weeks, each one with a Toronto Sunday, he journeyed to Montreal, looked it over, and then decided to backtrack to the Lakehead. He didn't know much about Port Arthur, but at least it would be a step nearer Calgary. There, on 14 August 1909, the *Eye Opener* reappeared, its character unchanged and its editor promising nothing more than to publish "from time to time." He wanted no misunderstandings and so he warned further:

> For the information of our Lake-town friends we beg to state that the *Eye Opener* is forbidden the use of the government mails. The postal department according to their regulations, were perfectly justified in doing this, on the ground that we published undesirable matter. In the public interests, we, from time to time, made some shocking exposures of the immoralities of certain members and ex-members of the cabinet. The facts are certainly unfit for publication and we don't blame the department a particle for trying to prevent their dissemination throughout the God-fearing country.

In moving to Port Arthur, Bob Edwards no doubt felt very much alone in the world and very much discouraged. But without seeking notoriety and without realizing how much he was getting, he was gradually emerging from a local figure to one of national and international note. Even *Collier's Weekly* editorialized about his last move, wished him success and hoped, "Bob will be as nice as he can, short of letting the *Eye Opener* get dull." On that point of dullness, however, there was no danger.

There was a challenging newness about the Twin Cities on the shore of Lake Superior, or so the editor was reckless enough to suppose. Certainly there should be business opportunities where the cities had water connections with remote parts of the world. Fort William and Port Arthur would be among Canada's greatest cities some day, he argued. He fancied the idea of "growing up" with a city and reasoned that Port Arthur, with no Reform League, would be congenial.

But the Lakehead City held him only a little longer than Toronto. He liked the place well enough, but there were problems. When an analysis of the personnel of the City Council showed certain aldermen to be "useless and dangerous" (4 December 1909), the people concerned objected to being told. Moreover, the newspapers of both Lakehead cities refused to co-operate by consenting to the use of their presses, and the *Eye Opener* had to be printed in Winnipeg. It was only reasonable, then, that if the printing was to be done in Winnipeg, the editor might as well live there. He was lonely for Calgary, and for Paddy and Cappie and the others, but it was too soon to go back. A move to Winnipeg would be in the right direction, and at the end of December, 1909, he began getting mail in that city. From 18 December 1909, through 1910, the *Eye Opener* was published with a Winnipeg dateline.[3]

If circulation had been the only consideration, the Winnipeg year could have been considered a success. But it was evident that Bob wouldn't be happy until he was back with Paddy Nolan, Winnipeg acquaintances notwithstanding. He was having bats with drink more frequently. It wasn't good. He knew the increasing attraction of the bar was dangerous, even though there was little evidence of such conviction in his writing. "One might as well laugh at an enemy."

Early in 1911 Bob reminded himself he had been absent from Calgary for nearly two years; that was long enough. Clouds formed a familiar arch over the mountains to the southwest, promising Chinook winds, that spring day when he landed back at Calgary and Paddy Nolan was at the station to offer a welcome. "Here you belong, you scoundrel," Paddy was saying; and Bob, a couple of years older, a decade wiser, and more enthusiastic than ever about the Valley of the Bow, vowed he would never leave again. And he didn't leave again, except for periods long enough for suitable fishing expeditions. He had turned his back on Toronto because it was too good, Montreal because it was too bad, Port Arthur because it was too dull, and Winnipeg because it had neither a Paddy Nolan nor a hotel rotunda like that of the Alberta.

Calgary was a bigger city by 15,000 people than when he had gone away, and its business face had changed somewhat. Daniel McGillicuddy[*] had moved away[4] and nearly everybody was glad that Bob Edwards was back. Making a deal with the *Albertan* to print the *Eye Opener*, the little man in the christie hat went about his unsteady editorial ways as though there had been no interruption greater than that of a long drunk. And demand for the paper? Instead of dropping as might have been expected, during the editor's two-year absence, it, like real estate sales, had risen sharply. With satisfaction Bob could say, "We sell more *Eye Openers* on the streets of the delightful city than we did when we were residing here previously." Circulation, which was at 15,000 when he left Calgary, reached a new peak of 26,000 just two months after his return. Excluding the Winnipeg dailies, the *Eye Opener* was first in circulation in the entire country from Toronto west.

[3] The move occurred in early 1910. The 1 January 1910 *Eye Opener* sported a Calgary dateline; the 19 February 1910 issue a Winnipeg one. The last known Winnipeg issue was 15 October 1910. The 21 January 1911 issue marked a return to Calgary—interim editions, if there were any, are no longer extant.

[*] Without mentioning any name, the *Eye Opener* of 21 December 1912 noted: "Hell got a new settler last week."—MacEwan

[4] McGillicuddy moved to Toronto, where he died on 11 December 1912. The 12 December 1912 *Calgary Daily Herald* made brief mention of the passing of this "Canadian newspaperman of some note."

For Bob Edwards, one of the best welcomes was in the circulation room of the *Albertan* two weeks after his return, when copies of his paper were ready for street sales. There at seven o'clock on the Saturday morning he faced his newsboys in familiar fashion. Nearly all who had sold *Eye Opener*s when he went away were present, their faces radiating breakfast jam and youthful joy at seeing their old friend again. He could call most of them by name and recall the special family needs of some. The delight was mutual: Bob Edwards would fight for any one of those boys. As he passed copies for the street sales—forty to the chap who was standing first in line, thirty to another, and twenty to a little fellow, he didn't forget the one who had always received twenty-five copies without the usual payment of two and one-half cents each, because his mother had a special problem in feeding and clothing her fatherless children. This was the man the Reform League was glad to see leave Toronto.

For each boy, Bob had a word of cheer as he passed out the papers, perhaps a joke of some kind: "Be on your way, lad, and be glad you didn't live a few thousand years ago when the Babylon *Eye Opener* was printed on bricks! Babylon *Eye Opener*, forty-five shekels—all about Sir Frederick Herod—Babylon *Eye Opener*!" (18 December 1909)

It was a strong admiration that persisted between the newspaperman and that gang which sold on the streets, and it should not be overlooked that a strikingly high percentage of those boys became leading citizens; a president of the Calgary Exhibition and Stampede, a couple of leading merchants, and a top executive would join in saying with obvious pride: "I sold the *Eye Opener*."

On only one other occasion did Bob Edwards see the East, and fortunately he so enjoyed the journey that he forgave Winnipeg, Port Arthur, and Toronto for everything. It was when a group of western editors took advantage of a CPR excursion. Alberta editors, Bob could explain with conviction, were generally too poor to travel beyond Medicine Hat on their own resources; but here was an opportunity with the railroad company generously placing a special car at their disposal. About twenty Alberta editors made the trip; and needless to tell, Bob Edwards, his trials with McGillicuddy forgotten, was the life of the party. At Winnipeg his old friend, Col. C. G. Porter of the *Winnipeg Tribune* and formerly with the *Calgary Herald*, entertained the group with an elaborate luncheon and a poker game, after which the host settled for the meal and entertainment with ten-dollar bills which some of the poker-playing editors had no difficulty in recognizing.

At Toronto "Mayor Tommy Church" met the train and directed the party to the museum, where the stuffed animals took on a peculiar fascination. Reaching down the neck of the carnivorous dinosaur, the mayor drew out a bottle of Scotch whiskey.

"Marvellous! Marvellous!" murmured the editors, gathering closer. Then according to Bob's telling:

> Everybody had a drink and pronounced the museum superior in every way to the British Museum in London and away ahead of the Louvre. The Megalasaurus, being extra large, was good for three bottles, though a small specimen of the dinotherium, six million years old and found in the Miocene formations, only yielded a pint of Seagrams. However, there was no kick about the arrangements. A visit to the wax works elicited much interest. In the breast pocket of Sir John A. Macdonald's Prince Albert was found a large flat oblong bottle of rather good stuff.

The editor from High River, who had just been reading Tupper's *Life of Sir John*, was deeply affected. Quite obviously, Mayor Church understood editors; Bob Edwards and other deep-dyed Westerners agreed that the East wasn't a bad place after all and Toronto improved with better acquaintance.

CHAPTER TWELVE
The Boom Years and Shadow

"All the speculation in the world never raised a bushel of wheat."
(10 February 1912)

"It's a waste of time telling a man he is a liar. If he is, he knows it."
(21 September 1918)

"Bankruptcy is when you put your money in your hip pocket and let your creditors take your coat."
(8 November 1913)

"Graft is still graft, even if they call it commission."
(2 December 1906)

RETURNING FROM THE EAST, Bob Edwards was just in time to witness the maddest scenes in Calgary's notable real estate boom, to see properties changing hands three and four times in a single month and always with profit for the sellers. People talked and thought about little else, and the possibility of a recession in values was something nobody seemed to consider.

It had begun, of course, years earlier; and if wealth had been Bob Edwards's ambition, he couldn't have taken residence in Calgary at a more opportune time than 1904. In March of that year, 500 city-owned lots were sold at an average price of $43, and real estate dealers like T. S. C. Lee and C. S. Lott were offering good building sites close to the heart of the business section on 7th Avenue for $200 each. Investment opportunities were everywhere, and some of the men with whom Bob sat in the lobby of the Alberta Hotel were amassing fortunes.

Values advanced slowly at first and then gathered momentum. By 1909 some of the $200 lots of five years before were selling at $1000 a frontage foot and going higher in this city that was to become "the Paris of North America." When the first issue of the *Calgary News-Telegram* came out on 28 March of the year just noted, the editor estimated the city's population of 29,265 would rise to 90,000 in three years and a quarter of a million in ten years. In the course of such expansion, every prudent person could become wealthy. All one had to do was to buy lots at a thousand dollars and sell them at two thousand. It was the spirit of the time. Along in December property salesmen were proposing city lots as the best possible Christmas presents—the kind that would be "worth twice as much before next Christmas."

By 1912 real estate prices and civic optimism were at precarious levels. The City Council, anticipating a population of half a million to a million, employed Thomas Mawson, an English architect, to draft appropriate plans. With little thought as to cost, Mawson set about to reconstruct the design of the city, even to change the course of the Bow River and build a multi-million dollar Civic Centre. In his report he noted that, "There is enough land subdivided now to house a population of at least five hundred thousand."

Areas farther and farther from the mid-point of the city were being surveyed to provide residential lots. The ridiculous extreme to which subdivision was carried was illustrated by Bob Edwards's story concerning a farmer looking for a site on which to build a city home. At the real estate office he explained his desire to get away from the hardships of country living, and declared an interest in selling the farm and buying a city lot. With characteristic impetuousness, the agent whisked him away to see some "good buys." Together they drove for miles, and finally, with well-practiced flourishes, the agent proclaimed: "There—wouldn't that be a lovely place for you and your wife to build your city home?" Then, after the slightest pause, the agent asked: "By the way, where is the farm you want to sell?"

"My farm?" the man from the country answered. "Why, we passed it a couple of miles back, nearer Calgary."

"Everyone has a lot in mind," Bob Edwards wrote at that time. "He wants to sell it or he wants to buy it." And salesmen didn't have to be the kind who could sell milkpails to homesteaders with oxen. According to Bob, a good conscience was not one of the qualifications sought in salesmen:

> Wanted by Calgary Real Estate firm: Explorers to conduct parties out to their parks and additions. Must have natural topographical instincts. Indian trackers preferred. Good opening for Arabs used to the desert. Camels provided that can go for a month without water. Must be able to put up a good line of guff. Compasses and chart of the heavens provided in case of accidents. Lies told on trips warmly backed up by firm, if not too raw. Pay on commission basis. Address: The William Miner Realty Co., Calgary. (18 November 1911)

Certainly, salesmen had it pretty easy; the rush to buy was like bargain day at a nylon counter, and Bob caricatured the situation with stories like the one about the unfortunate fellow who found it necessary to enter hospital at that particular time to

Lost on Prairie while trying to find location of Calgary Suburban lots he has bought.

have some molars extracted. With Dr. Scrunchen, dentist, and Dr. McMurder, and Dr. Slaughter, attending physicians, the patient's welfare was placed in jeopardy by the pressures of land deals.

The patient was ordered to stretch out on the oprerating table, and while one doctor administered chloroform, conversation turned inevitably to real estate. Scrunchen and McMurder became involved in an argument about the relative values of lots each one was holding. Nothing would do but they should go downstairs to study the blueprints.

Bending over the anesthetized patient, the nurse muttered something like, "Poor fellow;" and Dr. Slaughter, who had remained behind, exclaimed, "Oh, the patient!" but returned immediately to conversation about his Elbow Park lots, just fifteen blocks from the car line; and about some others, only nine miles from the post office.

Again the nurse reminded Slaughter about the patient. "Oh yes," he replied. "By jove, I almost forgot. . . . I wonder if I've given him an overdose of chloroform?" Then, as the dentist and the other doctor were slow about returning, Slaughter decided to remove the man's appendix, just to put in time, because the $150 fee would meet the second payment on some 21st Avenue lots. Slaughter tested the keenness of his knife on a hair plucked from his head, made an incision, and probed around for the appendix which the blighter didn't seem to possess.

At this point, Scrunchen and McMurder returned, McMurder having won the bet that his lots were closer to the car line. But what was Slaughter cutting up the patient for? The answer was, to get $150 for a payment on 21st Avenue lots. The explanation was fair enough, but it was then drawn to Slaughter's attention that he had cut his man open on the wrong side if it was an appendix he hoped to find. Slaughter admitted his error, explaining that he had been thinking about his Elbow Park property. It was easy enough to sew the patient up anyway, and then the professional men could get on with the extractions. But Slaughter's sewing was not fast enough for his colleagues, because they had property to inspect; and they decided to pull the teeth while the sewing was still in progress.

With two operations proceeding simultaneously, a race developed and Scrunchen had teeth flying in all directions. It was a close race; but the dentist was the winner "by a tooth," and the doctors grabbed their hats and started for Elbow Park. Some time later, the patient regained consciousness. He complained about a strange feeling in his abdomen and enquired if the doctors had extracted his teeth from that part of his body. But his complaining was only momentary, because his thoughts turned to his own property on 7th Avenue which, before he left the operating room, he was successfully selling to the nurse.

Time and again, friends came to Bob Edwards saying: "Bob, it's all very well for you to spend your time writing about Peter McGonigle and straightening out the Government, but we'd like to see you make some money. Now, here's a piece of property on which you couldn't miss."

"Make more money?" Bob would reply with obvious failure to comprehend. "Put the stuff in a sock? Why should I bother to make more money? I couldn't eat any more and I shouldn't drink any more." The fact was that he had no more regard for wealth than an alley-cat has for traffic laws. That he was close to bankruptcy much of the time worried his friends; but for himself, his pleasures came from self-assigned tasks and his writing.

At the very moment when an acquaintance was selling a lot on the corner of 8th Avenue and Centre Street for a bank building at $4000 per foot, and somebody else was selling a site for the new Hudson's Bay Company store at a reported three-quarters of a million dollars, Bob Edwards was celebrating the tenth anniversary of the birth of the *Eye Opener.* Starting exactly ten years before with a circulation of 250, "the rag embarked on a wild career, full of adventure by land and booze. In sending congratulations, do not enclose bottles, as we are strictly on the [water wagon]." (20 April 1912)

To honor the occasion, the editor had "the whole staff out to dinner which means he ate alone in the cafeteria food mill and forgathered amiably with the tomato catsup bottle and the cruet stand. There were no speeches."

At that particular point in the real estate frenzy, not many Calgarians would stop for an anniversary anyway; and even fewer would have time to enjoy, from the same issue of the *Eye Opener,* a bit of Edwards's comment about the tailors' strike then in progress. Here was a touch of the homely philosophy of a man completely detached from the craze for real estate profits:

> The tailors' strike in Calgary is really a blessing in disguise. We are now able to sally forth unashamed in our old duds of last summer and blame it on the strike. O, blessed strike! Please don't settle it till fall.

> After all, the only clothes that are really clothes are the old clothes. Men may be divided into two classes, those who have one suit of clothes and those who have more. With the purchase of a second outfit, a man's slavery begins. When one has but a single suit, it looks like him. When you see the familiar old coat and the vest and the baggy pants slung over a chair at night, you are tempted to cry, as Michael Angelo exclaimed looking at his completed statue of Moses: "Why don't you speak?"
>
> The one suit of clothes becomes creased to your personality. It is as much a part of you as your skin. Only the man with one suit of clothes may be said to be clothed at all. Those with more, wear uniforms. When you send clothes to a what-d'-you-call-'em—dyer and cleaner—to get pressed, you might say: "Remove my ego and steam away my characteristics. Iron out my personality. This suit is becoming like me. I cannot stand for that. I am ashamed." (20 April 1912)

Edwards, the philosopher, fraternized with men of wealth, but his interests remained unchanged and his resources consistently perilous by usual standards. He knew he'd never have much money. After commenting on the death of an acquaintance who had left a quarter of a million dollars, Bob made a prophecy notable for its accuracy:

> One thing we know. When our will comes to be probated, there will be no questions on the street as to where we "got it." All you'll hear will be, "What did he do with all the nickles he took in?" "What a pity he drank!" "Yes, it takes money to buy whiskey!" "They tell me that all he left was his kind regards." "Oh well, the estate can realize something on the empty bottles."

As a businessman, he was a poor one—perhaps the worst on Calgary's 8th Avenue. Business didn't attract him. The old *Eye Opener* was a hobby more than a money-making enterprise. He could write copy and read good books from sunset until Mary Fulham's pigs squealed for their breakfasts, and enjoy doing it; but making collections and paying bills were abhorrent necessities in the life of a man Bohemian in nature. Business, as he saw it, was cold, colourless and without humour; consequently, bills were not paid on time and many of the receivables were never collected.

In the first place, his failure to conform to regular schedules was unbusinesslike. The *Eye Opener*, conceived as a weekly but making its appearance rather like the Chinook winds, was evidence. When it received official rebuke because of irregularity, the editor, in most unprofessional manner, would tell his readers all about it, and, boyishly, promise to do better.

"The *Eye Opener*," he wrote, "had a slight ginning up from the postal authorities last week on account of the irregularity of its publication. It appears, according to the regulations, that a paper that passes as a weekly and receives postal privileges as a weekly, must come weekly, and not semi-occasionally. Our infuriated subscribers thus have cause to rejoice, for we shall have to come out once a week now whether we like it or not and whether there is anything to write about or not. It is a confounded nuisance but it can't be helped." (25 August 1906)

Many hard-working publishers finding it imperative to pursue sound business principles couldn't understand the *Eye Opener* phenomenon. There was Edwards—editor, publisher, manager, reporter, and errand boy, all rolled into one; and the more he neglected his work, the higher went the circulation. The *Eye Opener* might be under suspension by the railroad company or barred from the mails; it might miss several weeks because the editor wasn't in the humour to write copy, and yet demand did not slacken.[1] Edwards couldn't furnish the explanation; but as the tenth anniversary coincided with the peak in real estate transactions, he could supply the proof: "Today's issue is exactly 33,586."

For most of the time he didn't even have a subscription list, depending upon street sales at five cents a copy. Once in High River and once in Calgary he made half-hearted attempts to build subscription lists, announcing on the latter occasion that: "The subscription price should be $10 per annum but owing to slight irregularities in its appearance and occasional punk issues, we only charge one plunk." (22 December 1906) Probably the main reason he favoured street sales was that they gave the newsboys a chance to earn some money.

With a high rating in circulation along with the real estate prosperity of the period, advertising at $1.40 per column inch might have brought a fortune. But Bob would not solicit advertising and wouldn't even accept it unless he knew it was from a reliable firm whose announcement would not mislead innocent investors. Arthur

[1] It could be argued that Edwards's seemingly inexplicable success was, in fact, due precisely to his roguish ways. In the *Eye Opener* dated 22 August 1903, Edwards reprinted a groaner credited to *The Bee*, a short-lived Calgary satirical newspaper: "Why is Robert, of High River, like a Nun? Because he is not allowed to associate with mails." Even at this early date, Edwards cut an imposing enough figure to warrant such familiar namedropping. More telling, however, is how he basked in this notoriety. "Despite this horrible joke," he wrote, "the *Bee* man adds the shrewd observation, 'Of course Bob will come out of it with a bigger circulation than ever.' You bet he will."

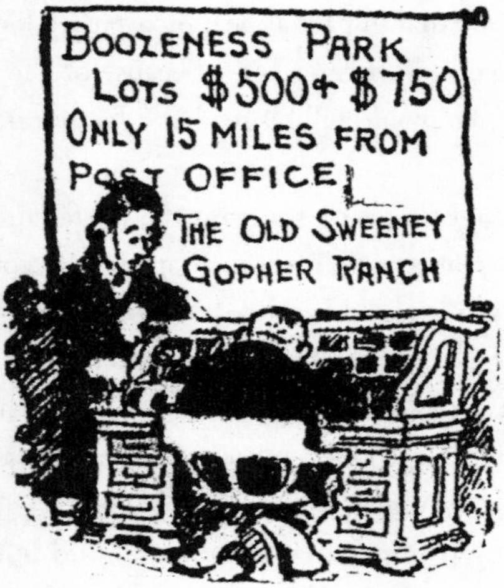

"Young man, can you write real estate ads?"

"You just bet I can, sir. I have published a volume of fairy tales and am author of a revised edition of The Arabian Nights."

"Well, consider yourself engaged. Get busy on Boozeness Park."

P. Halpen, who worked in the composing room of the *Albertan*, recalled one of Edwards's refusals to accept advertising from a Calgary real estate firm trying to sell lots in an ill-advised subdivision. Bob sensed a racket, and not only said so through his columns, but had his talented cartoonist, Charles Forrester, who was with him for the last six years of his life, sketch pictures showing gophers and longhorn cattle grazing on those remote lots. On a Friday noon, after the *Eye Opener* had been printed but not circulated, Mr. Halpen and a coworker at the *Albertan* were approached by a member of the real estate company and offered one hundred dollars for a copy of the paper. With such a copy in their possession, members of the real estate firm, presumably, would have sought an immediate injunction against sale of the issue. Halpen said, "No, we don't work that way, but if you'll wait till tomorrow morning, you can buy one on the street for five cents."

The papers were sold as usual and readers agreed that Bob Edwards had rendered another service in protecting the public from a real estate swindle.

Forrester, the ex-homesteader, confirmed that Edwards, "his mind stored with facts relating to the political history of Canada and his heart big and warm," wasn't much of a businessman. But he was a "terror to evil-doers and saved the public from having its pockets picked far oftener than we shall ever realize." (Written after Edwards's death, *Eye Opener*, 26 November 1922)

Somebody offering lots in a new subdivision or stock in a mining company would phone to place an advertisement; Miss Bertha Hart, who was the editor's devoted secretary from 1912, would turn to him and ask: "Will we accept it?" The reply was always the same: "We'll investigate; we'll not be party to anything that would tempt our working people to make worthless investments. We have our readers to think about."

"We could easily have trebled the size of the paper had we accepted advertising from all the companies who wished to place ads," the former secretary recalled. "But Mr. Edwards accepted very few." Many times, advertising from Vancouver and West Coast property dealers was refused because the editor considered the companies unreliable. If the situation seemed to demand it, he would lash out to expose the danger, for instance: "The *Eye Opener* takes this opportunity of warning all and sundry to have nothing to do with a gold mining company promoted by one James Malcolm, now in Calgary. Never mind why we issue this warning, but whoever you are, fight shy of it." (20 April 1918)

The editor's bookkeeping methods resembled nothing that a student of accounting would recognize. His "double entry" system of handling accounts consisted of stuffing bills to be paid in the left hand pocket of his trousers and what cash he had in the right, and hoping there would be enough on the right side to balance the demands of the left.

As for office records, the editor of the paper with the biggest circulation west of Winnipeg didn't even keep copies of all the *Eye Openers*. When, on 1 January 1910, he made an appeal for back issues, Dr. G. D. Stanley sent along copies of the earliest ones with a letter which stated: "During your stay in High River I was close enough to you to realize that the time would come when you would be promising big money—at least ten dollars apiece—for the first five issues of the *Eye Opener* so I tucked them away and bided my time. It happened as I anticipated. The papers go forward by this mail. Where did you say I could find those fifty bucks?"

In reply to his old friend, Bob said: "Many thanks for your kindness and congratulations on your profitable foresight. I need those copies badly and am happy to get them so cheaply. Just add the fifty bucks to the bottom of my old account and all will be paid at the same time—perhaps. In the meantime, the greatest of my real appreciation is your reward."

Early in 1913, as the notable real estate boom was fading, clouds filled Bob Edwards's sky. Death took his great counsellor and friend, Paddy Nolan; and just weeks later he sat at the ringside for the most famous boxing match in Calgary's history and saw Luther McCarty, acclaimed the "White Heavyweight Champion of the World," go down in the first round—dead. No amount of real estate fortune could have made the Bob Edwards of strong sentiment forget those two deaths, and throughout the summer men on the streets whispered: "What's wrong with Bob Edwards? He seems lost."

In his school days he had been considered a smart boxer, and through the years he followed the sport and wrote about it assiduously. Tommy Burns, who lost the heavyweight boxing championship of the world to Jack Johnson in 1908, was living in Calgary and operating two clothing stores on 8th Avenue. He and Bob Edwards saw a lot of each other, and Burns was promoting the 24 May fight between Arthur Pelkey of Calgary and Luther McCarty of Chicago. Negro Jack Johnson still claimed the world title, and his manager wired Burns asking for a matched fight with McCarty in Calgary. But Johnson, because of conduct, was in some disgrace at that time; and Burns and others were inclined to deny him the championship recognition. Burns would have nothing to do with Johnson but was anxious to see McCarty or Pelkey placed in position to challenge for the world title.

Anyway, all Calgary was worked up about the McCarty-Pelkey match. The great McCarty, with whom Calgary Pioneer F. B. "Bull" McHugh sometimes boxed in Chan's Pool Room when the big fellow worked in the city a couple of years earlier, was the favourite in the betting; but Calgarians were hopeful that their own Canadian, Arthur Pelkey, who had made a good showing against Jess Willard in New York, would distinguish himself.

On the morning of the match Bob Edwards met George Taylor, sports writer for the News Telegram, at the Alberta Hotel and together they journeyed by streetcar to the Manchester Arena where they had ringside seats. At 12:45 noon, the preliminary bouts over, the two heavyweights entered the ring for the event for which the sporting world was waiting. Tall and well-built—both fighters—they seemed perfectly matched, even though McCarty had the advantage of more ring experience and more publicity.

They shook hands; the fight was on—but not for long. At only one minute and forty seconds in the first round, McCarty reeled and fell to the floor. The crowd cheered madly, little realizing the seriousness of the knockdown. Referee Ed Smith counted to ten and signalled Pelkey to his corner. Bob Edwards sensed trouble and so did McCarty's manager, who called doctors. But artificial respiration, morphine, and brandy failed to do anything for the boxer. Luther McCarty was dead. As the autopsy was to show, he died from a hemorrhage caused by a dislocated neck, probably from a blow on the chin.

Bob Edwards was a Pelkey fan that day; but nevertheless, he was as much saddened as though he had delivered the fatal blow. He knew McCarty personally and liked the big fellow who had been an Oklahoma cowboy before becoming a professional boxer. The *Eye Opener* didn't go to press at the next usual time, because the editor was too unhappy to get it ready.

And as for the passing of Paddy, it probably affected Bob more than the death of his own brother Jack, back in Wetaskiwin days. It was on 11 February 1913, and

Paddy, of whom R. B. Bennett said: "The greatest criminal lawyer I've known," was only forty-nine years of age. By order of Calgary's mayor, flags on all civic buildings were at half-mast. There were two reasons for that: One was P. J. Nolan's passing; and the other was the news just received about the fate of Explorer Captain Robert Scott and his four companions who had perished near the South Pole.

P. J. Nolan had been a big part of Calgary, prominent in everything during the city's formative years. Men meeting on the street said the same thing: "Dear old Paddy has gone!" Everybody felt a sense of loss; but except for Mr. Nolan's widow, and son Harry attending the University of Alberta, nobody would miss Paddy more than Bob Edwards. Bob seemed to disappear for a time. He wasn't drinking; it was just that his world had lost much of its brightness when his big-hearted friend answered the final call, and he wanted to be alone. It was several weeks before Bob could bring himself to write about it; but when he did attempt it, readers saw the Edwards with a fine touch:

> Several weeks have elapsed since the passing away of our dear old friend, P. J. Nolan. . . . There is something tragic in the reflection that none of us shall ever in this world see his jovial face again.
>
> Brilliant though Paddy undoubtedly was in the court room, his brilliance shone with its most dazzling effect when he was completely ensconced in an armchair at home or at the club, surrounded by a group of congenial spirits. His humour was never vulgar and his shafts of wit never hurt. We have heard him relate myriads of yarns but never one that was in the remotest degree off color. His make-up was essentially refined and intellectual, and despite his light and jocular point of view, he was a profoundly religious man, punctiliously attentive to the duties imposed by his church.
>
> It is given to few men in the West to achieve a fame which spreads beyond the confines of a limited area, but Paddy Nolan was known far and wide across the Dominion as a famous wit, a great criminal lawyer and a whole-souled Irish gentleman. The mere fact of his being a citizen of Calgary imparted a certain renown abroad. . . . Calgary without Paddy can never be quite the same.
>
> His faculty of keeping a crowd in a sustained roar of laughter for hours at a stretch was a constant source of wonderment. . . . He never repeated himself. Paddy's well of fun never ran dry for an instant and the rapidity with which he could drive away the blues from the mind

of a worried friend was not the least endearing of his qualities.

The supreme characteristic of P. J. Nolan, the barrister, was loyalty to his client. No matter how obviously guilty his client might be, Paddy seemed to have the faculty of hypnotizing himself into the firm belief that the murderer, horse thief or whatever it might be, was perfectly innocent. To this very human trait may be attributed, in a measure, his astonishing success at the bar.

For example, he always believed and stoutly maintained in conversation with his intimates, that Cashel was innocent of the murder for which he was hanged. He made a trip to Ottawa at his own expense to try and induce the Minister of Justice to commute the sentence. Not only that, but he would not permit Cashel's body to be buried in the jail precincts. Again at his own expense—for he got no fees in this case—he had the body removed to a cemetery and given a Christian burial. No man had a more tender heart than old Paddy and he loved to take the part of the underdog.

Whenever we, the editor of the *E.O.*, happened to get involved in a libel suit, Paddy was always the first to rush to our aid. His advice in such cases was very sound. He would brook no interference nor allow any suggestions from a client. He had to handle the affair all himself or not handle it at all. . . . No question of fees ever passed between us. The only approach to remuneration that Paddy ever got out of the writer was a box of fifty cigars and on that occasion he jocularly declined to take even that until we had officially assured him that it had nothing to do with libel suits. We recall that about a week after making the modest little gift we happened to ask him how he liked the cigars and he replied quite gravely, "You mean those El Pewkos? They're fine. I've smoked 'm all but forty-nine."

Well might it be said of Paddy that in life he always left them laughing when he said goodbye. In this last goodbye of all, tears take the place of laughter. (8 March 1913)

Had Paddy Nolan lived a little longer, he would have seen his son as the first native-born boy to be accorded the high honour of a Rhodes Scholarship; he'd have seen another mad Calgary boom, gushing from the discovery of oil at Turner Valley; then the outbreak of the first World War; and he'd have seen his old drinking friend, Bob Edwards, passing one of his finest tests.

CHAPTER THIRTEEN
Society Notes

> "As a matter of fact, your neighbors think just as disagreeable thoughts about you as you think about them."
>
> (24 November 1917)

> "If a girl has a pretty face, no man on earth can tell what kind of clothes she has on."
>
> (6 October 1918)

> "Too many men salt away money in the brine of other people's tears."
>
> (30 March 1917)

SOCIAL DISTINCTIONS! BAH! Bob Edwards despised them as he would the hives. One thing his sojourn in Toronto and Winnipeg did was to make him want to expose the shallowness and folly in many of the displays by society people. The richness of clothes and the lavishness of euchre parties should not be the measure of men and women. Neither an expensive gown, a wealthy father-in-law, nor a proud record in pouring tea was enough to make a person better or worse than the neighbour next door. It was part of the editor's philosophy that, "You are only what you are when no one is looking." (11 May 1918)

Paddy Nolan had always agreed; if people must be rated, the basis should be a proper one. Achievement, public service, and good ideas are worthy of public commendation; but why pay more than passing notice to anything as inconsequential as pink teas and costly wardrobes? The new West with its fresh ideals about human behaviour was no place for social differences determined by wealth.

Money does strange things to people, Bob Edwards wrote.

> It has a curiously snobbifying effect in codfish society. Supposing the daughter of a comparatively poor man happens to be tall and rather thin, they call her long and lanky. But suppose her old man, while scrambling over the rocks with a prospector's kit, accidentally stumbles on what subsequently develops into a valuable mine, his daughter instantly, as if by magic, becomes divinely tall and graceful. Silly, isn't it? (19 February 1910)

Those society notes in conventional newspapers were offenders in fostering foolish notions. They glamorized false and empty values. "This is no country for society magazines. The whole idea is obnoxiously conducive to the propogation of snobbery of which there is already a preponderance." (8 March 1913)

One human trait the analytical Edwards could not stomach was snobbery. A repentant horse-thief he could forgive readily enough, but with a snob, a "stuffed shirt," or a hypocrite, pardon was more difficult. When he recognized these types on the street or in the "Society Column," he wanted to strike at them. The usual column of society notes might be a justifiable source of entertainment, but too many people took it seriously and something should be done about it. If he needed more incentive to do something, Mother Fulham furnished it when she complained that the daily paper was everlastingly reporting her name in the police court news but never in the society news.

And so the *Eye Opener* introduced a "Society Column," distinctive, of course, its notes well punctuated with overworked words like "delightful," "gorgeous," and "charming," as in the following:

> Last Wednesday night a charming dance was given at the charming residence of the charming Mrs. W. Sloshcum-Kachorker. Old Sloshcum-Kachorker, who had inadvertently got drunk at the Mariaggi that afternoon was unable to be present, but a pleasant time was had nevertheless. The rooms were tastefully decorated with flowers and ferns. Among those present were:
>
> A beautiful gown of blue satin with net trimmings and touches of gold.
>
> A gorgeous creation from Paris, Saskatchewan, of sequin trimmings and sage and onion stuffing.
>
> A charming gown of white crepe de chêne with apricote trimmings and apple dressing.
>
> A cream brussels sprout net over silk, trimmed with old point lace.
>
> A lovely gown of green satin, edged with point d'esprit and old rose silk, with touches of burlap.
>
> There were many more beautiful gowns present and they appeared to be having a good time. It really does not matter who were inside the gowns. (19 February 1914)[1]

[1] Edwards prefaced this entry by making self-effacing reference to his alcoholism: "By George, we must get off some society stuff this issue or bust a gut. It is the height of the season and owing to several unfortunate jamborees at the time when the big functions were being pulled off we have not yet been able to get in our fine work. But better late than never."

Bob Edwards had no quarrel with good clothes; the fact was that no man on Calgary streets, R. B. Bennett excepted, was more neatly clad. His well-pressed grey suit, christie hat, and wing collar came to be associated with the *Eye Opener*'s editor, like spots with a Dalmatian dog. But being well-dressed in a conservative sort of way was quite a different matter, and didn't lessen his urge to criticize those women whose highest purpose seemed to be in making fashion shows of themselves.

From the very beginning, the *Eye Opener*'s "Society Columns" were popular; no society notes published west of Toronto were read with more avid interest. Nor was entertainment the only reward, because these columns of ridicule led to an acknowledged improvement in the general tone of society reporting, giving the *Eye Opener* reason to announce: "We think we cured our local society editresses of some doltish habits." (21 December 1912)[2]

There was no sameness about the *Eye Opener* society notes. In addition to teas and recitals, the column reported births, deaths, marriages, and anything offering good local gossip, as the following items taken at random will show:

> Mr. and Mrs. Harry B. Binkley have returned from their trip to England whence they went on their honeymoon. Mr. Binkley looks as if he had come through a threshing machine, but reports a good time. He deplores the quality of the beer on the other side. The king begged to be remembered to the Canadian Rotarians and expressed best wishes for the success of the convention in Calgary. During his stay in London, Mr. Binkley attended a function at court, being driven there in a patrol wagon. (10 April 1920)
>
> Mrs. John T. Bugge sold her hogs last week and has purchased a sprightly new spring hat. Mrs. Bugge got the top price for her hogs and is looking quite chic. (12 May 1919)
>
> Mrs. James B. McToddy of Mount Royal, will not receive Friday. She was run over by a truck Thursday. (21 February 1920)
>
> Mrs. Peter Jawkleblotter has emerged from the kimona stage and will shortly be able to pour tea. It is a fine youngster and yells like a Laurier candidate addressing a hostile meeting on the North Hill. (24 November 1917)

[2] The actual quote is: "Well, we think we have cured our local society editresses of the 'poured-the-tea' habit. Still, they may revive it while we are off on our holiday."

John Moran of Sunnyside, who was killed last Wednesday by being run over by a Ford car, was a good fellow and deserving of a more dignified death. There will be a sale of empty bottles at the Moran residence Saturday afternoon at 2 o'clock to defray the funeral expenses. (1 September 1917)

Miss Bessie McGorley, the amiable stenographer, purchased a dam fine spring hat last Tuesday, which matches her red hair to perfection. (8 April 1916)

We regret to record the sad death of poor Mrs. J. B. Warble of Seventeenth Ave. W. It is said that she died of despondency and worry. When the sun didn't shine, deceased was miserable and when it did, she said it faded her carpets. (11 September 1920)

Mrs. Bucklewhackster of Riverside was hostess at a jolly tea last Wednesday. Autumn foliage brightened the pretty table at which Mrs. Bucklewhackster presided with her usual charming air of embonpoint. Mr. Bucklewhackster staggered in during the proceedings and kicked over the table, later on falling asleep on the sofa. Mrs. Bucklewhackster was deeply mortified and says she is through with pink teas for all time.

Miss Jessie Marshfield is staying in Banff for a few days nursing her alleged father, whose addiction to whiskey is most distressing to his friends, especially as he seldom has the price. (8 April 1916)

The family and relatives of Henry M. Beaglet of Fourteenth Ave. W., are rejoicing in his death by being run over by an automobile at the Bank of Montreal corner last Saturday night. Old Beaglet had lived long enough and won't be missed. There should be a law compelling drivers in automobiles to run over men like Beaglet when they catch sight of them. It was rather a bum funeral. The corpse was not the only stiff present. (11 September 1920)

Maude de Vere of Drumheller, arrived in the city Wednesday afternoon and was run out of town Wednesday night. It is a pity Miss de Vere is not a race horse. She is very fast. (20 August 1921)

The City of Calgary has been sued by Miss Susie Golightly for the sum of $7.50 compensation for loss sustained through defective paving. Miss Golightly stubbed her toe in an open crack last Tuesday and in stumbling forward, a bottle of Glen McSquirrel fell out of her muff and was shattered to pieces on the asphalt paving. . . . Mr. Brockington will represent the city. Considerable local interest is being manifested in this case. (13 May 1922)

Hank Borden, who was hanged last week in Lethbridge for a most atrocious murder is no relation to Sir Robert Borden, premier of Canada. Sir Robert expects the present session to be a short one. (30 March 1918)

The many friends of Martin M. Bingham will be sorry to learn that he fell down a steep flight of steps Wednesday and broke his neck. Mr. Bingham was in the act of lowering a case of Three Star Hennessey into the cellar when his foot slipped. It is understood that the Hennessey was three years old and will revert to his widow. The bereaved woman is receiving many callers. (8 July 1916)

Miss Annabel Pink de Petticoat gave a delightful piano recital at the Palliser Hotel one evening last week. Her interpretation of Bethoven's Moonshine Sonata was scholarly and remarkable for its technique. This charming artist remained perfectly sober until after the recital. . . . She got excellent notices the next day. (13 May 1922)

Miss Florence Smith, a charming debutante, had the honor of being presented at court one day last week. Her dress was a marvelous creation from Athabasca Landing and excited the envy of not a few of the grandes dames: She denied having sold any liquor in her house.

The family of Mr. and Mrs. W. S. Stott, Eleventh Avenue West, all had the mumps last week. A swell time was had. Mr. Stott will not be able to deliver his address today at the Rotary Convention, much to the relief of those who have heard him speak. (10 April 1920)

Poor old John McSwalligan, beloved by many friends and old timers, is the latest victim of the flu. Before passing away, Mr. McSwalligan divulged to his broken hearted family a secret cache in the house where ten gallons of F.O.G. whiskey were stored away. The sorrow engendered by the visitation of death was thus tempered with joy and gladness. The Lord tempers the wind to the shorn lamb. The number of people who have called to express their sympathy has been something fierce. (11 January 1919)

> A bouncing ten-pound boy arrived at the home of Mr. and Mrs. P. T. Gilpin of Fifteenth Avenue, West, last Tuesday. Mr. Gilpin has fired the hired man and engaged a more aged servitor. (11 November 1916)

The names of Cappie Smart, Paddy Nolan, R. B. Bennett, and others of Bob Edwards's friends appeared quite often in the famous "Notes." In most cases, as one may judge, the names were fictitious; but usually the agitated individuals at whom the jibes were pointed had no difficulty in recognizing themselves. Probably the people in Calgary identified readily enough the alleged hypocrite in the vitriolic death note appearing in the column:

> Simeon C———, aged 50 years, six months and thirteen days. Deceased was an ill-natured man with an eye for boodle. He came here in the night with another man's wife and joined the church at first chance. He owes us several dollars for papers, large bills to the grocers and butchers and you could hear him pray for six blocks. . . . He was buried in an asbestos-lined coffin and his many friends threw palm-leaf fans in his grave, as he may need them. His tombstone will be a resting place for owls. (*Summer Annual*, 1920)

More familiar were the names of certain out-of-town visitors reported after the Christmas season in one of Alberta's prohibition years:

> Mr. T. S. Hennesey, the well known star, was in the burg for the holidays, adding to the gaiety of the nation.
>
> Mr. J. Dewar dropped down to Calgary from Saskatoon and remained over the holidays, in large quantities.
>
> Mr. H. Walker arrived in Calgary from Maple Creek shortly before Christmas and is still in the city. (6 January 1917)

Sometimes the society notes as carried in the *Eye Opener* produced protest. The editor may have been close to libel now and then, and might have been in more trouble had the kindly Paddy Nolan not been looking over the editor's shoulder and counselling him. On one occasion a man about twice as big as Bob Edwards, and greatly incensed over something, burst into the office, saying: "For two cents I'd punch your nose—putting a thing like that in your foul 'Society Column.'"

"What's all the trouble about?" Bob enquired. With visible nervousness he picked up the recent issue; and the big fellow, shivering with rage, pointed to an item and shouted: "There it is; you can't fool me."

Bob read the item aloud: "Mrs. Alex F. Muggsy, one of our most delightful West End chatelaines, has notified her friends that her usual Friday musicale is called off for this week. Her husband, Old Man Muggsy, has been entertaining his own friends with a boozical for a change and is in an ugly mood." (21 February 1920)

"Is your name Muggsy?" Bob asked.

"No, it is not. But I know you meant me," the irate fellow answered.

"Now look here," Bob replied, mustering some courage. "You're here to tell me the story fits your recent conduct. That right? Well, don't you think you're damned lucky I didn't call you by your real name? And anyway, nearly everybody wants to get into the 'Society Column.' Here, have a cigar."

The big fellow said, "Thanks. That looks like a good one. By the way, who do you think will win the baseball game tonight?"

There were other types of *Eye Opener* notes, inspired by the conventional society pages: musical criticisms, cooking recipes, health hints, and domestic questions and answers.

Bob Edwards loved good music as he loved good books. His taste was not entirely orthodox, but then nobody would expect it to be. A player piano with a cabinet full of selected music was a conspicuous part of the furnishings in his Cameron Block suite; and when fatigued from reading and writing, he found rest in favourite selections. He attended all public concerts and frequently reported on them. Not all reports of musicales as they appeared in the *Eye Opener*'s society notes

Bob Edwards, c. 1912–1918.

were to be taken seriously, but there were those times when the editor waxed realistic—sometimes to make the musicians squirm:

> That a coterie of ladies and gentlemen of highly cultural musical intelligence, some of them possessed with beautiful voices, could put themselves to the bother of practicing, rehearsing and producing at infinite trouble to themselves, such a blithering conglomeration and inchoate mass of discordant notes . . . will always remain a mystery. As a piece of musical rubbish it stands alone like a sky-scraper.

As one might expect, affectation in musical performances drew Bob Edwards's sarcasm. Good music could stand by itself, and a talented musician needed neither long hair nor a foreign name. But was it that the people who occupied the high-priced seats wouldn't stand for plebeian names? Did they demand the:

> Moszkowskis, Chowskis, Powskis, Rowskis, Bowskis, Weinywaskis, Whiskeyflaskis, and all the rest of them? It would be interesting to know if musicians in foreign countries dose their audiences with compositions from the geniuses of far-off places, the same as is done here. Does a music program, say in Madrid or Vienna, ever read like this?
>
> (a) Etude F. Sharp—Sweeney of Saskatoon.
> (b) Capricia Kafoozlum—Higginbotham of Dunvegan.
> (c) Variations Symphoniques—McGonigle of Midnapore.
> (d) Humoresque—Cassidy of North Battleford. And so on.

And the cooking recipes? Perhaps readers of the society notes didn't clip and file them; but at least, nearly everybody read them. They were kitchen specials, tested in the "*Eye Opener*'s Research Laboratory." And always they had generous amounts of *Eye Opener* "pepper" sprinkled through them. Here are some favourites:

> Spinach—Do not comb your spinach. Just muss it up. Negligee appearance is essential. If two stalks of it lie parallel it is not fit to eat. After the spinach has been towsled and chucked about a good while, sift two handfuls of coarse sand over it and place on the stove to boil. Of course, stick in some water first. But don't forget the sand. Spinach without sand in it would not only be improper but illegal. Serve hot. (18 December 1909)

Mayonnaise—Take two ounces of butter, sift a pound or two of red pepper over it until the whole mass begins to smoke. Break an egg, if you care to, but do not waste it on the mayonnaise. Put it into a long glass, beat it up with a fork, add sugar, pour in a little milk and a heaping glass of whiskey. Sprinkle some nutmeg on top and drain to the last drop. After smacking your lips take the rest of the mayonnaise and set it away on the top of the shelf of the pantry and leave it there. (18 December 1909)

Xmas Plum Pudding—Take one quart of brandy, two handfuls of plums and raisins, a chunk of suet, some salt and a lot of flour. Knead the last three ingredients well together, pouring into yourself sufficient brandy to keep from getting tired. When to sufficient consistency, hang it on the clothesline and beat smartly with a yule log. Roll into a round ball, try and raise it slowly over your head with one hand to see if it is heavy enough and then saturate plentifully with brandy. Set fire to the mess and serve quickly. Return to the kitchen and put balance of brandy out of pain. (18 December 1909)

Bread Pudding—Gather up all chunks of bread that have been left on the plates for the past week and dump them into a bucket of water. Let them soak over night and in the morning pound into a pulp with the butt end of an empty beer bottle. Take a handful of plums and chuck into the mess. Stir with a big spoon and add a little sugar. Dump into a pan and stick it into the oven. As soon as it begins to look a trifle less disgusting, take it out and serve as Plum Pudding. (*Summer Annual*, 1920)

Other newspapers had questions and answers columns, often in the women's section. The *Eye Opener* was not going to be backward and so it too had a "Query Column," the following being a rather typical sample of its contents:

What was the date of the landing of Caracticus on the shore of Britain? Anxious Inquirer.

Ans.—Damned if we know.

How many Germans were killed at the Battle of the Marne? Constant Reader.

Ans.—A devil of a lot no doubt.

Can you give me a recipe for making rice pudding? Minnie.

Ans.—No, we can't.

Can you tell me how to get rid of vermin? Esmeralda.

Ans.—No.

What is the best way to straighten out bowed legs in a child? Mother.

Ans.—Can't say, I'm sure.

What is the exact age of Nellie McClung? J. T. P. Le Due.

Ans.—Don't know.

What is the population of Pekin? Student.

Ans.—Haven't the slightest idea.

Can you give me the correct recipe for making a John Collins? Old Subscriber.

Ans.—We certainly can. You take a tall thin glass and dump a lot of ice into it. Squeeze out a whole lemon and heap in a couple of spoonfuls of soft sugar. Dump in a frightful jorum of gin and fill the whole shootin' match up with soda. And there you are. Drink off while fizzing. Then prepare another while you have your hand in. (*Summer Annual*, 1920)

Folk would laugh at what Bob Edwards wrote and then might realize that he was making a point—maybe a protest at the sham of much of society's seriousness. "There's so much fun going to waste!"

CHAPTER FOURTEEN
Battle of the Booze

"Every man has his favourite bird; ours is the bat."

(13 November 1909)

"Yes, we agree, whiskey floats more troubles than it drowns."

(11 September 1920)

"Booze acts on the human character as developer on a photographic negative. It brings out the lights and shadows. It shows up the black spots. . . ."

(9 March 1918)[1]

WHISKEY WAS BOB EDWARDS'S GREAT WEAKNESS and periodically it was his master. It was one enemy he seemed totally unable to overcome. He knew what it was to regain semi-consciousness amid strange and filthy surroundings after heavy drinking, feeling as though there was lead in his head and rubber in his legs, hating himself and the thought of sobering up, and seeing another drink as the only possible remedy for his sufferings. He knew what it was to be beaten up while drunk and to have bouts with "snakes" and "pink elephants." "When one is driven to drink," he said, "he usually has to walk back." (4 August 1906)

Indeed, his experience surpassed the customary "snakes" and "pink elephants" which went with severe hangovers; he had encountered bears. It was during his years at Wetaskiwin when he was drinking heavily that Jerry Boyce and others wondered if a real scare might not inspire Bob to change his ways. It was worth a trial, and according to the plan, one of Jerry's half-tamed bears from behind the hotel was tied to the bedpost in Bob's room. Late at night Bob staggered in, struck a match to light the candle, and saw the outline of the bear. He stared, unconvinced, and muttered to himself that no pink elephant or black bear was going to fool him. He kicked at the indistinct form, believing it to be imaginary; and promptly the bruin struck back, tearing Bob's trousers and scratching his flesh to make the blood flow. Bob took to flight—didn't stop until he reached Jerry's room.

"What's the matter?" Jerry enquired.

"You'll say it's hallucinations," Bob replied, puffing like a broken-winded horse,

[1] The remainder of the quote is "...and the spoiled pictures."

Only Solution of the Whiskey Problem

"but, honest, Jerry, the hangover beasts around here are getting damned rough—one bit me—look there—blood!"

Several times he submitted to "cures," and following one of the treatments he appeared to have overcome the craving. But after about a year the temptations in alcohol were too much for his resistance, and he went back to the hospital. Once, at least, he abstained for two years; but the Alberta Press Association held its annual meeting in Medicine Hat that fall of 1906 and the hospitality was so intense that, "the writer, who has clung to the water cart for two long and weary years, was seized with a panic and ducked his nut." (6 October 1906) It was that occasion which inspired the remark that: "The water wagon is certainly a more dangerous vehicle than the automobile. At least, more people fall off it." (25 August 1906)

Some of those who considered themselves as friends of the editor didn't help him: "What a lot of booze is offered you when it becomes generally known that you are on the water wagon. During Christmas week the temptation to fall off was great indeed. One idiot who was lit up for a fair, entered the *Eye Opener* office waving a bottle of Scotch and blithering out, 'Dewar unto others as you would others Dewar you.'" (6 January 1917)

Bob Edwards was not a daily drinker, but periodically he took too much. After several days of intoxication he might be taken to Holy Cross or Western Hospital where he would remain until recovered. *Eye Opener* publication would be suspended during those spells; but on a few occasions when an issue was already well on its way his faithful secretary, Miss Bertha Hart, with help from friends like Arthur Halpen of the *Albertan*, managed to get it out.

Readers usually knew when the editor had been incapacitated by drink. Either the paper failed to appear when expected, or there was a full explanation in the columns. Perhaps he wrote about it too freely. Perhaps he was needlessly frank and honest about his own defects. Had he been less inclined to relate his alcoholic misadventures, the weakness would have been less conspicuous, and he would have escaped many noisy criticisms and insults from uncharitable tongues. But as friends said again, Bob was "a man without secrets."

As it was, a reader might have been misled by the mirthful way in which the subject of "booze" was treated. What was a reader to take from the frivolous account of the *Eye Opener* Road Race of 1906, for example? Old-timers who were around at that date appeared vague about whether or not the race was a reality. In any case, this was Bob's alcohol-reeking account of the epic:

> The *Eye Opener* road race of 1906 was in the nature of a novelty and afforded intense amusement to the populace. Contestants started from the corner of First Street and Eighth Avenue, underneath our office in the Cameron Block, to the shot from a pistol fired, as now, by Captain Smart of the Fire Department. On this occasion there were fifteen starters, all of whom had agreed to abide by the rather unique conditions. At the crack of the pistol they were off in a bunch, with a contestant from High River slightly in the lead and the Olds entry close up.
>
> Running west up the avenue, according to the terms of the race, the contestants raced up to the Royal Hotel, where each had to drink a glass of whiskey at the bar; thence helter-skelter up the street to the Alberta, where a snort of dry gin was the next condition laid down; from there they flew around the corner to the Dominion to put away a schooner of beer, speeding on and on from bar to bar the whole length of Ninth Avenue, drinking horn after horn, no two alike. A corps of umpires followed the runners the whole length of the course. Rounding into Eighth Avenue, it was noticed that only three were left in the race, and these just barely managed to make the Queen's Hotel. Only one emerged ten minutes later to finish the race. He had just

> one block to go, and it was indeed fortunate for him that Eighth Avenue is a narrow thoroughfare, for he came along bumping against the buildings on either side and stotting from one side of the street to the other. This was the only thing that kept him on his feet. He was the Macleod entry and had been training for just such an event as this for years. (25 December 1920)

The *Eye Opener* carried lots of levity about liquor, but it was not intended as a defence of either the drink or the editor's mistakes. To the curse of drink in his own life he confessed many times. It worried him and he wasn't fooling himself when he wrote humorously about it. But a long and mournful face or an unrealistic approach to a thing with some of the characteristics of disease would not make it better. Perhaps, he reasoned, there would be less of stilted thinking and more of sensible planning if people paused to laugh at the demon in whiskey. Moreover, there is a time for fun as there is a time for seriousness; and the person who will treat a serious topic seriously when seriousness would do some good, has license to treat it lightly at other times.

There was another and more determined reason for the jocular treatment of liquor questions; much of the humorous writing was Bob Edwards's scornful answer to the narrow way in which some pious prohibitionists approached the problem. The age-old liquor conundrum would not be resolved adequately by either the liquor interests or the fanatical prohibitionists, and Bob Edwards was ready to castigate both groups. Yes, and he would criticize a third group—the numerous people with independent views who seemed reluctant to speak above a whisper on the subject. Altogether too often people gave the impression that even the discussion of liquor was "forbidden fruit."

When people said, "It's too bad, but Bob is an alcoholic," he didn't deny it. He did say that "alcoholism isn't as contagious as leprosy but is equally vile." No doubt the constant flippancy in writing about booze made many readers think he was just another drinking man obliged, from time to time, to seek hospital care in order to recuperate from excesses. Certainly that manner of writing gave no clue to the mental agony that followed his periodic drinking bouts or the deeply thoughtful convictions which were his.

E. A. Shelley of the Alberta Hotel was one person who understood the weight of the cross Bob Edwards had to bear. Lots of times Bob came to Shelley's room after the latter had retired at an hour past midnight. "I'm fair choking for a drink," he'd say. "Will you get up and open the bar for me?"

Shelley would accompany Bob down the flights of stairs, unlock the door of the bar and pour the suffering man a drink. Holding the glass in two shaky hands, Bob would take down the contents in an unbroken drink. At once he would feel relieved and ready to return to his office to finish the night's work or perhaps sleep out the balance of the night in his chair beside the big rolltop desk. How could a man with such habits have lofty ideas about temperance? Even though he had two quarrels, one with the evils of alcohol and one with the intolerant attitude in which many prohibition workers conducted their campaign, how could such a person be magnanimous in his thinking?

The crucial test came in 1915. Nothing less would have convinced a multitude of sceptics. Calgary had been a battle-ground for "wets" and "drys" for years. Nowhere in the West were the liquor interests more vigorous, and nowhere were the prohibitionists imbued with more of crusading determination. The provincial referendum of 1915 promised to be the battle of the year, outclassing even the boisterous political frays for which that section was famous.

Where would the *Eye Opener*'s editor stand in this major test? Would he be on the side of the hotelmen, liquor wholesalers, and the rank and file of drinking people, many of whom he knew intimately, or would he, by any chance, be with the temperance workers and churchmen whom he had so often and roundly criticized?

About his influence in the community there could be no doubt. The fact of 10,000 copies of the *Eye Opener* being sold inside the city of Calgary alone every time the paper came off the press was enough to make both sides in any democratic contest covet the editor's support. Numerous people who would not admit admiration for him were visibly anxious to know his views and his reasoning.

The hotelkeepers who saw him drinking at their bars expected confidently that he would be on the side of the "wets" where he had lots of friends. They knew very well that if he followed unrestrained inclinations, he would be with them.

But Bob Edwards's sense of public responsibility was more highly developed than most people realized, and his conclusion was that the time had come when John Barleycorn should be struck down. The rumour went about the city: "Bob Edwards, of all people, is coming out in opposition to the liquor interests." It wouldn't have seemed more strange to hear that Henry Ford was advocating the use of horses to pull carriages.

Drinking friends were surprised, and the organized whiskey interests were worried. Well they might be. "This man is powerful," said the anti-prohibitionists; "but he's a drinking man and we must have him with us." A deputation was selected and instructed to call on him, its purpose being to win him back.

The delegation called at Bob's office, and politely the members related the amazing rumour that he might not be with them in this campaign. Bob listened with the subdued attention of a jurist. One thing of which the visitors could be sure was frankness; in stating his position, Edwards would not deceive or mislead.

It was his turn to speak. He told them what they already knew, that he had been a big consumer of spirituous liquors, but that having considered this issue studiously, he could not conscientiously oppose the new Alberta Liquor Act which, if approved by the voters, would mean no more liquor having an alcoholic content above two and one-half percent being sold in the province after 1 July 1916.

But members of the party believed they had a "trump card." One of them, so it is told, said: "Bob, you could use some money; wouldn't five or ten thousand dollars help you a lot?"

Five or ten thousand dollars! That was more money than Bob Edwards had ever had—more than he ever expected to have. Of course such a sum would help a lot. It probably flashed through his mind that the *Eye Opener* could have a building of its own with comfortable offices for an expanded staff; he could make a world cruise with a visit to the scenes of his boyhood in bonnie Scotland; he could give lavishly to hospitals and needy friends. There were many possibilities. But if such was his thinking, it was only momentary, because he replied with customary forthrightness, "Yes, I could use it, but I've never taken that kind of money and I would not accept it now. Gentlemen, my mind is made up."

It was but a short time until a delegation from the Temperance and Moral Reform League called on him. This time Bob Edwards opened the discussion.

"You're after my support? Well, the 'wets' would pay me well. How much is it worth to you?"

The reply was: "We're sorry, Mr. Edwards, but we have no money."

"That's fine," responded the editor, "because I'm not for sale. I'm with you. The next issue of the *Eye Opener* will make that very clear."

But a lot could happen in a Bob Edwards week; and as time was to show, the strife had only started. Bob wrote his editorial copy on Tuesday night. It was the analysis of one considering two sides of the question and concluding that drinking of hard liquor should stop. Here it is, perhaps the most influential editorial penned in the new West up to that time:

> Consider well. View the act and its consequences from every angle. Many hotelmen will be put out of business and placed in grave financial difficulties. They are to get no compensation. Engaged in an

occupation which is legalized and specially licensed by the government and the city, they suddenly find the earth opening up at their feet and a yawning pit of utter ruin being prepared for them to fall into, held the while at the mercy of rapacious land-lords, inexorable temperance workers and absolutely heartless bankers. Does this not excite your pity?

It does ours, but only to a limited extent, for a panorama passes before our eyes of women and little children in humble homes, shy proper food and clothing, lacking warmth in winter and bereft completely of the joy of living, going to sleep in misery and awakening to another day with the dull pain of hopelessness, innocent victims of the damnable traffic of booze; we see a multitude of downcast men, down-and-outers, panhandling for dimes on the street to procure more of that very booze which lost them every job they ever had; there appear in the picture men whom we knew in their more prosperous days, who before our very eyes day by day and year by year have kept gradually falling behind in the race until one almost forgets that they ever started at all; our mind's eye lights on poor devils of both sexes being yanked each night to the police station and chucked into cells, to meet further humiliation the next morning in the dock; we see in this mental panorama much wretchedness, but the most saddening is the pitiful vision of graves containing the remains of men, good men, who were jolly companions in their day, beloved by hosts of friends, but whose careers were brought to an abrupt and shameful conclusion by bad whiskey and by nothing else. In a word, there is Death in the Cup, and if this Act is likely to have the effect of dashing the Cup from the drunkard's hand, for God's sake let us vote for it.

Elsewhere in the same copy, he continued:

The Drys should have invoked the co-operation of the Dominion Government and brought about a condition where whiskey and kindred hard drinks were put in the drug class and labelled "Poison," with licenses granted for the sale of beer and light wines only. . . . The chief recommendation of the Act, of course, lies in the abolition of the bar. So long as there is a bar there will be treating and treating is

> the progenitor of every toot. . . . The jollity around a bar is absolutely bogus, booze-begotten jokes being invariably rotten. (17 July 1915)

The editor's copy went to the *Albertan* for printing. Thursday was the day on which the *Eye Opener* customarily went to press, with sales starting early Saturday morning. But about mid-way through the week, Bob Edwards yielded to his old enemy and lost all interest in publication. Indeed, it had not been overlooked by one of the plebiscite groups that if the editor could be led to intoxication, the *Eye Opener* would never reach the streets.

Nobody knew what happened from that time forward better than Arthur Halpen, the young Irishman who was assistant foreman in the composing room of the *Albertan* printing plant, normally located only a block from Bob Edwards's office (where Macleod Brothers store stood later). Thursday morning Jesse Rockley, manager of the Job Printing Department, came to Halpen saying: "Bob has seen his galley proofs but now he's half drunk; could you handle the make-up of his pages?"

Halpen replied that he was familiar with Bob's style and would do it.

Accordingly, the page proofs were made up and taken to the *Eye Opener* office, where the editor was sitting at his desk, christie hat on his head, and a smile of irresponsibility on his face. Partially drunk as he was, he insisted upon reading the pages and ordered Halpen to play the player piano in the office while he did it. After an hour or so of ineffective reading, the editor, in alcoholic recklessness, dashed his marking pencil across the pages as if to "kill" the entire issue. As far as Bob was concerned, the matter was closed; there'd be no issue that week. He took another drink.

In due course the drunken editor went to hospital as he had done many times before. The defaced pages which he, in his stupor, had repudiated, were taken back to the *Albertan* office; and the "wets" who had been spying breathed with some relief. To others who witnessed it, the most recent event appeared as the inglorious climax to a noble purpose.

But hope should never be abandoned, especially in Calgary. W. M. Davidson, the *Albertan*'s editor, was a loyal friend of Edwards, and he reasoned that once the type was set he had a mandate to see that the issue went to press. With Miss Hart, Arthur Halpen, and W. M. Davidson joining forces for the final effort, the page proofs were read and corrected and the *Eye Opener* went to press there in the *Albertan*'s temporary quarters in the basement of the Westminster Block, corner of 10th Avenue and 1st Street E., a fire having driven the printers from their usual location.

The *Eye Opener* would be published. To one side in the plebiscite issue this brought satisfaction; to the other, it brought fear. Two hotelmen visited the *Eye*

The Only Way to Save Her

Opener office on Friday and offered to bargain with Miss Hart for the purchase of the entire issue before it went into circulation. The object, of course, was to destroy the papers and prevent them from reaching the readers. Had they been successful, it wouldn't have been the first time that *Eye Opener* fans failed to receive their copies on the allotted day; but the reason would have been a new one. Miss Hart refused to enter into any "deal" and told her visitors very bluntly that Bob Edwards would never condone that kind of business.

Both sides seemed to be maintaining effective intelligence; and when the "drys" learned about the tactics attempted by their opposition, they appealed to Mr. Davidson. He agreed to see that the out-of-town papers were packaged and safeguarded, and that the balance of the issue for Saturday sale in Calgary would be given the security of his vault. That was a happy suggestion, and thus the precious supply for local distribution would not be exposed to risks which careless storage might invite. The possibility of a raid for the purpose of hijacking the issue was not being overlooked; and it has been told that several husky members of the prohibition forces, thinking that the *Eye Opener* office might be the object of an attack, volunteered to spend the night doing an inconspicuous guard duty. But there was no raid and no midnight clash between "wets" and "drys" to enliven the story. At seven o'clock on Saturday morning, Miss Hart was at the office to most the boys and see that they got their copies for the street sales.

Four days later, on 21 July, voters went to the polls and gave prohibition a substantial majority both in Calgary and in Alberta as a whole. The provincial result was expected, but the heavy prohibition vote in Calgary came as a surprise. On the Sunday following, the temperance forces held a big thanksgiving service at the Grand Theatre, with Rev. Robert Pearson as chairman. Bob Edwards wasn't present; he was still in hospital and probably wouldn't have been present if he had been out. But when he came out, he approved of all that his friends had done and thanked them for completing publication. Arthur Halpen received a present of twenty-five dollars.

Had anyone questioned Bob's earnestness in that 1916 crusade, such person should have turned back the pages of the *Eye Opener* to some notes written in other years, among them a New Year's message: "Swear off. Climb into the water wagon. Life is a one-sided fight for the man who is his own worst enemy. Swear off. If you make one hundred good resolutions and only keep one, you are just that much better off. But let that one be booze. The others will follow. We speak with authority." (16 January 1904)

Sure, he would indulge in frivolous chatter and humorous stories about whiskey and all its alcoholic relations; but at the proper moments he would declare himself, leaving no room for doubt. The force that went with his convictions and the folly of trifling with them were laid bare after a representative of a whiskey firm called upon him and presented a framed picture. The misguided emissary delivering the picture supposed he had won a supporter, but the story that appeared in the *Eye Opener* showed how wrong he was:

> The genial traveller for "———"[2] whiskey concern was in Calgary this week hustling up business for his firm. He presented the newspapers and his customers with a large colored picture of "———" race horses. The *Eye Opener* was favored with one of these pictures enclosed in a $7.50 frame on the distinct understanding that we were to give "———" a write-up. We shall do so.
>
> We consider "———" whiskey to rank very high amongst the numerous poisons now on the market. Not that it is any worse than

[2] In the original, Edwards names Seagram's.

> most whiskeys, but being the most drank, it creates more havoc throughout the country. It has put more men in their graves than a corps of census sharps could enumerate in a year and has put thousands upon thousands of good men on the hog. "———" wealth is built on the folly of others and each of his race horses represents a hundred or more wretches who have died of delirium tremens brought on by mopping up an overplus of his rotgut. We have no more respect for a man in "———" business than we have for Radcliff the hangman, or the murderers whom Radcliff hangs. They are all in the killing business. "———" racehorses and his wealth cut no figure in our eyes. We have helped him buy too many of his fliers and so has almost every other fool of our acquaintance. (30 July 1904)

During Bob Edwards's life and after, it was difficult or impossible to convince many people that he was fundamentally opposed to liquor. But at no time would he even accept advertising for drink other than beer, and he had to remind would-be customers of the fact now and then: "For the information of those wholesale liquor firms which have sent along ads for publication in the *Eye Opener*, would say that the only booze ads we care to accept are those for lager beer."

His theory was that if beer and light wines were made available, complete prohibition of whiskey would be practicable. Even after 1916 he was fearful that total prohibition would beget a flourishing generation of bootleggers; and when his fears were fulfilled, he was one of the first to advocate that "There is just one way to put the bootlegger out of business and that is to place the whole business under control of the provincial government." (11 September 1920) Then he added that the revenue might be applied to the improvement of our roads.

Had he lived another thirty-six years, he would have been among the first to recognize that the liquor problem was still unsolved. Of what reforms he'd propose, one can only speculate. Whatever they might be, the ideas would be bold ones, and his own. Nobody would make him think like the masses, or squeeze him into dull conformity about liquor or anything else—not Bob Edwards.

CHAPTER FIFTEEN
The Cruel Fate of Willie Hohenzollern

"There is enough going on in Europe just now to make the exploits of Xerxes, Alexander, Caesar and Napoleon look like holiday operations of the boy scouts."

(30 March 1918)

"If it's all the same to history, it need not repeat itself any more."

(31 May 1919)

"Well, at all events, the Canadian navy will be able to lick the Swiss navy. This is one comfort for which we should be thankful."

(19 February 1910)

WHEN THE "BATTLE OF THE BOOZE" reached its climax in and around Calgary, World War I was nearly a year old and assuming its ugliest form. Canadian troops were at the Western Front, experiencing bitter fighting and winning glory at Ypres. But casualties were high and anti-German feeling was mounting everywhere. The enemy had resorted to the use of poison gas; and if more were needed to fan the flame of hate, the submarine sinking of the British liner Lusitania on 7 May 1915, with a loss of 1,198 lives, furnished it.

Bob Edwards wanted to join up, but he was fifty years of age and the army wouldn't have him. But, "Every Canadian should be equally under the burden;" and those who refused to render some essential service "might well be treated as Indians and disenfranchised." (6 January 1916) If he couldn't go to war, he would do some fighting at home—for the boys in Europe's vermin-infested trenches. That he did with determination of purpose. As far as he was concerned, nothing would be too good for Canada's war-widows, and for the soldiers upon their return. He became their finest champion.

Every time a contingent of soldiers left Calgary to go overseas, Bob was at the station to say farewell. Many of the lads of his acquaintance went away and many never returned. With tears in his eyes he set down his New Year sentiment:

It brought on quite a heartache at the close of the old year to sit down and have a quiet think about the various old friends and acquaintances who departed from Calgary so gaily for the front, to whom we waved

> goodbye at the depot and wished good luck and safe return, but whom we shall never, never see again in this world. Nevermore shall those brave chaps walk Eighth Avenue on a Saturday night nor drop into Pantages to seek a hearty laugh. . . . What a confusing phantasmagoria. . . . (6 January 1916)

War is hateful business at any time, and Bob Edwards suffered with every battle fought in France and Belgium. But constant seriousness would be a mistake. Soldiers and civilians needed fun; they needed to laugh and gain release from worry, even more than in peacetime. Herein Bob Edwards recognized opportunity for service, and the *Eye Opener*'s new and bigger task was to ease the tensions of the war years.

From the time the first Canadians saw active service, hundreds of *Eye Openers* from every issue were being sent overseas; and had a poll been taken among the boys "over there," that man Edwards would almost certainly have been voted "Favourite Editor."

Members of the 31st Battalion reading the Eye Opener *in England, 1915.*

In 1915 he was proposing a battalion of bartenders from Alberta. The periodically drunk editor had just declared himself for prohibition, and it was in keeping with his campaign to contend that: "The bartenders have shown such success in killing off men at home, they ought to be able to kill off at least an equal number of the enemy abroad." And then, while the bartenders were being recruited, the Canadian Government should strengthen its navy by recruiting hotel chambermaids from the towns of Alberta; "their skill in handling vessels of all descriptions" might be the very thing to turn the tide of naval warfare.

Following these suggestions, Bob received a letter from a friend of long standing, "Peace River" Jim Cornwall, a man who had gone into the north in 1898 and for a time packed the mail on his back over the three-hundred-mile trail between Edmonton and Peace River. Now, as Lt.-Col. Cornwall, he was taking command of the 218th Battalion, Irish Guards, and was writing to exchange good humour with Bob. The idea of drafting the bartenders and chambermaids because of their technical experience was a good one, he reasoned; and now, if Bob would accept the Command of the new naval unit of Chambermaids, the war would be shortened; and sooner than anybody expected, the Allies would be facing the problem of punishing Kaiser Wilhelm, who was blamed for all the bloodshed and agony.

Cornwall, ever anxious to receive a Bob Edwards letter, invited his views. Should the hated Kaiser, like Napoleon, be banished to some remote island? Should he be hung like any common murderer, or would it be better to give him a lifetime sentence as janitor at the Nevermore Hotel in Midnapore, brought to fame as a favourite Peter McGonigle rendezvous?

Bob made it clear that he would willingly act as a one-man tribunal before which the Kaiser, at war's end, would be hailed for trial and sentence. No mercy would be shown, Bob promised. The very limit in punishment could be expected by the accused. It would be severity without precedent, and a new chapter would be written in court history. In the subsequent issue of the *Eye Opener*, Jim Cornwall and others were able to picture a penitent Kaiser sitting in the prisoner's box and a severe-appearing "Judge" Bob Edwards handing down a vengeful sentence from his exalted place on the bench. Readers hardly needed to be reminded that it was the "Judge" speaking:

> Willie, stand up. You have been adjudged guilty of so many atrocities that the court has difficulty in keeping track of them all. Any one of them qualifies you for the scaffold. It is my duty, however, to say to you that the jury has gone entirely beyond the limits of its jurisdiction in recommending that you be cooked alive in boiling oil, and you need therefore labor under no fear that this recommendation will be carried out. I should disapprove of it myself, inasmuch as death by boiling oil is too speedy for such as you.

A brief moment of agony in a vat is no expiation for a prolonged series of ghastly crimes. For you, Willie, a species of living death, characterized by lingering torture, is the proper caper. The sentence which I am about to impose consists of a variety of novel tortures, to follow one upon the other in close succession, after which, should you survive, you shall be condemned to live in a prohibition province for the balance of your natural life. Inhumane and brutal as this sentence may appear, you must remember that you have forfeited all claims to mercy at the hands of your fellow-men.

Owing to the exceptional nature of this case, the Minister of Justice has allowed me carte blanche. You will get all that is coming to you, Willie. I am no Judge Beck, so you need not flatter yourself that you are going to get off with a hundred dollar fine. When you leave the precincts of this court, you will be conducted to a lonely hall on the North Hill, where you will be addressed for twelve consecutive hours by Dr. Michael Clark on the inequities of a protective tariff. Thus will Louvain be avenged.

After being brought around by the doctors, you will be introduced to a group of oil men, all of high business repute in the city, who will proceed to gnaw into the Hohenzollern fortune by selling you Monarch shares at $20, Alberta Petroleum Consolidated at $10, Dingman at $76, Black Diamond at $9 and so on, after which you will be conducted to the Calgary Stock Exchange to study the blackboard and see how you stand. During the dark watches of the night, a talkative oil expert (preferably Owens) will sit at the footboard of your bed and deliver a learned and involved disquisition on anticlines, Dakota sands, Clagget-Benton shale, faulty formations, broken bits, inadequate casing and wet gas. If this does not settle accounts for the Dinant atrocities, nothing will.

Denied all sleep during the night, deprived of drinking water . . . you will be taken at seven o'clock the following morning to the Palliser Hotel where a long Collins in a very tall, thin glass, with lots of ice, will be set before you. This you will be permitted to gaze upon but not to drink. The horror of your position will thus be vividly impressed on your mind and, if you have any decency left, bitter regrets for past infamies will agitate your soul and smother you in remorse. No punishment will be too severe to atone for the devasta-

If Wilhelm were plain Bill Smith

tion of Belgium and the dastardly crimes committed against helpless women and children.

For the torpedoing of the Lusitania, I confess I am somewhat at a loss how to decide upon an adequate punishment. However, I think that compulsory residence in Cochrane for a week, Okotoks for two, Didsbury for three and Macleod for one solid month should perhaps meet the case. May God have mercy on your soul, Willie.

On your return to Calgary, the court directs that you deliver an address at the Canadian Club luncheon. Not only are you to deliver a glowing panegyric on the English race, but you are to eat the grub at the luncheon. This function will cost you fifty cents and may possibly reconcile you to the high cost of dying. In the afternoon, you will be taken to Pantages, where a specially engaged monologue artist will crack weird jokes for a couple of hours about jitney busses and Ford cars, at which you are directed by the court to laugh. On coming out of the theatre, a stiff horn of whiskey will be handed to you and deftly withdrawn when you reach for it. The long evening of this day is to be spent listening to John Mosely on Prohibition. Willie, I feel sorry for you. I do for a fact.

At this stage of the fulfilment of your sentence it might perhaps be as well to have you examined by a physician, in case of collapse. If pronounced fit, the physician will put you on an operating table, open you up, remove bladder and unadulterated gall, and sew you up again, after leaving a sponge and a pair of forceps in your stomach. Every afternoon for a fortnight thereafter you are to box four three-minute rounds at top speed with some husky gentleman who has been banged about in a German prison camp for six months or so. This will remind you of Hill 60.

When Sunday comes around, an official appointed for the purpose will hand you a ten-dollar bill and tell you to go out and have a good time. At the close of the Sabbath, you will return the money you have not spent on riotous living. The same tenspot will do you for each Sunday. There is nothing that will more forcibly recall to your mind the spectre of Death on the battlefields of Europe than a Calgary Sunday. Poor Willie.

In conclusion, the court directs that you take your meals at a cafeteria, except on legal holidays when, weather permitting, you will have a grass lunch at Sarcee Reserve.

Should the prohibition Act have passed in the meantime, you will take up permanent abode within the confines of the dry Province of Alberta. No motion of appeal, no plea for pity, no modification of this order will be entertained. I can hold out no hope of mercy. Failing the passage of this Act, you will be transferred to the already dry Province of Saskatchewan where Premier Scott will no doubt be willing to aggravate your temper with two-per-cent beer. Dearly will you thus have paid for the destruction of Rheims Cathedral and the ruthless cutting off of limbs.

Finally, Willie, you will be good enough to face the jury and sing Allies Uber Deutsches. (12 June 1915)

As far as anybody knew, the Kaiser never learned about the "judgment" read against him by the *Eye Opener* Court. That was unfortunate.

CHAPTER SIXTEEN
"Had Moses Been a Methodist"

"One kind of hypocrite is the man who, after thanking the Lord for his dinner, proceeds to find fault with the cook."

(5 October 1916)

"Some men are good because they find it cheaper than being wicked."

(22 May 1915)

"The man who uses religion as a cloak in this world may have more use for a smoking jacket in the next."

(22 May 1915)

"To do right is easy when sin ceases to be a pleasure."

(21 February 1920)[1]

"About the only people who don't quarrel over religion are the people who haven't any."

(17 July 1920)

"A good many people do not believe in the efficacy of prayer because the Lord gives them what they deserve instead of what they ask for."

(23 March 1912)

BETWEEN THE CHURCHES and the *Eye Opener* there was repeated irritation, and the events of 1916 brought the strained relations to a breaking point. Much of the trouble arose from a ministerial determination to restrict Sunday activity to little more than church attendance.

The editor's ideas about the dullness of Calgary Sundays were made quite clear in the sentence passed by "Judge" Edwards upon Kaiser Wilhelm. For a bachelor like Bob the days were long ones. Frequently he walked in the country with his Airedale dog and sometimes took his gun along to shoot gophers on the ranchland of William Nimmons, southwest from the city. (The ranch buildings were close to the present 17th Ave. and 14th St. W., and a favourite Nimmons slough in duck season was situated about the present 22nd Ave. and 21st St. W.) That was all very well until the

[1] The issue is incorrectly dated 1919. It seems Edwards often had that trouble at the beginning of the year.

guardians of the Seventh Day learned about it; and then, on a Monday morning, a Mounted Policeman called at the Cameron Block to report a complaint and order Bob to desist from shooting gophers on Sundays or face a formal charge. Such wicked behaviour would have to stop.

There was no more Sunday shooting, but there was an increase in editorial sniping at those straight-laced churchmen who imagined: "The Sabbath was invented to allow smug Methodists to put on plug hats and caper along the street with hymn books under their arms, by way of gaining spiritual strength to rob people on Monday, and of drowning their arrant hypocrisy in an uproar of preposterous doxologies, badly sung." (20 April 1912)[2]

A hypocrite, according to Bob Edwards, is "a man who isn't himself on Sundays."

Actually, the controversy about Sunday conduct had begun at High River soon after Bob went there. When the Lord's Day Profanation Act was declared invalid by the Judicial Committee of the Privy Council in 1903, Bob Edwards had some comment:

> Sergeant Dee of Okotoks, will be unable to arrest boys for shooting glass bottles with a toy pistol on Sunday and Rev. Campbell will not be in a legal position to threaten people with arrest for using a polo stick on that holiest and dreariest of days. . . . Sunday was intended as a day of rest for people who work hard during the week, to most of whom indulgence in healthful outdoor sports would be the truest rest. Nor would it interfere materially with church attendance. There are always people anxious to hear how the Israelites crossed the Red Sea thousands of years ago. The craving for the latest news will always exist. (8 August 1903)

Church insistence that there be no Sunday sport was a prohibition Edwards could not comprehend. Recreation could be restful. By what authority, then, did church people seek to ban relaxing recreation on Sunday? "The joy-killers have the wrong idea," he wrote.[3] If outdoor sports on Sunday were irreligious or immoral in

[2] Bob's invective was specifically directed at the Lord's Day Alliance. This passage concluded with a topical kiss-off: "It is a pity some of them had not been on board the Titanic."

[3] Again, MacEwan goes light on the fingerpointing specifics. Actual quote: "The Lord's Day Alliance kill-joys have the wrong idea altogether. The only argument to justify the prohibition of outdoor sports and indoor amusements on Sunday would be that they were irreligious or immoral in their nature. If undesirable on Sunday, they should be equally undesirable during the week. We merely mention these things by way of suggesting to the ministers a possible cause for popular antagonism. Our guess may be a wrong one, but may be worth pondering over."

their nature, they should be prohibited; but "if undesirable on Sunday, they should be equally undesirable during the week." (6 May 1916) And if golfers were permitted to play, unmolested, on Sundays, those who preferred baseball shouldn't be confronted with the "Thou Shalt Not." The fact that those who played golf had more wealth, on the average, than those electing baseball and gopher shooting, was no reason for a double standard.

When Bob Edwards went to Sunday service, as he did quite often, he sat in a back pew at the Central Methodist Church; but it was with that particular denomination that he found the most fault. "Two-thirds of Canada is Methodist ridden," he said; and Methodists specialized in joy-killing. "Had Moses been a Methodist, he would undoubtedly have had five hundred 'Thou Shalt Nots' in his Commandments instead of ten." (6 May 1916)[4]

As the editor voiced his criticism in 1916, the gulf between church and *Eye Opener* widened and produced a nasty whispering campaign. Folk who were obliged to admit that the editor's stand on liquor the year before had fooled them, were now saying in muffled voice: "Bob is an atheist—yes sir, an atheist." Some of the ministers said it too.

There were other reasons for the mutual unneighbourliness of church and *Eye Opener*. One was the editor's impatience with what the church was achieving. The church, like civilization, has "too many glaring inconsistencies." Church people send missionaries to China to convert the Chinese and "try to get them into the Kingdom of Heaven, but they won't let 'em into this country." (24 October 1903) Then, too, a strict and puritanical upbringing at the knees of Scottish aunts had made Bob Edwards critical. As a boy he was required to submit to unending religious instruction, and attendance at the kirk was with a punctiliousness that would have gratified John Knox. Nobody read a paper or secular book on Sunday, and the family attended a kirk in which the minister considered it sinful to have organ music on that day. In addition to the requirements of church attendance two or three times on Sabbath, the Edwards boys were obliged to memorize paraphrases, psalms, hymns, and the Shorter Catechism on a Sunday "diet of cold mutton." (2 February 1920) Perhaps there had been an overcharging with prescribed churchiness and moral law and not enough opportunity for a young fellow to reason his relationship to the church, to his Creator, and to the world about him.

In the years that followed, however, Bob Edwards did his own thinking and his religion was his own. It had to be an intensely personal thing, not something to be

[4] Bob continued: "You never hear of a Roman Catholic priest trying to take the joy out of the lives of his parishioners, do you? No, you don't." Make of this what you will.

paraded like a stylish hat or a clerical collar. It should be worked out between a man and his God and not necessarily tailor-made by one of the religious specialists who could not agree upon form and style.

Nor did a man have to be noisy about his religion in order to serve God. Sensationalism and emotionalism were not religion, and it was Edwards's view that itinerant evangelists who excited the people left nothing that local ministers could not provide equally well.

When evangelists Crossley and Hunter visited Calgary, Bob attended some of the meetings and then offered a bit of advice to the well-meaning visitors:

> Gentlemen: The parable tells of the sower who went forth to sow and some seed fell on rocky places. Well, Calgary is a rocky place for sowing your seed. At the same time we wish you well, and have no desire to ridicule. Yours is a good work if properly conducted.
>
> . . . Now, about card playing. I listened to you, Mr. Hunter, proclaim with uplifted hand, "If I were a pastor of this church and knew that a member of this congregation played cards in his house, I would turn him out of the church. I would turn him out and let him die in the street."
>
> Now come, come, Mr. Hunter. You do not mean a word of that. This superheated style of banality spoils the general effect.
>
> Nobody is going to cut out the little game of whist or pedro or cribbage in his home because you don't like it. If you had gone after the pirates who throw the harpoon into a stranger at two in the morning, we would understand your wrath. But I can assure you, much as you may dislike it, the harmless pack of cards is here to stay.
>
> . . . As regards your remarks about bartenders, I really must enlighten you. The bartender, from the nature of his business, must be a temperate man. Otherwise, he could not hold his job. At least half the bartenders in this wayward city of Calgary are teetotallers. Almost all are family men with homes, wives, children and all the domestic trimmings.
>
> All in all, the bartender leads quite a good life, jogging along impervious to all the slings and arrows of outrageous evangelists. And I warn both of you boys that if you took to hitting the bottle, the bartender would be the first man to advise you to cut it out.
>
> The people you should get after in this town are those absorbed

Crossley and Hunter shooting off their mouths.

in money-making to the exclusion of everything else. A man will cheat his best friend to make a dollar. These are the people to rail against and convert. . . . The chase after the dollar is the real besetting sin, ranking far above little peccadilloes.

You, Mr. Hunter, said that men who attended balls and danced with their arms round a lady's waist were dirty rascals. That is not a pretty thing to say. A great many people dance, and very badly too.

Before closing I would remind you that you will not find our western audiences quite as emotional as the Ontario brand. Scars gained in the struggle for existence have raised bumps of commonsense to predominate over emotions.

To tell the truth, I doubt if we need you. We have pastors out here who are struggling along very well, meeting life as it is and drawing a few erring souls into the Kingdom. Upsetting religious equilibrium by intemperate ravings seems to lack something in substance.

Yours very truly,
Bob Edwards, the *Eye Opener*.

There it was—the real besetting sin; it wasn't shooting gophers on Sunday, but rather the mad chase after the dollar. Greed for money stood in the path of a better and higher order of things. Even in the church, the constant cry from the pulpit was for money, money, money.

> The clamor of the soul becomes inextricably mixed up with the long, loud scream for money. Supplications for divine mercy are subordinated to the building fund and worshippers find themselves worrying more about meeting the interest on the church debt than about the salvation of their souls. (21 February 1920)

Why not be honest and acknowledge the Almighty Dollar as supreme? Why not a prayer to the Almighty Dollar such as Edwards proposed just after some perfunctory Thanksgiving services when the churches and the *Eye Opener* were feuding in 1917?

> Almighty Dollar, thou art worshipped the world over; thou hast no hypocrites in thy temple or false hearts at the altar; kings and couriers bow before thee and all the nations adore thee; thou art loved by the civilized and savage alike with unfeigned and unfaltering affection. We continue to regard thee as the handmaid of religion and the twin sister of charity. O Almighty Dollar, be with us we beseech thee, attended by an inexpressible number of thy ministering angels, made in thine own image, even though they be but silver quarters. Their light shall illuminate the vale of penury and want with heavenly radiance. . . . Almighty Dollar, thou art the guide of our footsteps and the goal of our being. Guided by thy silvery light, we hope to reach the golden gate and triumphantly enter while hands harmoniously sweep the golden harps. Almighty Dollar, thy shining face bespeaks thy wondrous power. In my pocket, make thy resting place. I need thee every hour. And now, Almighty Dollar, in closing this invocation we realize and acknowledge that thou art the god of our grandfathers, the twofold god of their children and the threefold god of their grandchildren. Permit us to possess thee in abundance, is our constant and unwavering prayer. (13 October 1917)

The people who said he was an atheist were hearing quite a lot about themselves.

They were being reminded that their faith was not well supported by works. They were told about a prominent Calgary churchman, one loud in condemnation of gambling and drinking, who turned a hungry man from his door; and about one Smythe, ". . . a prominent member of the Presbyterian Church who in fullness of his Christian spirit, had one of our brightest newsboys summoned to appear before the magistrate for selling newspapers on Sunday. Now what are we to do with a lobster like that? This lad, Harry Bell, is a lone newspaper boy. His parents do not live in Calgary and he hustles his own living."

The church had more to do than worry about a friendly baseball game on Sunday or an editor's stroll in a gopher-infested field. There were some barnacles to be rubbed off. And most of all, churchmen should guard against putting words of their own choosing into the Almighty's mouth.

The fact was that Bob Edwards was not an atheist, and anyone who suggested such a thing was guilty of injustice. Never did he ridicule anything bearing the marks of religious sincerity, although he had no hesitation in "roasting" those he believed to be hypocrites, those "psalm-singers" whose weekday conduct was ill-becoming.

Man needs a faith; of course he does. He needs spiritual wings on which to rise above the clay of worldly things. Bob Edwards would be one to agree, and the first to add that "faith without works" will furnish uncertain wings on which to rise. But religion, he contended, is not to be divorced from reason. There was St. Paul's injunction to "prove all things." A man's belief should stand the test of unemotional examination. Mankind's inherent instinct through all the ages pointed to a Supreme Being; it was as natural for man to seek to know the Deity as for a newborn calf to search for milk.

To one all-good and all-powerful God, the spirits of mankind could rally, and Bob Edwards would join in belief. But a multiplicity of denominational sects and religious factions, many with a blind conviction that others were wrong, weakened the religious fabric. For any group of denominationalists to suppose that it alone possessed the full truth was doctrinal conceit. Was it reasonable that a great and just God would choose to reveal himself to a small segment of mankind and leave the balance of his children in darkness? Was it understandable that the Almighty would declare the truth to the "prophets" of one group of His people and deny by circumstances the same enlightenment to the leaders of other religious groups? Honesty and fairness were characteristics of Bob Edwards's God, and it did not seem too much to expect the same in those people who sought to serve that God. The Edwards spirit reached up for the God who had given people of all races and colours an equal chance to know him and be drawn to Him. It was a concept that rejected religious dogmas based on "chosen people," with revelations of enlightenment for a few; and he believed, like Robert Burns, that "Every honest, upright man, of whatever sect, will be accepted by the Deity."

Scholarly Bob Edwards was well versed in church history and made it his purpose to know something about all the great religions: Christianity, Mohammedanism, Buddhism, Confucianism, Vedaism, and the Hebrew religion. Running through all, he noted, was that golden thread; each had its Golden Rule standing for goodwill and linked with faith in a sovereign God.

Charity, honest dealing, and goodwill were thus close to the core of Bob Edwards's religious creed, and no faith would be worthy of its name without these. It was easy for him, therefore, to make the so-called "down-and-outers," the hungry and the unemployed, his special interest. He did, indeed, become the eager champion of the underprivileged.

There were thus two places in early Calgary where a man who was down on his luck could get a meal or money with which to buy it: one was the Salvation Army and the other was the office of Bob Edwards. Bob knew what it was to be destitute and hungry, and he knew how cold the gutter was when one awakened to find himself in it.

That somebody would one day be piecing together the bits of evidence to find the real shape of Bob Edwards's religious beliefs would have surprised no one more than the editor himself. Significantly enough, however, those "bits" make a definite pattern, showing that, drinker, cynic and denominational critic as he was, Bob Edwards was far from being a godless man. He had strong convictions, and now and then summed them up in terms that must have astonished and confused his antagonists. He meant it when he said that religion, being a very personal affair, should induce people to "go down on their knees in the quiet of their chambers and hold communion with their God." (21 February 1920) No churchman could criticize that.

Of course, nobody would expect Bob Edwards's prayers to conform to the conventional pattern. Like his views on most topics, his supplications would be his own, as evidence that prayer which appeared more than once in his columns. It was Bob Edwards's Prayer and it follows:

> Lord, let me keep a straight way in the path of honor—and a straight face in the presence of solemn asses. Let me not truckle to the high, nor bull-doze the low; let me frolic with the jack and the joker and [sometimes] win the game. Lead me unto Truth and Beauty—and tell me her name. Keep me sane but not too sane. Let me not take the world or myself too seriously, and grant more people to laugh with and

fewer to laugh at. Let me condemn no man because of his grammar and no woman on account of her morals, neither being responsible for either. Preserve my sense of humour and of values and proportions. Let me be healthy while I live, but not live too long. Which is about all for today, Lord. Amen. (4 August 1917 and 20 August 1921)

Dr. George Kerby, formerly minister at Central Methodist Church and then principal of Mount Royal College, asked Bob for a copy of that prayer when they met on the street soon after the end of World War I. Bob was pleased to accommodate, and a few days later Dr. Kerby called at the *Eye Opener* office, placing a small package on the editor's desk. Between the two men there had been differences in 1916 and at other times, but, happily, respect and friendship survived. The dynamic little Methodist, with pince-nez spectacles riding his Etruscan nose and chin-whisker carefully cropped, now recalled to the editor the times he had met him on the street and had been handed a ten-dollar bill for some needy and deserving person. Then he mentioned having talked that very day with a blind man who told of receiving an envelope containing money regularly for five years from a Calgary editor some people called a sinner. "Such deeds," Dr. Kerby said, "are not reported in the *Eye Opener*."

Dr. George W. Kerby, c. 1911.

Dr. Kerby was making a speech, as though he had rehearsed it. "I need not say again that your writing, at times, has offended me and I am still opposed to Sunday shooting. But I've come to the conclusion that when we all stand for the last judgment, you'll have more in your favor than most of your critics. I've brought around this box of bullets for gophers. As for the days on which you use them, I'd quite willingly leave that to your conscience."

CHAPTER SEVENTEEN
"A Certain Newspaperman Got Married"

"Not all women are as bad as they paint themselves."

(12 April 1913)

"The woman with the ideal husband very likely wishes she had some other kind."

(6 December 1913)

"If men could read woman's thoughts, they would take many more risks than they do."

(*Summer Annual*, 1920)

"The saddest and funniest thing on earth is to hear two people promising at the altar with perfectly straight faces to feel, think and believe for the rest of their lives exactly as they do at that minute."

(4 December 1909)

"A woman's indifference has reached the limit if she no longer listens when her husband talks in his sleep."

(22 May 1915)

"A girl should never marry until she is fully competent to support a husband and then she shouldn't marry that kind of man."

(11 September 1920)

TO CALGARY SOCIETY Bob Edwards had all the characteristics of a confirmed bachelor. By his philosophical standards, as everybody knew, freedom was the sweetest and richest of endowments. That was the reason he could not work for someone else; that was the reason he had left employment in Winnipeg; that was one reason for his many years of bachelorhood.

Marriage would necessitate regularity of habits, and regularity tended to stifle creativeness. No artist, composer, or writer could hope to express himself clearly within the confines of time schedules. Men about him might become automatons, but Bob could not see himself arising every morning at 7:15, shaving at 7:30 without exception, breakfasting exactly thirty minutes later, opening the office punctually at 8:30, lunching at a fixed time whether hungry or not, dining again at 6:30, retiring at 11:00 whether tired or not, and repeating the monotonous program day after day.

Doctors and family specialists could recommend regularity in living habits all they liked, but they were not for Bob Edwards. He would eat when he was hungry, go to bed when he felt a need for sleep, work all night if he felt so inclined, and go fishing for a day or two when the urge struck him. He said he could not adapt himself to regularity, and he would not expect a woman to bring herself to his way of life.

But it wasn't true that he didn't like the ladies. He radiated nervous good nature when they were present and boyishly backed away. Of course he liked the ladies, but for steady companionship they were his second choice. He was a man's man. But such controversial topic as "women"—"no two the same and no one the same for long"—could not escape his pen.

Though somewhat cynical when writing on the subject, he was ever the gentleman in the presence of a member of the opposite sex, whether she was "the Colonel's lady" or just "Rosie O'Grady." As underprivileged men came to him for counsel and help, so did underprivileged women. He was more interested in the welfare of the nurses than the prosperity of the doctors; he contended that the pay and treatment given to domestic maids were no credit to the society of his day; he was a friend to the waitresses and the chambermaids and wrote a good deal about and for them.

Anyone attempting to take advantage of one of these girls occupying a lowly position would have Bob Edwards to deal with. That was proven in the case of a restaurant waitress whom he found depressed when he went to breakfast one morning.

"What's the matter, lassie?" he enquired.

The pent-up urge to relate her troubles to someone she could trust was very great and she told her story. She had been swindled—had lost all her hard-earned savings of several years.

"How did this happen?" he enquired anxiously.

With tears in her eyes, the girl explained that two local men in real estate had persuaded her to invest her savings in lots they were selling. It was the boom period and speculation was the order of the day. These lots, however, were found to be worthless. It was heartbreaking to think that all she had worked for during the years was now lost.

Bob was moved—angry. It was the kind of thing that infuriated him. But he said little. He made a note of the names of the real estate sharps and left, saying: "Don't worry; leave it to me. I think I can do something."

Bob walked directly to the office of the smart salesmen, introduced himself, and offered some advice about returning the girl's money.

The reception was no better than one might have expected. "Who do you think you are, Bob Edwards, that you can tell us how to handle our affairs? Now get out of here!"

The next issue of the *Eye Opener* told the story with all the details except for the names of the two agents. It was made clear, however, that if the parties concerned did not return the money taken for the worthless lots before the next issue of the *Eye Opener* went to press, the names of the swindlers would be used to decorate the front page.

Two days later Bob lunched at the restaurant at which the girl victim worked and found her in smiles rather than tears. She had an affectionate hug for the man who was a friend of needy people. Yes, her money had been returned.

For the restaurant waitresses generally, he had a tribute: "Of all the birds that inhabit the dressed lumber forests known as 'burghs,' none is so fly, so smart, so much admired as the waitress. This lovely creature is indigenous to the West, and although not as sweet and persistent a songbird as the chambermaid, she has a bobolink twitter which few other birds possess. It is the prevailing impression that the waitress is a modern acquisition introduced by the hotelkeeper to distract man's mind from the rotten grub."

When Bob Edwards first went to Calgary, women were still without the franchise. They could work and worry with the men but they could not vote. Gradually, however, "Votes For Women" became a burning issue, though not as riotous in the new provinces as in England, where the militant mothers in the Suffragette movement went as far as to attempt blowing up St. Paul's Cathedral.

Bob's manner of writing, of course, didn't always make his convictions clear; and women might wonder where he really stood when he yielded, as he did very often, to the temptation to be facetious:

> Woman should vote. Certainly she should. . . . She says she has as much practical sense as man has. Then she starts out to prove it in public. Watch her get ready to go out to prove it. She adds to the few hanks of hair adhering to her scalp, a lot of coarse stuffing and supplements it with a wig consisting of a lot of hair sausages. Did not St. Paul say that the glory of a woman is her hat?
>
> Then she hermetically seals herself with a time lock into a hipless corset and a strap contrivance to keep her stomach flat. Afterwards she uses a shoehorn and forces herself into a one-piece dress. She then gets in front of a mirror and reaches for a hat that looks like the roof

of a merry-go-round, covered with feathers and fruit and flowers and birds and buckles and long stick pins and starts out to prove her common sense.

In that set of snaffles and martingales and hobbles which would make a man scream for the bartender and bite himself in a dozen places, she sallies forth and immediately remembers that it is Mrs. Winkle's receiving day. Into Mrs. Winkle's she accordingly drops and helps to "pour tea." After vivisecting the characters and reputations of all such friends as are not present, she finds that it is time to return home to see about her husband's evening meal. . . . Of course woman should vote, whenever she pleases. Anyway, she will some day." (1 January 1910)

But regardless of levity, Edwards, the great reformer, firmly believed that women should have the vote and prophesied that it would not be long until they would have it. Were not women the driving force in men's lives? Was there not a woman at the back or at the bottom of every important event, good or bad, even though the illustration Bob used was not for telling at a Mothers' Day service? He recalled that Bill Halliday, with whom he had shared a house when living at Strathcona, had drawn exactly the same conclusion, although the words as well as the observation were strikingly like those of Edwards himself. Anyway, this was Bob's telling:

Up at Strathcona a number of years ago, old Bill Halliday, the Scotch tailor, since dead, had his well cleaned out one day because the water was getting so rank that he could not even wash in it. He never drank much of it at any time. When the water was all pumped out, the decaying body of a squaw was found at the bottom, having been there for some weeks.

"Yes, yes," mused Halliday, peering down the well, "I might have known there was a woman at the bottom of it." (16 January 1904)

Before long, women did get the franchise; and then Bob Edwards, who was one of the first westerners to come out in support of the principle, was one of the first to urge women to go into politics. "It is our firm conviction," he wrote, "that blending of women's ideas with those of reasonably thoughtful men will some day bring about an era of common sense." (30 March 1918)

However, not so serious were his reasons when he wrote: "We actually need

women in politics. Women could never possibly participate in any graft system, owing to their inability to keep a secret. As publicity is the remedy for most political ills, women in politics should function admirably. (Hear, hear!)" (18 March 1916)

"Mr. Edwards, why don't you get married?" He heard that question more than once from prominent socialites.

"Because," he would reply, "I'd hate to contribute to a woman's tears. You must understand, no man makes as good a husband as either he or his wife expects."

But cynical as he was and single as he seemed likely to remain, matrimony was a desirable state—for others. Had he participated in a local debate in High River in 1903, he would have upheld the case for marriage, arguing that:

> He who is married has something tangible for which to save. Moreover, he has a home and in this respect alone, has an edge on the poor devils of bachelors whose leisure hours are perforce spent in crowded hotel offices or in the unlovable precincts of a bum boarding house. The only advantage enjoyed by the bachelors is that there are no tidies on the backs of their chairs and no perambulators to fall over when arriving home from a St. Andrew's banquet.
>
> Many a man has been drawn into the boozestorm and other dissipations for which he had no natural bent, simply because he was lonely. By marrying a sensible young woman who does not run too much to pink teas, the inconsequent bachelor reforms unconsciously, becomes of real use, and even stands a fair chance of some day being asked to give a reading at a church social. . . . By all means marry, and God bless you.

He advised young people to marry; but as the years passed, folk thought of him only as the perpetual bachelor—"one who'll never marry." But the year 1917 spawned some surprises for Bob's friends. The first was an automobile which he bought in April. His longest trip during the season was to the Millarville Race Meet, thirty miles southwest; but he taught his Airedale dog to ride with him and was enjoying the new adventure, even though the parody which brought word about the new car to *Eye Opener* readers might suggest otherwise:

The Ford is my jitney,
I shall not want;
It maketh me to lie down in wet waters;
It soileth my clothes.
It leadeth me into deep waters;
It leadeth me into the paths of ridicule for its namesake;
It prepareth a breakdown for me in the presence of mine enemies;
Yea, though I walk through the valleys, I am towed up the hills.
I fear great evil when it is with me;
Its rods and its engines discomfort me;
It anointeth my face with oil,
Its tank runneth over;
Surely to goodness, if this thing follows me all the days of my life I
shall dwell in the house of Ponoka forever.

(2 June 1917)

Why young men are afraid to marry.

After the appearance of these lines about his car, there was a lapse of four weeks without an issue of the *Eye Opener*, and then, in the paper of 30 June 1917, the unpredictable editor furnished a hint, followed by an explanation of a really major change in his life: "You recollect that we wrote considerable about Ford cars after we got one. Should we perchance happen to harp about women in this issue, just draw your own conclusions." (30 June 1917)

On the same page there was additional detail, set down in characteristic style:

> A certain newspaperman in Calgary got married the other day. He is pretty well known, especially to the old timers and much sympathy has been expressed for the bride. On the eventful morning he arose at seven o'clock, having spent a somewhat restless night, and donned a black suit which had been laid out for him. After receiving the ministrations of his spirituous adviser, the condemned man partook of a hearty breakfast which consisted of ham and eggs, cookies and coffee, after which he smoked a cigar with apparent relish. To the last, he stoutly maintained his innocence. At the appointed hour, the Rev. Dr. Kerby adjusted the noose and the distinguished criminal was launched into matrimony. The happy couple left by the afternoon train for Hootch, where they will spend the honeymoon. (30 June 1917)

Miss Kate Penman, daughter of Alexander and Mrs. Penman of Glasgow, Scotland, was the lady who became Mrs. Bob Edwards. She and Bob had met four years before—just weeks after her arrival in Calgary. A copy of the *Eye Opener* was the first paper she bought, and after reading it she said to a companion: "I'm going to meet the man who writes that way." In a few days Charles Taylor arranged the meeting, but Bob was bashful in the presence of the strange girl and didn't say much.

Kate Penman, buxom Scottish lass, was twenty years of age; and with money supplied by her mother, her plan was to attend business college and fit herself for office work. The plan was carried out, and upon completion she worked in R. B. Bennett's law office and then in the Land Titles Office.

Actually, the *Eye Opener* report of the wedding, in the issue of 30 June, was in readers' hands in advance of the ceremony on that date. With Bob's long-time friend Rev. George Kerby officiating, Mount Royal College was the place set for the quiet wedding, and 6 PM was the hour. To make it like a lot of other weddings, the bride arrived late—nearly half an hour—but the nervous groom was able to compose himself sufficiently to remark: "What've you been at, Katie? Did you stop in to see a Charlie Chaplin show?"

After the wedding the newlyweds dined, attended the evening performance at the Calgary Exhibition, and took the early morning train for the west to honeymoon in the British Columbia Interior and at Vancouver.

Soon after their return to Calgary, Bob and Kate rented a house (919 4th Ave.

W.) and there they lived until in 1921, they contracted to buy a home (112 4th Ave. E.) not far from Bob's office.

Matrimony was a test, sure enough. It was not easy for the eccentric editor to accept meals at regular hours. At lunch time he nearly always thought of something more important than food. When bachelor friends invited him out for an evening, he could not accept with the former abandon. But gradually he accepted it and liked it.

All his life Edwards was involved in controversy, and even in marriage he did not escape completely. But the all-important point was that Bob Edwards was happy—happier than he had been since before losing his great companion, Paddy. When his Kate was visiting her old home in Scotland in 1919, Bob was lonely; and not waiting for her to make her own reservation, he booked a passage for her return and cabled to hurry home. "When a man is in love for the first time," he said, "he thinks he invented it." (24 November 1917)

CHAPTER EIGHTEEN
"Deformed Babies Must Be Straightened"

"Never trust a man whose dog has gone back on him."

(19 February 1910)

"When you feel like doing a foolish thing, remember that you have to live with your memory."

(30 March 1917)

"There is nothing better than a good woman and nothing worse than a bad one."

(25 May 1918)

"If your luck isn't what it should be, write a 'p' in front of it and try again."

(13 January 1912)

WAR AND POST-WAR YEARS can be expected to improve the climate for reform. So it was in 1918 and 1919. Returning soldiers had to be rehabilitated, labourers were restless, and western farmers were inclined to "raise less wheat and more hell." Drought reduced the crop of 1918; and before the harvest was completed in that year, the influenza epidemic took hundreds of lives to add to rising tensions. Across the West, Bob Edwards the reformer was enjoying a broader audience.

It wasn't that his style or purpose had changed. Perhaps, due to additional maturity or a wife's good cooking, the quality of his writing was at its best; but he was still a one-man newspaper staff, writing voluminously, courageously, and sometimes recklessly. The fact was that more people were thinking in terms of reform and more were saying, "Bob is right about that."

A. L. Smith, who later represented Calgary in the House of Commons, urged him to pack a slightly refined Peter McGonigle into a novel, but Bob had no visible ambition to be a great author. During hours of seriousness he was increasingly absorbed with the social challenges about him.

There was really nothing new about his zeal to correct society's wrongs. If he wrote more about his views, a better audience was the reason. Throughout the life of the *Eye Opener*, Bob Edwards advocated abolition or reform of the Canadian Senate, "that impotent relic." As early as 1910 he recommended adoption of the European system of controlled racetrack betting—pari-mutuels, they called it, with the government taking a percentage of the betting turnover for charity. Views might differ about the moral significance of betting on races, but it was always Bob's contention that betting within a structure of order and control was not "half as harmful as the stockbroker's board by which the public is induced to speculate in margins." And for years ahead of the politicians, Edwards was arguing for old age pensions, travelling libraries, minimum wage laws, hospitalization, and school books with Canadian stories in them. Nobody about him had heard of the "welfare state," but his ideas on the subject of social security would have sounded appropriate at the middle of the twentieth century. For many of his proposals the new West wasn't ready.

The Lords are Stormed at—

Anyone who said that Bob Edwards lacked feeling on those subjects didn't know the man. He might try to keep his humanitarian side hidden; but it became clear that nobody had more sensitive sympathies for the unfortunate, the ill, and those who felt the hardships of poverty. The poorly paid domestic servant girls, hired men on farms, war widows, sick people, nurses in training, struggling farmers, and victims of the drink habit had no more sincere and vocal champion in those years; just as the grafters, hypocrites, and bluffers had no more persistent tormenter. Hearing that the nurses at the General Hospital who contracted the "flu" while nursing patients with that sickness were docked their wages for the period of their illness, Bob Edwards was horrified. "Unfortunately, it is true," he wrote. "And the girls thus docked while off sick for a week or so are receiving a monthly wage of $10." The only story the editor recalled to rival this degree of meanness was about a railroad construction worker who was blown skyward in a dynamite blast and was "docked by the foreman for the time he was up in the air." (7 December 1918)

It was his impatience for a better deal on behalf of underprivileged people that had led to his resignation from the chairmanship of the Advertising Committee of the Board of Trade, some three years after coming to Calgary. The city businessmen, he believed, were "soaking" the incoming settlers, paying small wages and unfair prices for farm produce.

"I am sorry," he wrote in submitting his resignation, "but I cannot lend myself to an organized project which contemplates bringing in settlers under false pretenses . . . wages are low and remain low, damned low . . . You must let people live after they get here." (23 February 1907)

While our Senate is Merely Laughed at.

There were other topics about which *Eye Opener* readers learned much; one of these concerned knighthoods and titles for Canadians, a controversial issue in that period. Edwards would go along with Plato in approval of an aristocracy based on service to the nation, but for hereditary aristocracy he had no patience whatever. A titled person, sometimes a social misfit, whose only claim to eminence was a distinguished ancestor or wealthy father, could arouse no enthusiasm in this man.

Traditions were fine if they were good ones, but tradition for tradition's sake was not for Bob Edwards. A thousand years of British titles didn't make anything contributing to class distinction one bit more attractive to him. And so he registered determined opposition to the creation of hereditary titles in Canada, thus limiting the degree "to which snobdom may be allowed in this democratic Canada of ours."

Wealth and title carried no license for special privileges; if anything, they should

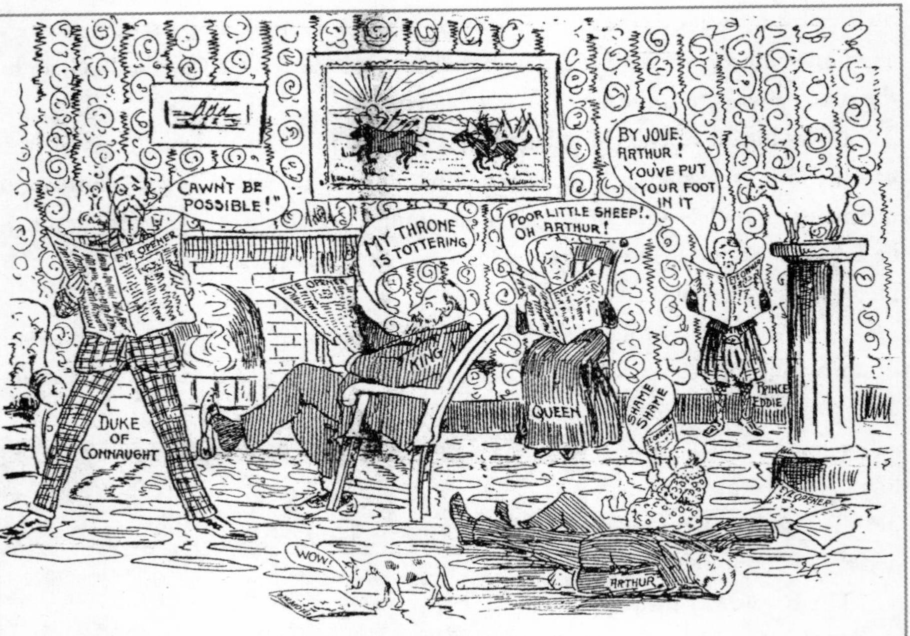

The Eye Opener at Windsor Castle

impose extra responsibilities, he contended; and most western readers agreed with him. When Prince Arthur of Connaught shot mountain goats out of season during a visit to Western Canada, the Edwards wrath was kindled. To those who would have hushed up the ill-advised hunting expedition because the offender was an aristocrat, Bob Edwards said, "No; this illegal action deserves the same rebuke and penalty that would be meted to any other hunter, farmer, doctor or Indian." (7 April 1906) When another visiting nobleman explained in Bob's hearing that his title was not of the "mushroom variety," his father having been a Baron and his grandfather a Baron, the editor remarked in an undertone: "A pity his mother wasn't barren too."

"Oh well, what's the use?" he wrote, concluding an editorial argument against hereditary titles and knighthoods for Canada: "In a few years we shall all be lying in our coffins under mother earth where the vanities of this world will cut little if any ice. In hell where most of us are going, we shall all be equal, and in Heaven, there shall be no knight there. So drink up and let's be going." (20 April 1918)

And formal ceremony with morning coats and top hats was out of place too, especially in Calgary. An air of naturalness is always the best dress; and if one must make a show, why not be original? The Calgary white hats and distinctive western clothes of a later period would have won Bob Edwards's acclaim, even though a black christie hat was a standard part of his attire.

There were times when the "free-wheeling" and progressive Edwards seemed to stand alone in his crusades, but at war's end there were two men from whom he drew unfailing strength as well as encouragement. One was Rev. Robert Pearson, the sportsman idol of every local boy big enough to carry a baseball bat, and general secretary of Calgary's YMCA for ten years prior to enlisting in 1915. The "two Bobs" had met for the first time in 1904 at Banff, to which place Pearson had gone as a Methodist missionary and Edwards as a hospital patient with a recurring disorder.

Pearson was one of those ministers who didn't wear "a graveside expression," and who did live his religion every day to win Bob Edwards's lasting admiration. He more than any other seemed to reinforce the Edwards notion that poverty must not be allowed to stand between sick people and the best possible medical care and treatment. That meant hospitals and good doctors; but unfortunately not all the practising physicians were "good ones." For the devoted medical men who were conscious of the vital nature of their tasks in handling human lives, Bob Edwards had nothing but respect. When complacency raised its ugly head, however, he was unforgiving; an academic degree in medicine was not a license to commit manslaughter, and Bob's conviction was that careless doctors should be required to stand by their mistakes:

> We would like to see incorporated in the Medical Act, a clause compelling every physician who loses a patient, to ride in an open vehicle at the funeral, immediately behind the hearse. In this way, everybody could tell which were the careful, competent, successful physicians and which were the dubs. It would, moreover, be a direct incentive to members of the so-called "noble profession" to take some pains with their cases and, when necessary, call in other doctors for consultation, thus minimizing the chances for sad consequences of professional mistakes. (15 August 1908)

The "two Bobs" agreed that governments, acting for the whole of society, should assume more responsibility in assuring the best treatment for all sick folk. Disease and injured bodies are everybody's concern. Here was Torch-Bearer Edwards on that subject in 1916:

> The unrestricted capacity of the public treasury must be used to bring to the people, with the utmost economy, every known benefit of medical science, for the prevention of disease and deformity. We must

> safeguard childbirth so that no mother need dread or fear it. We must attack and prevent as far as possible those diseases which interfere with a child's right to be well born; deformed babies must be straightened, the ravages of accident "repaired" by every artificial device available, contagious disease obliterated, wasting diseases prevented—all this must be done for every citizen without regard to his station or wealth, and paid for by all the citizens for each other.
>
> The provision of the local or district hospital is the first in the chain of public institutions necessary . . .The *Eye Opener* commends this to the electorate as the most important question which the Provincial Legislature has to consider this year. (6 January 1917)

The provincial system of free public hospitals didn't come fast enough to suit him. With sarcasm born of growing impatience, he wrote: "Now that we have the horses and pigs fixed up cosily, and plenty of experimental farms to keep the alfalfa alive, and plenty of paved streets for the automobiles and plenty of fire protection to save our precious business blocks, let's have enough free maternity wards to accommodate the women. It's pretty late but better late than never." (16 September 1916)

How deformed babies were to be straightened, Bob Edwards didn't profess to know; but at least he was prepared to accept nothing less than science's best efforts. If doctors didn't know how to correct or improve those twisted wee bodies, they had better get busy and find out. "Honest Bob Pearson" was nodding his enthusiastic approval, wishing there were more such editors.

The other influence in Bob Edwards's life in those years was Missouri-born Henry Wise Wood, farmer at Carstairs and rapidly becoming the undisputed agrarian leader of the time. Wood's earnestness and humility, coupled with a bulldog firmness of purpose, attracted Bob Edwards. The man was no radical, but he was convinced the farmers of Canada were carrying too many non-producers on their backs and that co-operation held the best hope for betterment. This long-legged, lean-bodied, bald-headed farm philosopher began calling at the *Eye Opener* office soon after he became president of the United Farmers of Alberta in 1916. There in Bob's untidy office, sitting like a statue, with long-stemmed pipe in one hand and a burnt match in the other, he would "try out" his ideas about farm co-operation, wheat marketing by pooling the entire crop, and the wrongs of protective tariffs which farmers were feeling painfully at that time.

Wood was a member of the first Board of Grain Supervisors in 1917; and it is believed that after the general election when the Union Government was elected in that same year, Henry Wise Wood was invited by Prime Minister Sir Robert Borden to become Canada's Minister of Agriculture. Wood's decision to refuse that offer, in order that he might continue to pilot his beloved Alberta farm movement, may or may not have been discussed with Bob Edwards; but certainly Bob was invited to express his views on many of the public issues taking the farm leader's attention.

Political upheaval was sweeping rural Canada in those years of 1918 and 1919. In April of 1918 there was the announcement of cancellation of exemptions from military service for those in the twenty- to twenty-two-year category who had been granted occupational essentiality. Farmers, already tried by labour shortage, saw this move to take their sons from the farms as a direct violation of a promise made to them during the 1917 election campaign. Coupled with this there were fixed prices for wheat, tariff obstacles in marketing cattle in the United States, and rising implement costs due to the Canadian tariff policy. Farmers found themselves in a squeeze, and more than ever before felt the need for a stronger voice in government. Henry Wise Wood agreed that the farmers must have that voice and so did Bob Edwards. The only question was how political action should be achieved—by group action through an organization like the United Farmers of Alberta, or through a new and distinct political party. Woods favoured political action by the organized farmers rather than by organized politicians.

T. A. Crerar entered the Union Government as Federal Minister of Agriculture in 1917; but two years later, in protest against a high tariff policy, he resigned and with a group of supporters formed the Progressive Party. Here were "Farmers on the March." Alberta farmers too, were making political progress. In January 1919 the UFA decided in favour of action at "the next election." Wood's plan for political participation was accepted, and one who was prominent in the farm movement at that time has testified that Bob Edwards was as much interested, "as though his future depended upon the price of wheat."

Politics, however, was just one of the subjects to concern Wood and his friends at that time. Markets seemed uncertain. When the price of wheat started to fall after the Canadian Wheat Board of 1919 ceased to operate, Philosopher Wood began talking about the growing necessity for farmers to handle the marketing of their wheat through their own co-operatives, or pools, like those organized by California growers to market fruit. The idea was a bold one, but Bob Edwards was one of the first to encourage Wood to pursue it.

How many of Wood's policies crystallized while he conversed with Bob Edwards, and were strengthened by Bob's agreement with them, will never be known; but after one of the farm leader's visits, the *Eye Opener* was likely to carry

Whipping Them Into Line

some reflections of the conversations in the form of pithy agricultural items, for example: "Did it ever occur to you that some fine day the farmers of Canada might go on strike to force the government to remove the duty on agricultural implements? This would be some strike, if they all struck together. All the other strikes would be skim milk alongside this one." (5 April 1919)

At the same time it was noticed that some of Wood's public statements about hospitalization and medical care sounded strikingly like Edwards's. Bob would have the Federal Government back a national program of research to find a means of combating cancer; and though years had to pass before much was done about it, one of Bob's contemporaries saying about the same thing was Henry Wise Wood. The Edwards influence was difficult to measure.

It might have been expected that the political turn of events in 1921, which found Bob Edwards and Wood's United Farmers of Alberta on opposite sides in the Provincial Legislature, would separate the editor and the farm leader. But it didn't. Both men were honest and courageous; both were reformers. In their respective ways their influence on the life of Western Canada was very great indeed.

Unfortunately, Bob Edwards didn't live to witness the launching of the ambitious Provincial Wheat Pools in 1923, with his friend and fellow-reformer, Henry Wise Wood, as a distinguished figure in them then and for many years thereafter. Bob Edwards wasn't a socialist, but he was a co-operator; and had he been alive he would have been a Pool supporter through the good years and the bad ones.

CHAPTER NINETEEN
Mayor For a Day

"Lloyd George who says the world is on the eve of a glorious peace, is evidently not in touch with the mayoralty situation in Calgary."
(21 September 1918)

"What really makes it worth while to be an alderman is the delight it gives one's family."
(8 March 1913)

"One trouble with being efficient is that it makes everybody hate you so."
(18 March 1916)

"The great man of today in Canada is made up of one part achievement and nine parts printers' ink."
(19 February 1910)

BOB EDWARDS ENJOYED POLITICS at all its levels and on various occasions was asked to stand for election. But he preferred to be on the sidelines, from which point it was always "open season" on politicians. As it was, he could say he had been drawn into active public life on two occasions, having been Calgary's "Mayor for a Day" and Member of the Provincial Legislature for the year and a half prior to his death.

On his occupancy of the Mayor's Chair, there is little more than Bob's own account of the adventure. Time and again, with tongue in cheek, he contended that Calgary would never have perfect civic government until the city was ruled by a commission composed of the local newspaper editors. "They are the only . . . men who know how things ought to be run." (9 February 1907)

Following the universal pattern, Calgary editors regarded criticism of governments as their special prerogative, with local governing bodies as the most inviting targets. Nobody fired more editorial criticism than the editor of the *Eye Opener.* When the day came for him to take over the duties that went with the office of mayor, however, he admitted that being the critic was easier than being the mayor.

Calgary's Mayor Mike Costello, it seems, was impressed by the statements that editors were the men who knew how things ought to be run, and he had a good memory. In May of 1916 the Mayor was invited to Ottawa to "interview the Dominion Government in connection with the unemployment situation." The rest of the story does not appear in the minutes of City Council, but the various editors did receive invitations to "take over," and if one accepts the *Eye Opener* account, nobody derived much glory from it unless Mayor Costello was the one. This is Bob Edwards's account of his long and terrible day:

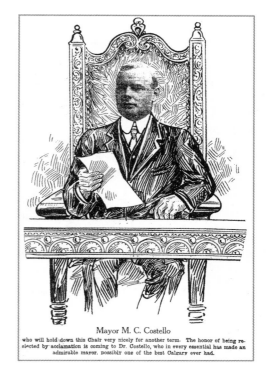

Mayor M. C. Costello
who will hold down this Chair very nicely for another term. The honor of being re-elected by acclamation is coming to Dr. Costello, who in every essential has made an admirable mayor, possibly one of the best Calgary ever had.

> Mayor Costello, finding that he had to be out of the city for a few days, called around at our rooms this week with a most alarming proposition . . . "Since I have been in office, Bob," said he, "it has often struck me that you newspaper editors appear to know how the affairs of the city ought to be run much better than either myself or the commissioners, or even the council for that matter. This being the case, it has occurred to me that an opportunity should be given the gentlemen of the press to run the show themselves for a spell, just to give us poor devils a few pointers."
>
> "Great idea," said we.
>
> "I have to be out of the city for at least four days, leaving, in fact, early tomorrow morning. This will give you, Davidson, Thompson and Wood a day apiece at the city hall. The mayor's room will be at your disposal, also the stenog, and I think, Bob, that you had better take the first day as acting mayor, seeing that you are the most harmless of the bunch. Are you on?"
>
> "You bet your life. I'm on."
>
> "Can you start right in tomorrow morning at 10 o'clock?"
>
> "You will find me Johannes in the Spotto—Johnny on the spot."
>
> "All right that's settled. The rain ought to help the crops some eh?"

The mayor then left to put his proposition before the other three moulders of public opinion. The following morning we were up bright and early, just like a murderer on the morning of his execution. The prospect of putting in the day as acting-mayor of the City of Calgary did not look quite as alluring in the grey dawn of morning, so we toddled quietly over to the Palliser and quaffed a deep Collins. And then we had another just to keep it company.

As no man was ever known to bother about breakfast after partaking of a series of Collinses, we found ourselves at 10 o'clock seated in the mayor's chair on an empty stomach, but feeling remarkably fit withal. The stenog was very gracious. A great pile of letters lay heaped on the desk and eyeing them dubiously, we enquired of the young lady—"Am I supposed to read all these letters and answer them?"

"Oh, certainly."

"Well, you'll have to excuse me for about five minutes. I had an appointment with a man at exactly four minutes past ten and it's just about that time now. Would you mind opening the envelopes and stacking the letters so I can read 'em quickly?"

"Not at all. I shall have them all ready for you."

As we passed into the Queen's we noticed a couple of droughty city hall employees passing out, wiping off their chins and looking unnaturally brisk. So it wasn't to be wondered at that the first question we put to the bartender was: "Have you any gin left?"

"Yessir, lots of it."

"Well, make me a Collins."

On returning to the mayor's cosy sanctum, a formidable stack of letters was staring us in the face. There seemed to be more of them than the envelopes had originally indicated.

"Ho, there," we cried to the stenog, emboldened by the last Collins. "Is it customary for the mayor to read and answer his mail the same day as he gets it?"

"Why of course."

"Then here is where you see the custom broken. There will be another pencil-pusher occupying this chair tomorrow and you can just slip this stack on top of his stack. He will be none the wiser."

"Just as you say sir."

"Well, I guess I'll have a smoke now. You don't mind?"

"Oh dear no! They do nothing else around this place. Sometimes I think the building is on fire. By the way, there are some gentlemen waiting to see you in the ante-room."

"Show 'em in."

Entered three ferocious looking men who proceeded to range themselves around the desk, nonchalantly flicking their cigar ashes on the beautiful crimson carpet by way of indicating that they as ratepayers, had helped to pay for it.

"Be seated, gentlemen. What can I do for you?"

"We have come to do for you, Costello," began the most ferocious of the three grimly. "The foreman of the job we were on in East Calgary has just fired us and taken on two Germans and one Austrian. This comes of your rotten decision to keep on hiring the enemies of our country in preference to Britishers. We've come to do you up, Mr. Mayor, and if you get out of this room alive, you'll be playing in big luck."

"But look here," we cried in dismay, "I'm not Costello at all. I'm only. . . ."

"That'll do now—don't give us any of that guff. The only way to din anything into you city hall fellows is to beat you up. So here goes."

With that, the spokesman, a very large person, sprang upon us and banged our head on the desk. He then proceeded to slam our puny body all over the room, finally dropping us on the floor to get a better hold, after which he gave an excellent imitation of Gotch toying with a fourth-rater.

Happily Detectives Richardson and Ritchie chanced to be passing the window and saw our body hurtling through the air from one side of the room to the other. Rushing up the city hall steps they quickly effected a rescue and escorted the three ferocious gentlemen to the cells.

This was a poor beginning.

"Is it always like this around here?" we enquired of the stenog, who, to our surprise, seemed to take the incident as a matter of course.

"Oh, that's nothing," she replied carelessly, pounding away at the typewriter for all she was worth.

After staring at the fair lady for a few minutes, we re-entered the office and started gathering up the tables and chairs and putting them back in their. proper places. This done, the stenog popped her head in and said a man would like to see us.

"Just one man?"

"Yes."

"Is he a big man?"

"Oh no, rather a little chap."

"Show him in."

The newcomer was all smiles and deposited his hat carefully on the floor.

"Bli' me," he ejaculated, gazing with unfeigned delight at the crimson carpet, "but this is certainly a bloody swell joint."

"Ain't it though!" said we, passing over a cigar. "What can I do for you?"

"I want a job wukkin' for the city. My pal joined the soldiers, but Gawbli' me they wouldn't tyke me 'cos I was too bloody small. A blawsted shyme, wot?"

"What nationality are you?"

"Austrian."

"Well get to hell out of here!"

"But look 'ere old chap, I was told that if I said I was an Aus—"

"Get out!"

"But man alive, 'ave a 'eart, 'ave a 'eart!"

"Scoot."

A few minutes of peace followed. Then came the inevitable knock on the door. More callers. In they trooped, a deputation of five, more or less sober. The most respectable looking of the bunch bowed gingerly and began:

"You are acting-mayor, I believe, during Mayor Costello's absence?"

"I am."

"As such, I take it, you have large powers and are allowed considerable latitude?"

"I guess so."

"Well don't you think this would be a splendid opportunity, a propitious time, a psychological moment to issue a permit for a segregated area within the city limits?"

"I certainly do—it's a great idea!"

"You're the stuff, Mr. Mayor! We gentlemen have formed a syndicate and propose to run the district according to Hoyle and free from all turbulence."

"I thoroughly approve of your scheme, gentlemen, and I shall give you all the assistance in my power. These Austrians and Germans living in Calgary should have been segregated long ago and it is very creditable to your sense of patriotism that you are taking up the matter so earnestly."

"I fear you misunderstand me, Mr. Mayor. We do not propose to segregate any Austrians or Germans. The segregated district we propose to run. . . ."

"Oh, that's it, is it? Just wait till I ring up the chief of police. Here, hi! What's the hurry? Don't run away like that."

We sank back in the chair and touched the bell for the stenog. The look of concern on her face as she perceived our wretchedness, touched us deeply.

"You don't happen to know," we said, "if Mayor Costello keeps a bottle on the premises?"

"I hardly think so. I've never seen one."

"Well, you'll excuse me if I run up town for a brief moment? Thanks, that's very good of you. I won't be long. Don't cry for I'll soon be back. If any callers should come, send them to Mr. Garden."

"Very well sir, won't you see the gentleman who is waiting outside? He seems a very nice person."

"Well, if it doesn't keep me too long."

A tall, gaunt man stepped briskly into the room and shook us by the hand.

"Delighted to meet you Mr. Mayor, delighted to meet you. You are the greatest mayor that ever graced the precincts of the city hall and I am proud to shake you by the hand, sir. Your countenance beams with the divine light of . . ."

"Here, hold on, hold on! Who are you and where do you hail from?"

"Who me? I am a cousin of General Von Kluck and was directed to you for a civic position, preferably that of lineman on a wireless telegraph lay-out, if you have one. I just arrived from the North this morning."

"From what town, pray?"

"Ponoka."

As soon as this enthusiastic gentleman was safely landed in a cell, we bade the faithful stenog farewell. She was sorry to see us go.

"Won't you be back this afternoon?"

"No!" (22 May 1915)

But however much Bob Edwards criticized civic administration, his thinking was most progressive and he suggested numerous changes that the city adopted to advantage. He was one of the first to advocate "two or three salaried men to act as an executive or a commission," to take the rough and routine work off the shoulders of the city council. A city's affairs must represent big business and "no one surely will deny that the affairs of a great western city like Calgary deserve the exclusive attention of somebody." (9 February 1907) Calgary and other cities adopted the principle of city commissioners as administrators.

CHAPTER TWENTY

"A Statesman Is a Dead Politician"

> "The difference between American and English politics is shown by Mr. Chamberlain having the gout. Over in the States, a man who expected to appeal to the masses and suggest extra taxes on the grub pile wouldn't dare to have the gout."
>
> (24 October 1903)

> "If you want work well done, select a busy man; the other kind has no time."
>
> (*Summer Annual*, 1922)

> "From an Ottawa dispatch we learn that no work will be done this year on the Hudson's Bay Railway. We had no idea they were still puttering away on this line. Sir John A. Macdonald started the road in the first place and it is expected that Gabriel the Trumpeter will be invited to drive the last spike on Judgment Day."
>
> (21 September 1918)

ALL HIS LIFE Bob Edwards was a politician of sorts; but not until 1921, when the provincial election was called, did he yield to the urging to stand as an active candidate. Few people had a finer grasp of political history, but through the years he believed he could serve the best democratic purpose by remaining on the political sidelines—teasing, criticizing, and cajoling, and always effectively. Writing about the political scene was one of his greatest enjoyments and not even a good horse race was more fun than watching an election. "As one crosses the roaring forties of one's years," he remarked, "one's notion of real excitement is a good general election."

Readily it may be said that he loved politics much more than politicians loved him. He made life uncomfortable for many of them. The trouble was that they didn't always know when he was serious, and more than once some political figure threatened action for libel. One of those occasions was when Provincial Premier Sifton was the target for the remark that the biggest liars in Alberta are "Robert Edwards, Gentleman, Hon. A. L. Sifton, (Premier), and Bob Edwards, Editor of the *Eye Opener.*" Perhaps Bob should have been worried about the report that the Premier was taking steps to sue him; but he immediately announced a proposal—that "Robert Edwards, Gentleman," associate himself with "A. L. Sifton, (Premier)," in joint legal action against "Bob Edwards, Editor." Assuming such ridiculous proportions as the affair was, the premier was glad to forget it.

Writing political stories and speeches was a pastime in which he indulged quite frequently. Cappie Smart or Charlie Taylor might find him sitting alone at the bar, "capturing some wild ideas before they became outlaws," perhaps setting down a "Throne Speech" for Lieutenant-Governor Bulyea in opening the Alberta Legislature. Needless to say, it wasn't a "Speech" the Lieutenant-Governor would use; but when Bob noted that "the chap who composed the speech from the throne must have written it in a hurry on the back of an envelope, with someone hollering at him from the adjoining room to come and have a drink," he was inclined to write one he considered no worse. Such a speech, written in august terms, might propose a Legislative Reception Committee to extend an appropriate welcome to Halley's Comet, expected to appear shortly; a bill to compel hotel keepers to sell five drinks for half a dollar; and friendly relations with Turkey for the purpose of: ". . . obtaining the residue of the deposed Sultan's harem as wives for the lonely settlers in Alberta. Arrangements are under way for their passage from the Bosphorus to this country and on their arrival they will be given a course of training at the Government Cooking School at Cooking Lake to fit them as helpmates for the hardy tillers of the soil."

Some of Bob's most vitriolic political attacks were upon the Canadian Senate. It was not, in his view, an essential part of a democratic administration and therefore there was no point in maintaining it. A lot of uncomplimentary remarks have been directed at the Canadian Senate, but few more caustic than Bob's:

> As a home for decayed politicians run on purely benevolent lines at $2,500 per, the Senate could lay claim to being a success. Indeed, were they to throw off the mask and admit once and for all that the place is but a Cabman's Shelter, a Refuge for fallen political prune-eaters, a Haven for the discredited, a Home for pensioners who don't need the money, an Exhibition of ill-visaged wax-works and chamber of horrors, the country at large would think more of them. It is the hypocrisy, the bogus prestige and the spirit of make-believe which pervades the red chamber, making it redolent of pompous humbug and aristocratic mystery, that irritates the people so much. (22 December 1906)

Bob was generally regarded as a Conservative in politics, but that was due largely to his admiration for Frederick Haultain, premier of the North West Territories for nearly eighteen years and doughty fighter for Provincial Rights. It was the Edwards conviction that during his years in the West, the Conservative Party could boast more able parliamentarians and statesmen than the Liberal Party. But "Statesman" was a term he used sparingly, at least until that day when he discovered exactly what it meant. After attending the funeral of a well-known local politician and listening to the eloquent oration about the dead man's greatness, Bob wrote: "Now I know what a statesman is; he's a dead politician. We need more statesmen."[1]

But however Bob was tabbed by people around him, he was ready to criticize Conservative and Liberal Parties alike. The main difference between them, he noted, was, that "one is in and the other is out." And then he added: "Politics has not ceased to make strange bedfellows; at least, the politicians of both parties continue to share the same bunk. You know the kind of bunk we mean." (5 October 1912)

Perhaps his strongest sympathies were with Labour, and time after time he voiced the sort of sentiment that came at a later period from J. S. Woodsworth. When he ultimately threw his hat into the provincial election ring in 1921, he was standing as an Independent with a strong Labour bias.

After some years of Liberal domination at both Ottawa and Edmonton, it was obvious that the editor found most to criticize in that party. Certainly, the Liberals figured most prominently in *Eye Opener* stories, typical of which was the one about Dr. Shearer, eastern Liberal and Methodist, who went to visit a convict under sentence of death in an Ontario Penitentiary and could not resist the urge "to convert him to Laurierism." The conversation went this way:

> "Ah, my poor fellow," began the reverend doctor, grasping the murderer's hand, "I am grieved to see you in such a plight. They tell me there is no hope for a reprieve."
>
> "No hope?"
>
> The doomed man sat on the edge of his cot and stared vacantly at the floor.
>
> "None whatever, my dear sir. The Minister of Justice has carefully considered your case. In going through your past record he finds that you always voted Conservative. There is yet time to repent, however. I have brought with me that wondrous book from which so many have drawn consolation, Willison's *Life of Laurier*. Allow me to read you a passage."
>
> The distracted man sighed and looked lovingly at a patch of sky

[1] This is one of Edwards's most quoted (and mis-quoted) quips. But hanged if we can find the issue in which he quipped it.

which he could just see through the bars of the tiny window, while Dr. Shearer reverently read the touching chapter which deals with the Canadian navy.

"Hark," cried the poor fellow, nervously. "What is that knocking sound outside?"

"That? Oh it's only the workmen setting up your scaffold. I noticed them as I came in. The contractor is an active Grit and must control some seventy-five to a hundred votes at the very least. He gets all the scaffold jobs around the jail, they tell me. But let me turn to the beautiful chapter which tells of Clifford Sifton and Potiphar's wife . . ."

Canadian fleet giving Dr. Shearer and Gypsy Smith a whiff of the ocean breeze. They are both seasick, but refuse to take any brandy. Very foolish of them.

"Don't, don't," pleaded the agonized prisoner. "Spare me that! Tell me sir, is there no hope for a reprieve? The governor of the jail held out such bright hopes for me yesterday, and now everything seems to have gone on the blink."

"My poor fellow," said the doctor, deeply moved, "put your trust in Laurier and he will aid you. Are you willing to accept him? He is your only hope."

The condemned man, cornered like a rat in a trap, pondered a while and finally said with an air of resignation, "I'll go you."

"Very well, my good man, then it is as good as settled. There is more joy over one Tory that repenteth than over 99 Grits that are solid anyway. I shall wire the department of justice within the hour. Buck up! All will be well."

The poor chap sank back on his cot in a swoon.

Sure enough, early next morning, the governor came rushing in to the condemned man's cell, waving a telegram. "Wake up! Wake up! Your sentence is commuted to three years and nine months."

"Good eye!" quoth the murderer, sitting up in his cot.

"And when are the next Dominion elections?"

"In another four years, I fancy."

"Well," said the murderer, rolling over for another snooze, "I'll be there." (5 April 1919)

Through the years, *Eye Opener* policy was to support the "best man" regardless of party. While still in High River, the editor had advised his readers to forget how their fathers and mothers voted and do their own thinking. He was through with party ties and would support the candidate best qualified, whether Liberal or Conservative. At that time he went to some length to brief his High River readers about constituency representation:

> It seems a pity that in our Councils, Territorial and Dominion, there are so many lawyers, doctors and editors, and so few business men. . . .
>
> The average business man may be . . . very patriotic while in the balmy atmosphere of banquet speeches and champagne, but his patriotism does not seem strong enough to allow him to spare any time from his business to work for the country he so much adores. It is almost impossible to induce any prominent business men out this way to run for the Assembly. They "cannot spare the time." What is the result?
>
> This is a country of agriculture and stock, and agriculturists and stockmen certainly come within the category of 'business men,' no less than do manufacturers and storekeepers. . . . It is from this element that a fair proportion of our western representatives should be chosen.
>
> A fair sprinkling of the professions gives tone to any parliamentary body but there is no crying need for a cloudburst.
>
> Nor would preachers fill the bill as legislators. They would be forever introducing impractical measures. . . . Accustomed all his life to dealing with topics of the time of Israel and King David and handling questions of an intangible nature, the preacher could hardly handle questions of current moment. So we may leave the preacher out as a legislative possibility.
>
> From agricultural centres, practical agriculturists of approved mental equipment should make the most effective representatives; certainly not a lawyer who is out for the office only as a stepping stone to higher things.

> From stock centres, an experienced stockman (not necessarily a bronco buster) who has a thorough understanding of the stockman's requirements, is the right and logical kind of representative to have; certainly not a doctor who only knows the difference between a horse and a cow because the horse has no horns. (5 September 1903)

Study proves that Edwards's political ideals were high, even though he continued to make jokes about governments and poke fun at legislators. A candidate for public office, he felt, should possess three qualities in particular: intelligence, honesty, and courage. His urging was to "raise the standard of truth and fight for it." (30 April 1904)[2] When he finally accepted the challenge to go actively into politics, his declaration was to "go in clean and come out clean."

And so, after a lot of coaxing, Bob Edwards consented to be a candidate for the Provincial Legislature in the election of July, 1921.[3] Liberals had been in power since the province was created in 1905; and Premier Charles Stewart's administration was receiving criticism, mainly because of the "staggering provincial debt" of around twenty-four million dollars.

The United Farmers of Alberta, under President Henry Wise Wood, were out to evict the "party system" and win political laurels for themselves. Nobody expected them to gain landslide success; but many people were ready to agree with Bob Edwards that if they were successful in turning the Stewart Government from office, "it would be a tragedy in one sense and a comedy in another."

Edwards's decision to enter the contest was not that of a man seeking personal advancement; nor was it that of one bitterly opposed to the Stewart administration, because he announced that if elected he would support the Liberal Government in any reasonable measures.

He was one of twenty candidates for five seats in the city of Calgary. He was

[2] Quote was in specific reference to Conservative candidate S. McCarthy: "He has only to raise the standard of truth and fight under it, to win out."

[3] On at least one previous occasion, Edwards was encouraged, albeit unsuccessfully, to run for office. In 1905, the local typographical union proclaimed Edwards their legislative candidate, spawning a brief spurt of BobMania. "For the sake of those who will be elected it is to be hoped that Edwards will not be elected," declared no less an authority than "Old Man" Simpson of the *Cranbrook Herald*. "He has brains, he has courage and he has a tongue like the sting of a wasp, and a pen as facile as the downy end of an ostrich plume, with a point as sharp as a serpent's lancet. If he occupied a seat in the first house of Alberta he would have all kinds of fun with the weak kneed and grafting government." (Simpson was quoted in the *Calgary Daily Herald*, 27 September 1905.) Edwards apparently declined the challenge: the idea quickly, quietly disappeared from headlines. John R. Boyle, a fellow MLA (25 November 1922) speculates that Edwards's reluctance to seek public office stemmed from his fear of public speaking and overall shyness. In "Bob Edwards and I," Robert Pearson raises the possibility that this shyness stemmed from self-preservation, an attempt to avoid the temptations of social drinking. One also wonders whether Edwards's alleged speech impediment, so ruthlessly mocked in McGillicuddy's "Nemesis" letter, limited his public ambition.

running as an Independent, and his campaign was as unique as people who knew him might have expected. It was a campaign conducted "Bob Edwards" style, and it led to his election with a big vote.

It was a time of rip-roaring political speeches, and it was supposed that nobody could win an election without a lot of high-powered oratory. While opponents were working night and day, Bob Edwards made a single speech; it was an address that lasted exactly one minute. That lone speech was in response to a personal request from a group of returned men meeting in Paget Hall. He accepted that invitation only because he felt he could not refuse any reasonable request from the veterans who had chosen him to be a patron of their association every year since its inception.

What he told his audience during that period of sixty seconds on the platform was to forget about the election until after the races, because that was what he intended to do. He added, also, that no political candidate should be allowed to make more than one speech per campaign.

Friends said, "All right, Bob; but if you refuse to accept a speaking campaign, for Heaven's sake use your pen to sell yourself to the electors." He did accept an invitation from "my old friend, Editor Davidson," to run a "one-minute message" on the editorial page of the *Morning Albertan*, daily for about ten days prior to the election. The same privilege was extended to other Independent candidates; and according to Edwards, "Although none of us says anything especially sparkling, the public does not have to read it."

In his first message he announced that there would be no public meetings on his behalf and no speeches.

> My views on every imaginable topic under the sun are already perfectly well known to all. I have been discussing and handling public questions for a very, very long time in this province and you must admit that I have never stalled or fourflushed on any one of them. Indeed, I think I can safely lay claim to the distinction of having delivered the longest address of any man in this community by means of the fact that I have been addressing Calgary audiences steadily for a period of over twenty years. (*Albertan*, 4 July 1921)

As the campaign advanced, Edwards became increasingly convinced that the electors were losing interest in attending political meetings anyway. "They positively decline to allow themselves to be bored by speechifying and blethering candidates who tell them nothing they don't already know and who tell it badly at that."

Not Wanted--Too Respectable

Bob Edwards was being perfectly natural. He never could be otherwise.

In one of his brief messages in the morning paper, his main plea was on behalf of the Labour candidates opposing him; strangely enough, the only candidate in a field of twenty running in Calgary to poll a bigger vote than Edwards was Labour Candidate Alex Ross. One message from Bob's pen was devoted to endorsation of Duncan Marshall who was running at Olds. There was just nothing that an experienced politician could recognize as conventional about the Edwards campaign. Another morning, in response to the pleas of worried friends, he explained that Candidate R. C. Edwards, whom some people evidently did not identify, was the same mortal as Bob Edwards about whom nearly everybody knew something, good or bad.

It was fortunate, he admitted, that candidates are expected to talk so much about themselves, because they wouldn't dare tell anything except the most uninteresting parts of the story. As for himself, he was born in Edinburgh, "about a hundred years ago," and educated at St. Andrews, "where they breed golfers." One of the boys from Clifton Banks School, which he attended, became Field Marshal Lord Haig. How he became a Field Marshal instead of a golfer or a poor editor after attending that school, "God only knows." Bob Edwards admitted he had lived in Alberta for twenty-six or twenty-seven years, had agitated for provincial autonomy, had done some other things good and bad; but that was enough about himself.[4]

The big issue which he discussed in some detail concerned liquor; and let there be no mistake about it, liquor and what Alberta was going to do about it was a big issue at that time. Again he took a stand in opposition to hard liquor, just as he had done six years before when the *Eye Opener* was credited with having been the biggest single factor in carrying the prohibition vote in Calgary. But all the liquor problems had not been solved, and the Edwards stand was that of one who opposed extreme measures and believed that only a reasonable compromise could bring a reasonable solution.

[4] These biographical details appeared in the *Albertan* of 12 July 1921.

"The gradual disappearance of whiskey can be brought about," he wrote, "by providing and making accessible to everybody a cheap form of mild stimulant and by no other means. . . . Prohibitionists can take it from me that they will never make headway in the direction of true temperance until . . . they meet Human Nature half way. Fine rain we had, eh?"

One might have expected Edwards to use the pages of his own paper to further his chance of election. In his initial "minute message" published in the *Morning Albertan*, he announced: "On this page, each morning, I shall make an abbreviated talk to the electors, until my own paper comes out on the 16th for the final wallop."[5] But Bob changed his mind about that. In his *Albertan* column on 15 July, there was a countermanding message: "I am not publishing the *Eye Opener* tomorrow. It is all written but in reading over the proofs, I find it contains a bewildering variety of cogent reasons why you should vote for R. C. Edwards on the 18th. I could not very well charge people 10 cents for reading my own advertising. Certainly not."[6]

Moreover, he did not wish to be in the position of having an advantage in the contest for votes. The issue, ready for the press, was scrapped.

His was a campaign completely new in an area where political contestants were traditionally bitter; but the electors liked it, and on election day, 18 July 1921, Edwards polled the second-highest vote in the field of twenty candidates.[7] In addition to Edwards, the Calgary vote elected Alex Ross and Fred J. White from Labour; R. C. Marshall, Liberal; and Bob's particular friend who had induced him to run and later became his legislative desk-mate, Rev. Robert Pearson.

Over the province, the United Farmers of Alberta were swept into power, winning thirty-eight of the sixty-one seats; and in the days which followed the election, Herbert Greenfield was chosen to be leader and premier. Probably no group was more surprised at the UFA successes than the leaders of the new party. They might have been even more surprised if they could have known they would remain in office in the province until 1935, to be superseded by yet another new political movement—Social Credit.

A month after the election, the *Eye Opener* reappeared, carrying its own report about the editor's success at the polls:

> This is the first appearance of the genial *Eye Opener* since the eventful Election. It was some election.

[5] *Albertan*, 4 July 1921. Edwards went so far as to capitalize "FINAL WALLOP," making his retraction all the more disappointing.
[6] Edwards wrote, "Cert'nly not"—an important distinction, perhaps, in cinching his casual Everyman tone.
[7] Edwards's 6,141 votes placed him a close second to Alex Ross's 6,842.

> Three months ago the editor of this paper had no more notion of becoming a member of the Alberta Legislature than Mr. Greenfield of becoming premier of the province or Mr. Brownlee of becoming attorney-general or Alex Ross, minister of public works. Fate or destiny was obviously on a wild spree, tossing some men aside, destroying others and pitchforking sundry extremely astonished individuals into the seats of the mighty where they now lie sprawled gasping, blinking their eyes and wondering whether it was a cyclone or just an earthquake.
>
> As for our success at the polls—well, now, what the devil are we going to say about that? That we deeply and gratefully appreciate the kindness shown on every side, goes without saying. . . . No speeches were made on our behalf; no meetings held.
>
> One temptation we are going to guard against while attending sessions of the House is that of using this paper to poke wanton fun at fellow-members. . . . This would never do at all. What we do chance to write about the proceedings in the House or about the members will be done in accordance with good taste and in as happy and good-natured vein as is compatible with a torpid liver. (20 August 1921)

Quite naturally, people wondered if the successful flight into political life would change Bob Edwards. "What difference will this make in the character of the *Eye Opener*?" they asked, considering the possibility that it might assume a new air of respectability. For the answer they did not have to wait long, because almost at once they were reading about post-election experiences as only Bob Edwards was likely to find them. There was, for example, the account of a Calgarian who, with tears in his eyes, bustled into the *Eye Opener* office, congratulating the editor on his great victory, the dialogue going like this:

> "By George, ol' man," he cried, "you certainly put one over that time! Right over the plate! By golly, if I had a snifter handy I would drink your health right now! By gum, I tell you, I feel like going off on a bat! I do for a fact. I won a ten-spot on you to be elected, but lost fifteen that you'd be at the head of the polls. I'm out five, otherwise I'd have brought up a bottle to celebrate. However . . ."
>
> "Well, let us have a jolt anyway," said we, reaching for a drawer.
>
> "By golly!" he shouted. "Where's the glass—where's the water?

Don't break the cork whatever you do! Oh hell! Well, push it down in the neck of the bottle and hurry up! By gum, that's pretty smooth stuff! Say, I won't be satisfied until I see you premier of the province. You're a great man. When you go up to Edmonton I want you to give 'em hell."

"Give who hell?" we mildly asked.

"Oh, everybody, nobody in particular. I met a man down the street as I was coming up and he said you were a comer in the political field and now that you were started nothing could stop you. I won't give you his name—you know him all right—but he said you would wind up at Ottawa as a front bencher of a new party."

"Did he say what kind of party?"

"He mentioned something about the Wets . . ."

"Oh, tut, tut! Have another touch of this Scotch and I'll fetch some fresh water from the tap. In the meantime, have a cigar."

After downing another stiff snort, he resumed the conversation with renewed zest.

Hell of a note—what?

"By golly, I was glad to see you near the top of the poll. I bet $25 that you'd be at the top—Oh that's all right—I'm glad you won, anyhow. We all were. I was with a bunch of fellows last night and they all agreed you should be given a swell job, something like Canadian Ambassador at Washington or High Commissioner at London, where your eminent qualifications of education, culture and refinement . . ."

"Were they sober?"

"Well, no, not exactly, but their hearts were in the right place. You'll be surprised to know that the women almost all voted for you. They did for a fact. I was talking to a dear old lady this morning, one of the most prominent church women in the city, and she told me confidentially that although she did not entirely approve of the *Eye Opener*, she thought that Mr. Edwards was the finest Christian gentleman that ever came down the pike. In fact, she . . ."

"Ever came down the pike? Surely she didn't say that."

"Well, words to that effect. She felt genuinely sorry when I told her that I had lost $75 on you to head the poll and introduced me to a rather pretty young dame who is visiting her. She wants to meet you."

"Which one? The young one?"

"Yes, she said . . ."

"Never mind what she said—this is worth another drink! Help yourself."

"I hate to drink up all your whiskey: If I hadn't lost such a big wad of money on betting that you'd head the poll, I'd have brought up some myself. This is pretty good stuff. Where did you get it? By golly, it's different from some of that bootleg stuff I was hitting up the other night. By the way, a prominent bootlegger in this city told me in confidence that they are going to send you round a case of real stuff so that you can set 'em up to the Attorney General at Edmonton once in a while. The local bootleggers need a represhennarive at Edmonton and it was the general conchensh—conchenshus of 'pinion that you were their man. By golly, I believe this shtuff has gone t' my head. It's buzzin' 'way to beat the band."

"Oh well, finish the bottle and then we'll go home."

"Don' you ever take a drink yourself? Oh well, here's lookin' at you. Not bad stuff, but I've tasted better. With the $260 I losh on you toppin' the poll, could have bought half a dozen cases—five anyhow. I think you made a poor run at that. Is this all the booze you got left? You're a poor fish. Next time you run, I'm not going to vote for you arall, norarall. I met a feller on shtair comin' up here and he tol' me in confidence you were a poor fish. Thaz wot he said—a poor fish. He said you were no good, no good arall, an' I agreed with him—in fact I corrobrr—corroborated him."

"Get to hell out of here," we roared.

"Orl right, ol' sport! But you're a poor fish, remember that, a poor fish. Goo-bye." (20 August 1921)

But however lightly he may have taken the campaign and election trials, the new

Member for Calgary accepted his responsibilities with earnestness of purpose, and while he lived he served his constituents faithfully.

He sat through one session of the legislature and died before the next. In "The House" he did not speak often; all his life he dreaded the thought of being called upon to deliver a speech, and the prospect of having to address the provincial legislators filled him with fear. In the course of his "maiden" effort[8] he started slowly and haltingly; but he seemed to overcome all nervousness, and members of the legislature listened to a masterpiece. As the self-appointed "Minister of Boozological Problems," his principal message was a plea for "sensible and practical liquor laws." It was a pet theme, admittedly. Unrestricted sale was wrong; in fact, he concluded for the benefit of fellow legislators, any sale of liquor was wrong, but so was any program that transferred the whiskey business to the bootleggers and allowed them to flourish. Bob had editorialized in support of prohibition sufficiently that no one could question his intent, but the growth of bootlegging convinced him that the province should continue its search for a better system. That "bootlegging may be considered the major industry in Alberta" (29 July 1922), could bring nothing but shame to all conscientious citizens of the "Fair Province."

Basically, yes, he believed that whiskey was a diabolical culprit. He would like to think that its manufacture and sale would one day be halted. But the only means of achieving that end would be by providing beer and making it readily available. Beer would satisfy the craving of those who would otherwise consume liquor of hard variety; it would foster conviviality without danger of drunkenness. His proposals for low-alcoholic beers were merely compromises, but they were advanced with the earnestness of a man seeking to perform a public duty.

In proposing the sale of "light stuff to check the consumption of heavy stuff," Bob Edwards was giving expression to a concept in the philosophy of public administration in democracy, that, "The science of politics consists of compromise. Without the spirit of compromise, the conflicting views of good citizens cannot be reconciled." (*Morning Albertan*, 15 July 1921)

[8] Edwards delivered this speech on 20 March 1922. The ur-text forever lost, a reconstructed version appears in *Irresponsible Freaks, etc.*

CHAPTER TWENTY-ONE
"More Joy in Heaven"

> "One reason the *Eye Opener* has so many high ideals is that Calgary is over 3000 feet above the level of the sea."
>
> (1 August 1908)

> "The price of this paper is one dollar a year. It ought to be five but we knock off four for irregularity."
>
> (17 February 1917)

> "After a man has passed through his baptism of booze, so to speak, he is either ready for big business or the discard. If he survives and is worth while, nothing can stop him but if he is weak . . . he will not survive. Booze has been a great eliminator."
>
> (9 March 1918)

JUST BEFORE BOB'S LAST ISSUE of the *Calgary Eye Opener* went to press in 1922, a middle-aged man with dishevelled hair, dirty face, and a wild stare in his eyes, called at the office. Stains and grime discoloured the front of his roll-neck sweater, while coat and trousers made shapeless by twenty-four-hour occupancy day after day bore but little resemblance to the costly suit which came originally from a fashionable English tailor. That such a figure would be calling to see Bob Edwards was not in itself unusual, because he was not one to discourage eccentricity, particularly if it were a reflection of natural inclinations or honest convictions. One of the fascinations about frontier personalities was diverseness. The "average" people never reached the frontier; those who came and settled were "different." It was their right to be uncommon, to think for themselves even though they shocked the neighbours now and then. It was perfectly obvious that the new West gathered and held more than its share of social monstrosities as well as moderate eccentrics, and quite a few of them made the *Eye Opener* office a port-of-call.

Well, as this particular caller with a skid-row odour and a scholarly English accent advanced to the editor's desk, he introduced himself by saying: "I'm Bertie. You see, damn it, I'm really Percy but either way I'm that bloody fool remittance man you knew at High River about twenty years ago. Remember? Nobody told me but I know frightfully well that my damn foolishness gave you the idea for your Bertie Buzzard-Cholomondeley stories. Now be honest, Old Thing. Isn't that so."

Bob smiled and reached to grasp the man's cold and trembling hand. "Yes, I remember. You were a damned fool, all right, and I wasn't much better. But before you ask for a drink, sit down and tell me where you've been."

A rarely seen portrait of Bob in a jolly mood.

Things had gone badly with Percy. That much was immediately evident. The money from home stopped coming; and having been raised as a complete stranger to useful work, Percy was more than ever an object of pity. His only approach to practical training was part of a year at the High River School of Agriculture which Bob, in 1903, exposed as a fake. It was supposed to be a place to which English boys of the problem type could be sent to learn "fahming" at $500 a year. When Bob first drew attention to that school farm east of High River, there were "eight or ten semi-halter-broke pupils of the Little Lord Fauntleroy variety, sloshing around the place in the first flush of bucolic enthusiasm." (24 June 1905) Percy was one of them, but interest in farm life didn't last long. Like most of the others, Percy had lots of money and the laborious side of farming had no chance against lures and companionships about the bar. But when money came no more, Percy, not knowing how to do useful work, was in a bad way. Now, his only resemblances to the younger Percy who had treated all comers at the Astoria Hotel were his tongue and his craving for liquor.

"Jolly fine to see you again, Mr. Edwards," he said in a voice that didn't seem to belong to his neglected appearance. "But I simply must have a drink. Haven't got a bloody bob to buy one but I knew you'd have a bottle."

But Percy was due for a bitter disappointment. Bob was obliged to inform him: "There isn't a drop in the office." Then to make the bad news convincing, Bob pulled out each one of the drawers from the big roll-top desk, revealing complete absence of bottles. "Hasn't been a bottle there since last Christmas," he added.

The barrenness of those desk drawers which had long harboured liquor was enough to sadden any visitor so parched for a drink, but Percy was intelligent enough to be curious about the shocking change.

"What are you trying to tell me?" he asked. "That you've cut it out? I never thought it would happen to you. How in the devil did you manage it?" Percy's astonishment would have been no greater had he discovered the Bow River flowing westward into the mountains.

This wasn't a topic Bob wanted to discuss at the moment; immediately his old thirst was back. At his throat he could feel the flames of desire which nothing but alcohol could extinguish. It would have been so easy to yield—to give Percy five dollars and say: "Go round to the bootlegger and get us a big bottle." He reached into his pocket and grasped his wallet, paused, then withdrew the empty hand and said: "No—I'm not drinking. It's been a hell of a battle and I don't want to lose it now. Of course I had a good man with me—Reverend Bob. If you don't know Bob Pearson, I'm going to take you round to meet him. Now, look here Percy; I know how you're suffering. I know all about it. I'll tell you where you can get just a wee snifter for yourself and then we'll see Pearson."

The other Bob—Rev. Bob Pearson—with whom Edwards had shared living quarters at Edmonton and a desk in the Legislature, could tell about the terrific struggle starting months earlier, in the course of which Bob Edwards was the victor. The editor had quit drinking on various occasions through the years, but always the craving overpowered the good intentions eventually. There was but small reason to believe that another attempt to beat the devil in alcohol would be any different. There was, of course, nothing usual about the man Edwards, and even the compelling nature of his thirst seemed unique: In acknowledging a most uncommon physiological weakness for drink, he explained that it was additionally sad "when a man cannot take a horn without going off on a week's bust." (7 December 1918)

But when Edwards considered the trust placed in him by Calgary voters, and the loyalty of Bob Pearson, he promised in that Methodist minister's presence that no matter how the old enemy gnawed at his insides, he would drink no liquor during the session of the Legislature—and perhaps none thereafter.

Is it possible, thought Pearson, that this will be the great triumph? It promised to be quite a battle. It was clear that Pearson commanded Edwards's admiration and respect; Edwards would do anything in his power for a friend. He'd do anything for Bob Pearson, ex-University of Toronto football player and champion of clean sport. Pearson was the right man at this time. He was no prig about liquor or anything else. He was a man's man—one who understood Bob Edwards, recognized the conflict between two powerful forces within the man, one reaching frantically for a drink and

Rev. Bob's Notion of a Truly Ideal Forward Movement

the other trying desperately to reject it. Outwardly, of course, Edwards seemed to live in constant conflict with the man within—writing humorously and thinking seriously, wearing a mask of frivolity but harbouring a spirit ready to wage war against wrongs, no matter what the odds against him. To most people the Edwards behaviour appeared hopelessly complex, but Pearson recognized one basic principle which helped him to understand the man; the real Edwards character in every case of apparent conflict was the one adhering passionately to honesty. When Bob Edwards offended somebody it was probably because his honest nature compelled it; when he struck at hypocrisy it was because that trait was incompatible with honest living. And now, to be honest to a rededicated conviction and purpose, Bob Edwards would have to quit drinking.

Because of the unceasing effort to ward off the old enemy, the period during which the Legislature was in session became an unhappy one for Bob Edwards. So conscious was he of his weakness, so worried that he might not have the will to say "no" when liquor was offered, and so fearful that one drink would lead to a prolonged drunk, that he refused all social engagements while in Edmonton and thus denied himself much of the fun that went with legislative work. When most members congregated for an evening of relaxation, Edwards was not with them. He was in his room, reading or writing; but usually that staunch friend who steeled his resolute purpose was with him.

Among the spectators were the usual skeptics who speculated that, "Bob may do it for these few weeks, but at the end of the session—look out; there'll be an awful spree." Well, the session ended and there was no spree. Pearson and Edwards, equally proud of the record, returned to Calgary together, and then the editor confided to his friend that the adventure in abstinence was just beginning.

Listening attentively while Edwards recounted this story of his hard-won triumph over liquor, Percy was impressed. For minutes he sat in silence, but then shook his head. The ambition to try to "cut it out," even with Reverend Bob's help, wasn't there. The thirst was upon him and he had to be going—somewhere. This was the life he had made for himself, and he could scarcely imagine any other into which he would fit. And so, after the temporary relief of that "one wee snifter," and a visit and a meal with the two Bobs, he moved away, aimlessly, to rustle his "necessities of life," sleep in all the clothes he owned and lead a wasted life. Too bad, but that's the way it would be.

As for Bob Edwards, he did persevere in his new way, though not without moments and days of suffering. But there was the reward in victory and the suffering was diminishing. Booze had been his weakness for many years and booze his self-chosen trademark. He made people laugh at the cursed stuff. He would continue to joke about it—might as well. He would tell his readers, for example, that the latest stunt is "fountain pens filled with whiskey. We just bought a dozen and expect to do some spirited writing during the coming year." (*Summer Annual,* 1922) But the fact remained that triumph over alcohol was what he acknowledged as his greatest personal achievement, and it continued to bring him his finest satisfaction.

Said Pearson one day in 1922, a twinkle in his kindly eyes: "Bob, I have an idea there is more joy in Heaven over one old boozer who is big enough to overcome the habit than over ninety and nine Methodists who never took a drink."

CHAPTER TWENTY-TWO
"We Shall Never See His Like Again"

"It's as easy to recall an unkind word as to draw back a bullet after firing the gun."

(11 November 1916)

"There never was a man as great as the average dog believes his master to be."

(4 August 1917)

"As one journeys through life and the shadows begin to fall eastward, one reaches the solemn conclusion that too much of the world's wisdom is uttered and too little lived."

(5 October 1918)

"Never judge a man by the opinion his wife has of him. Be fair."

(10 April 1920)

ON 29 JULY 1922, Bob Edwards published what proved to be his last issue of the *Eye Opener*. He was then a sick man; and late on the 14th of November following, the message went over the wires from Calgary: "Bob Edwards is dead."

As though they had lost their best friend, thousands of Canadians repeated something resembling the statement of Alberta's Lieutenant-Governor, Hon. R. G. Brett: "Big hearted, genial, and lovable Bob has passed"; or that of Rev. Robert Pearson: "We shall never see his like again."

Still now was the spirit of that human paradox at whom terms like "rebel," "drunk," "sinner," and "saint" had been hurled during a tempestuous life: scorner of money who might have left a fortune instead of a mortgage on his house; journalistic relic of a freer age who without fear of business failure could close his shop for a few weeks when the fish were biting; cultural "monstrosity" whose writing ranged from the low-brow satires about English aristocracy to high-brow criticism of drama, which the *Bookman* of New York would describe as "a model for our more pretentious critics."

Strange and fascinating mixture of human traits of course he was, this staunchest and kindliest of friends and hardest-hitting of opponents. A man of strong opinions, he was patient with humble folk, impatient with others. Even if they couldn't understand him, most people could like him. "He was fond of children," men and women told each other as they paused on Calgary avenues to reflect upon his passing. He was an admirer of the Mounted Police, a patron of fairs and exhibitions, and one who acted charity more than he preached it. And perhaps he wasn't alone in disliking "stuffed shirts" and hypocrites, especially when they appeared in pulpits and public office.

Early in 1921 his health had begun to fail, and doctors ordered a rest at sea level. Accompanied by his wife he went to the West Coast,[1] and the *Eye Opener* lapsed into another period of quiescence. That holiday seemed to help him, and he returned to Calgary convinced he could resume the role of editor. On 30 April, the *Eye Opener* appeared again, with apologies to readers of "the extra-ordinary rag" for the long period between issues.

A few months later the editor acquiesced to the demand from friends that he contest the provincial election; and although far from having the best of health, he presented a bold front and managed to keep most worries about himself to himself.

After the election and political victory, there were many days in which Bob Edwards did not come to the office; and the *Eye Opener* was more irregular than usual. Sitting through his first and only session of the Provincial Legislature, colleagues noticed that he was not well. He didn't complain; but his close friend and fellow legislator, Rev. Robert Pearson, knew something was wrong—something more than the agonizing days of abstinence from booze. The two "Bobs" were living together, eating together, and working together there at Edmonton; and Pearson had every opportunity to observe the failure in health as well as the terrific strain[2] under which Edwards was living in order to remain sober during the period of the legislative session. Only Pearson knew the fight that his friend was waging—resisting the almost overwhelming temptation of a Collins in the morning, saying "no" to an invitation to have a drink at noon, and rejecting the release that a man of his habits would get from a Scotch at night. And then, to make matters worse, Bob Edwards contracted a severe case of influenza during the session of the Legislature, and it aggravated a heart weakness identified some months earlier. He was never well thereafter.

Tempestuous as were his years in Alberta, the funeral on 17 November 1922, was that of a man whose friends were legion. The remains were borne to the graveside at Union Cemetery on the shoulders of six stalwart Mounted Policemen; and in

[1] Edwards made brief mention of the trip in the 30 April 1921 *Eye Opener*.

[2] In "Bob Edwards & I," Pearson recalls how Edwards avoided social engagements because he feared the temptation to drink would be too great. He also claims Edwards went on a bender shortly after delivering his 1922 pro-beer speech in the provincial Legislature; Pearson suggests Edwards was hurt at public joking that he was drunk during his speech.

the large crowd that congregated there, all walks of Alberta life were represented. His Honour, Lieutenant-Governor Brett was present; also Acting Premier George Hoadley and Minister of Labor Alex Ross, representing the Government of Alberta. The service, simple and beautiful, was conducted by the dead man's great friend, Minister-Sportsman-Soldier Rev. Robert Pearson. It was part of Bob's last request.

Speaking of one he had learned to love and understand, Rev. Pearson said:

> He whose memory we hallow today was one of the most widely known men in the Dominion of Canada and I doubt if there is anyone in Canada who had more intimate friends. By that I mean friends who love you, want to see you and show appreciation by some act of kindness. Men distinguished in the state and in business, as well as men celebrated in arts and sciences sought eagerly to meet face to face with R. C. Edwards and have an opportunity of talking with him.
>
> As a friend, there was never a more loyal one. He was always ready to fight the battles of those in whom he believed. . . . His pen was powerful in defence of those who suffered injustice. . . . When he believed anything, nothing could turn him from his cause. On many an occasion he had the opportunity of rich reward if only he would swerve from what he believed and on one occasion he discussed such a situation with me. He said, "Would it not be wonderful at one fell swoop to get all that money?" He thought for a moment and then added, "no, the old paper will never be used for any such purpose."
>
> His qualities of mind were such as are given to few. He had a sense of humour that is very seldom attained and hardly has been surpassed. . . . Had he been more ambitious, his works might have been placed beside [those of] the great writers of the world. . . . Though his humour and satire were of the brightest order, they were directed more to passing comment than to a work that might live. . . . We shall never see his like again.
>
> Like Cervantes who turned his satire on knight errantry and the snobbery it occasioned and made it ridiculous, so our friend turned his satire on snobbery of the present period and tried to make it vanish. Or like another Scot, Robert Burns, his sense of humour helped to banish many a foolish custom and helped people to gain a correct perspective. (25 November 1922)

William Toone, newsboy for the Eye Opener*, 1909.*

Rich and poor, educated and illiterate, capitalists and labourers, all found common ground at the graveside and few eyes were dry.

There were other tributes—many of them:

"The editor of the *Eye Opener* was a genius and while his humour was specifically of one locale and one definite period, he was an artist of undeniable form. . . . There never was an *Eye Opener* in which the genius of its editor did not shine in some inimitably brilliant sketch or anecdote . . . a man of sterling qualities, true to his friends and possessed with courage to stand by his convictions . . . he often showed to the world the mask of frivolity, yet behind that mask was reverence for all that was pure, high and beautiful. Hypocrisy he could not endure."[3]

Some of the finest tributes were from less scholarly men who talked only in terms of deeds. "He paid the hospital bill for my Missis when she was sick;" or, "He sent us a turkey that Christmas when I wasn't working." Another Calgarian who visited him a few days before his death recalled that he was obviously very ill but said: "You go to my wallet for a five-dollar bill and give it to Nick; he's out of work you know."[4]

It is said that a man can be judged by the friends he makes. It was more complex than that in Bob Edwards's case. Although his enemies were mostly in one stratum of society, he drew his friends from every level. Barristers, bartenders and bums called him "Bob." In one of the last mail deliveries prior to his death there were letters from two friends: one was Prime Minister Arthur Meighen enquiring for advice on a certain matter of public policy; and the other, "Kid" Mulligan, New York fight promoter, seeking Bob's opinion about a circuit of boxing matches for the West.

Some time after his funeral, Mrs. Edwards ordered a stone to mark the grave on

[3] From the *Morning Albertan*, reprinted in the 25 November 1922 *Eye Opener*. MacEwan omits the tribute's rather damning qualifier: "It is unfortunate that his written humor was all in the ephemeral form of current periodical writing and contained so little which can be preserved."

[4] These tributes may be composites, but are likely accurate in spirit. Dr. R. G. Brett wrote of Edwards, "The main and yet the least known characteristic of his life, was his generosity to the poor, and many a family in Calgary will mourn his loss and miss his Christmas hamper." (25 November 1922)

the side of the cemetery knoll, close to the Macleod Trail. The spot, some folk noted, commanded a view of two well-known breweries, but in that there was nothing more than coincidence. On the widow's instructions, the stone carried this epitaph:

Robert Chambers Edwards, M.L.A.
Editor
Sept. 12, 1859 – November 14, 1922
Sweetest Memories Will Ever Linger
Katie

Bob's birth date as shown on the tombstone is at odds with that accepted by the press and the editor during his lifetime, purporting to make him sixty-three years of age at the time of death instead of fifty-eight.[5] That, however, is of small importance, because Bob Edwards would have been the last to worry over a mere age discrepancy of five years.

But what of the bottle of whiskey which was supposed to have been buried with the editor's remains? The story has been told in different ways until many people supposed it to be pure legend. The man in the best position to relate the facts was Albert J. Hart, who sculptured and set up the gravestone.

It was shortly after the funeral that the widow visited Mr. Hart's office to discuss gravestones. She wanted a nice one for Bob's grave, and before she left made a selection and declared her choice for an epitaph. From her stocking she produced a one-hundred-dollar bill and gave it as first payment on a stone priced at $210. She made it clear, too, that she would return with a few things she wished to have deposited and sealed within the stone.

What she brought back for deposit in the crypt which Mr. Hart made in the base of the stone, were a copy of the *Wetaskiwin Free Lance*, a copy of Bob's last *Eye Opener*, a copy of his third and last *Summer Annual*, and finally, his old pocket-flask filled with whiskey. The instructions were carried out; the papers and the whiskey were lodged safely within the recess in the rock and sealed against the fingers of interested humans, with six inches of concrete. The stone was then erected at its Union Cemetery location on Calgary's south side.

After several years the stone was returned to the monument mason's premises for repairs, a corner having been chipped. There it remained for a few more years, final

[5] See notes to Chapter 1. Was Bob's widow trying to set the record straight? Perhaps. However: the tombstone conflicts with both Bob's birth certificate and the date recorded in the memorial issue of the *Eye Opener*. A slippery eel to the end (and beyond).

payment having never been made. In 1938, however, when admirers of the late Bob Edwards noted that the stone was still in the shop, Harold Riley, Sr.,[6] proposed that friends subscribe the balance of payment and thus ensure that the grave be adequately marked. On 27 June 1938, the *Calgary Herald* carried an appeal; and on the very next day it was announced that an anonymous friend had offered the necessary final payment on the stone,[7] and that the Bob Edwards's resting place would be marked without further delay. Old friends were pleased, yet they knew very well that Bob's finest monument would be the memory of that one who loved truth in the daily practice of living, and whose life was an open book.

The Bob Edwards funeral was scarcely over before people began asking: "What will become of the *Eye Opener*?" For all practical purposes, it died with its creator. An attempt was made to prolong its life, but with indifferent success; and a sale was made to American interests. Accordingly, the files, such as Bob had at the end of his life, were moved from Canada.

Not many copies of the distinguished paper survived the years. The editor was not one to be meticulous in the keeping of business records, and even his personal files were far from complete. In 1949 the *Calgary Herald* appealed to people having copies of the *Eye Opener* to submit them for microfilming.[8] As a result of the appeal, some sixty-three issues were filmed and assured of a place in the permanent records. There were other issues, a few here and a few there, most of them receiving no special care and becoming yellow and fragile and illegible. Folk realized all too late that copies of the *Eye Opener* would one day be regarded as prizes just as many were late in realizing that the editor, with all his faults, was doubtless Alberta's most original and intriguing journalist.

To quote again about "the day they buried Bob,"—this time from an unidentified writer: "As the last words of the burial service died away, the cold harsh wind suddenly ceased, as though stilled by an unseen hand. Then the first snowflakes of an Alberta winter descended gently, slowly enveloping Mother Earth in a soft blanket of white." (25 November 1922)

That November day so clearly marked an ending: a unique and vibrant personality had finally laid down his pen, closing forever a distinctive chapter in the history of Western journalism.

[6] The *Herald* article identifies Riley as secretary of the Southern Alberta Old-Timers' and Pioneers' Association.

[7] The *Herald* claimed that "Half an hour after the [previous day's] paper was published, a close personal friend of the late Robert Chambers Edwards made arrangements [with Riley] for the tablet to be put back on the grave." The anonymous benefactor was described as "a well-known Calgary citizen."

[8] The 31 October 1949 article characterized the *Eye Opener* as "part of the history of this community of the west." It stated that donated issues would be combined with issues held by the *High River Times* (publisher of the *Eye Opener*, 1902–1904) and those "from a local collection."

EDITOR'S AFTERWORD

Making History with Grant MacEwan and Bob Edwards

GRANT MACEWAN'S BOOKS, laid one atop the other, make a tall stack. He was the West's most prolific popular historian, having authored forty-nine distinct published titles and several unpublished ones, as well as innumerable newspaper articles[1] and occasional pieces.

Looking at that daunting pile of Western stories now, it's difficult to imagine that when Grant MacEwan arrived in Calgary in 1952 after his defeat as a Liberal candidate in a Brandon by-election, his future as a writer was less than assured. His first four books, textbooks in agriculture and livestock, were successful in their field, but MacEwan yearned to make his mark in more popular topics.

His first two books of popular history, *The Sobdbusters* (1948) and *Agriculture on Parade* (1950), were received with little enthusiasm. His next book, *Between the Red and the Rockies* (1955), did begin to establish him as a respected writer in history. However, he had yet to taste real popularity.

MacEwan could hardly have arrived in Calgary at a better time. The city was changing rapidly during the 1950s with the influx of money and new residents occasioned by the discovery of oil at Turner Valley a few years earlier, but the old town was not yet obscured by towers of glass and steel. As MacEwan worked to secure himself a place in the foothills city, he talked incessantly with Calgary old-timers. With his uncanny personability he ferreted out their stories of pioneer days, and particularly of newspaperman Bob Edwards, who had first caught MacEwan's fancy when he read about him in Robert Gard's book of Alberta folktales, *Johnny Chinook*.[2]

In Edwards MacEwan found the ideal subject for historical biography: a man with a balance of the qualities of sinner and saint. A man who encapsulated the spirit of his age, through whom not only his own story, but the larger story of his place and time, could be told.

Eye Opener Bob is both the prototype for and the pinnacle of MacEwan's writing. It is here that he hit his stride. Nearly all of MacEwan's later works would follow the pattern set in this book: solidly researched biography, fleshed out with anecdotes of

[1] It is tempting to measure the amount of newspaper writing he did in column miles rather than column inches.

[2] *Johnny Chinook: Tales Tall and True From the Canadian West* (Toronto: Longmans Green, 1945; Edmonton: Hurtig, 1967) was clearly a source for MacEwan's treatment of many of the episodes in *Eye Opener Bob.*

varying veracity, and enlivened with conversations mostly invented by the author.

In *Eye Opener Bob* the streets of early Calgary come alive under MacEwan's pen, and the colourful characters whom Edwards seemed to draw like a magnet to himself were the very stuff of which Calgary was made. When I first read *Eye Opener Bob*, it turned a switch in my head and my perception of my adopted hometown has never been the same; I'm sure a great many of its readers will vouch something similar.

Thomas Nelson & Sons, the publishers of MacEwan's first six books, rejected the manuscript, which was originally entitled "Boozological Bob—Alberta's Prize Personality." The University of Toronto Press, who had published *Between the Red and The Rockies*, also passed on it, as did McClelland & Stewart. It was considered just too regional a book. Finally it found a home—with a textbook publisher: the Institute of Applied Art, which was the only book publisher operating in Alberta at the time.

Despite this unlikely beginning, *Eye Opener Bob* was an instant smash success in Alberta and across the West—the very first such success in the province, and possibly the first anywhere on the Prairies. Without the benediction of the national cultural centre of Toronto or the colonial magnates in London, a book published in the West, about the West, and solely for the people of the West found its way into the hands of thousands of readers.

In 1974, the Western Producer, publishers of the majority of MacEwan's subsequent books, reissued *Eye Opener Bob* in another hardback edition. By the mid-1980s it was out of print and has remained so until now—all but unavailable to the hundreds of thousands of people who have emigrated to Calgary since that time. Brindle & Glass is pleased to reissue *Eye Opener Bob* for the first time in paperback.[3]

The temptation to "clean up" MacEwan's text has been mostly resisted; aside from James Martin's notes and silent correction of references, no attempt has been made to render this biography more authoritative than MacEwan himself made it. Archival photos and images from the original *Eye Opener* have been added; and obvious typos have been emended. Otherwise, this new edition reflects "Eye Opener Bob" as Grant MacEwan envisioned him, and as he has captured the imaginations of thousands of readers to date.

Far from a mere "first," a historical curiosity, *Eye Opener Bob* is as vital and ongoing a part of the cultural heritage of Alberta as is Boozological Bob Edwards himself. This is a book for the ages—treasure it.

Lee Shedden
Calgary, May 2004

[3] A paperback edition was published alongside one of the original hardcover runs in the late 1960s, but it seems few were printed; for all intents, this is the first trade paperback edition.

Unless otherwise noted, the images are from the *Eye Opener*, and were scanned from original issues in the MacEwan/Foran collection, or from microfilm in various collections including the Glenbow in Calgary and the McLennan Library at McGill University. Quality may vary accordingly.

p. 6: September 27 1910; p. 14: "Wetaskiwin Looking West from Elevator," City of Wetaskiwin Archives 78.15.100 #20166; p. 16: "General View of Wetaskiwin", City of Wetaskiwin Archives 88.40/7 #40005, F. L. Talbot Fonds; p. 24: April 4 1902; p. 28 May 5 1917; p. 37: June 30 1906; p. 41: I didn't write down the date, d—mmit, but sometime in 1905; p. 50: MacEwan collection; p. 51: Glenbow Archives NA-1528-1; Glenbow Archives NA-2854-91; p. 59: September 2 1905; p. 61: sometime around 1910, oh, is it that time already, I must be going, dum de dum; p. 63: March 31 1911; p. 64: Glenbow Archives NA-654-3; p. 66: Glenbow Archives NA-654-4; p. 70 Goshonly knows what issue this came from; p. 75: Glenbow Archives, NA-1351-2, after an *Eye Opener* illustration of issue February 24 1906, AKA the "Rolled Oats Edition" (don't ask); p. 82: September 18 1909; p. 92: University of Alberta Folklore and Local History Collection 96-93-716; p. 96: from "Officers of the Dominion Exhibition" Glenbow Archives NA-2913-4; p.104 November 21 1908; p.114: once again, no citation. Very strange. I'd say 1911; p. 118: November 18 1911; p. 129: Glenbow Archives NA-5624-1; p. 134: May 22 1915; p. 141: May 5 1919; p. 145: Glenbow Archives NA-3868-25; p. 148: January 6 1917; p. 154: are you still reading this? Good for you. Have a drink; p. 158: Glenbow Archives NC-24-194; p. 163: Glenbow Archives NA-3818-11; p. 164: May 4 1912; p.168, 169: January 1 1910; p. 170: April 21 1906; p. 174: August 9 1919; p. 177: October 23 1915; p. 186: March 31 1911; p. 190: February 22nd 1919; p. 193: Glenbow Archives NA-2920-5; p. 197 Glenbow Archives NA-937-12; p. 199: February 21 1919; p. 204: Glenbow Archives NA-3522-18; p. 210: MacEwan/Foran collection. And that's the truth.

John Walter Grant MacEwan, born in 1902 near Brandon, Manitoba, was one of Western Canada's most prolific and popular writers. In all, he authored forty-nine books, many of which, including *Fifty Mighty Men*, *John Ware's Cow Country*, and *Memory Meadows*, are much-loved classics. This remarkable man, who has been called "the Western Canadian of the Twentieth Century," died in 2000 at the age of 97. *A Century of Grant MacEwan*, a selection of his writing spanning his entire career, is available from Brindle & Glass.